Regency Furniture

Plate 1. The Rose Satin Drawing Room, Carlton House, from *History of the Royal Residences* by W.H. Pyne, Vol. III, 1817, showing the suite of seat furniture made for the Chinese Drawing Room by Francis Hervé with new crimson upholstery. This furniture and other fittings, including the chimneypiece with its clock and candelabra were moved to the Rose Satin Drawing Room c.1811 when extensive remodelling of the ground floor, including the Chinese Drawing Room, was in progress.

REGENCY
FURNITURE

Frances Collard

Antique Collectors' Club

First published 1985
Reprinted 1987, 1995

ISBN 0 907462 51 0

British Library Cataloguing-in-Publication Data
A catalogue record for this book is available from the British Library

The endpapers are reproduced from a fragment of early nineteenth century wallpaper (reduced), handprinted today by Alexander Beauchamp of Gloucester

Designed by John Lewis FSIAD

Printed in England on Consort Royal Satin paper from Donside Mills, Aberdeen, by Antique Collectors' Club, 5 Church Street, Woodbridge,Suffolk IP12 1DS

Antique Collectors' Club

The Antique Collectors' Club was formed in 1966 and quickly grew to a five figure membership spread throughout the world. It publishes the only independently run monthly antiques magazine, *Antique Collecting*, which caters for those collectors who are interested in widening their knowledge of antiques, both by greater awareness of quality and by discussion of the factors which influence the price that is likely to be asked. The Antique Collectors' Club pioneered the provision of information on prices for collectors and the magazine still leads in the provision of detailed articles on a variety of subjects.

It was in response to the enormous demand for information on 'what to pay' that the price guide series was introduced in 1968 with the first edition of *The Price Guide to Antique Furniture* (completely revised 1978 and 1989), a book which broke new ground by illustrating the more common types of antique furniture, the sort that collectors could buy in shops and at auctions rather than the rare museum pieces which had previously been used (and still to a large extent are used) to make up the limited amount of illustrations in books published by commercial publishers. Many other price guides have followed, all copiously illustrated, and greatly appreciated by collectors for the valuable information they contain, quite apart from prices. The Price Guide Series heralded the publication of many standard works of reference on art and antiques. *The Dictionary of British Art* (now in six volumes), *The Pictorial Dictionary of British 19th Century Furniture Design, Oak Furniture* and *Early English Clocks* were followed by many deeply researched reference works such as *The Directory of Gold and Silversmiths,* providing new information. Many of these books are now accepted as the standard work of reference on their subject.

The Antique Collectors' Club has widened its list to include books on gardens and architecture. All the Club's publications are available through bookshops world wide and a full catalogue of all these titles is available free of charge from the addresses below.

Club membership, open to all collectors, costs little. Members receive free of charge *Antique Collecting*, the Club's magazine (published ten times a year), which contains well-illustrated articles dealing with the practical aspects of collecting not normally dealt with by magazines. Prices, features of value, investment potential, fakes and forgeries are all given prominence in the magazine.

Among other facilities available to members are private buying and selling facilities, the longest list of 'For Sales' of any antiques magazine, an annual ceramics conference and the opportunity to meet other collectors at their local antique collectors' clubs. There are over eighty in Britain and more than a dozen overseas. Members may also buy the Club's publications at special pre-publication prices.

As its motto implies, the Club is an organisation designed to help collectors get the most out of their hobby: it is informal and friendly and gives enormous enjoyment to all concerned.

For Collectors —By Collectors —About Collecting

ANTIQUE COLLECTORS' CLUB
5 Church Street, Woodbridge, Suffolk IP12 1DS, UK
Tel: 01394 385501 Fax: 01394 384434

—————— or ——————

Market Street Industrial Park, Wappingers' Falls, NY 12590, USA
Tel: 914 297 0003 Fax: 914 297 0068

Acknowledgements

I would like to thank Clive Wainwright who originally suggested that I should write this book and who has provided a great deal of encouragement and many illuminating discussions. My other colleagues, Simon Jervis and John Hardy, also made valuable contributions as did Peter Thornton, whose interest and knowledge particularly in the field of historic interiors has been most stimulating and instructive. I am very grateful to the following for their help over various problems: Geoffrey de Bellaigue, Pamela Brown, Stephen Calloway, John Compton, Dr. Rosalys Coope, Belinda Couzens, Peter Day, Mrs. June Dean, Mrs. Elaine Evans Dee, Mrs. A. Edmonds, Kate Eustace, Christopher Gilbert, Susan Hare, John Harris, Jill Lever, Martin Levy, Sarah Medlam, Christopher Payne, Pamela Reekie Robertson, Norris Wakefield, Charles Walford and Lavinia Wellicome. Dr. Gordon Glanville kindly read the text and made many useful and knowledgeable suggestions but the final result is not of course his responsibility. I am very grateful to Victoria Keric for turning a mass of confusing drafts into clear and accurate typescript, to Jill Champion for helpful and expert editorial work and to John Steel whose patience and interest in this project has been most encouraging. Finally I must thank my husband, Anthony, whose support, understanding and practical assistance throughout has been much appreciated, and to whom I dedicate this book.

Contents

List of Colour Plates

The Great Room, Wynnstay. Watercolour from an album in the Prints and Drawings Department, Victoria and Albert Museum, c.1810, showing tiered bookcases on the left and a what-not in the middle.

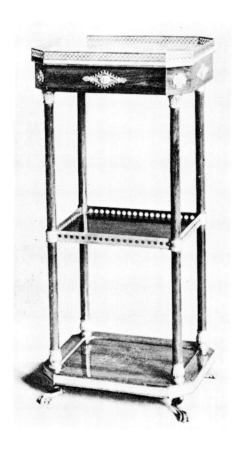

What-not of rosewood with ormolu mounts, one of a pair formerly in the Boudoir at Southill furnished by 1800.

Introduction

The term 'Regency' is often used not only to describe the constitutional position in the nine years between 1811 and 1820 when the Prince of Wales ruled as Prince Regent during the illness of his father, George III, but also the development of architecture and decorative arts at the end of the eighteenth century and the beginning of the nineteenth century. Margaret Jourdain, in her pioneering work, *Regency Furniture 1795 to 1820,* deliberately limited herself to the period just before the political establishment of the Regency until just after the accession of the Prince Regent as George IV in 1820. Her book, by ending abruptly at 1820, was unable to include the various developments of the period up to 1840, including much of the work done at Brighton and Windsor for George IV, the resurgence of interest in French inspired decorative arts and the importance of the illustrations and contemporary comments of Ackermann's *Repository of the Arts.* The growing number of pattern books were produced by cabinet makers and designers in response to demands from the new middle class who 'possessing or having cultivated a taste for beauty, ornament is added to their apartments, either by elegance in the architectural finishing, or by introducing fine furniture, pictures &c. and generally in both ways.'[1] Bryan Read's comprehensive *Regency Antiques* deliberately included the simpler types of domestic furniture ignored by Margaret Jourdain for that of the grander houses and provided an excellent coverage of these pattern books of the 1820s and 1830s while Clifford Musgrave in *Regency Furniture* illustrated many very fine pieces by well known craftsmen, some from the very good collection in the Pavilion and Museum at Brighton, as well as examples of the styles prevalent between 1800 and 1830.

This book, by covering the period from c.1790 to c.1840, is intended to show the development of the different trends which epitomise the Regency in all its eclectic aspects, from the neoclassical influences of Sheraton's Drawing Book and the Anglo-French taste of Henry Holland to the more substantial but still attractive pieces produced in the 1830s after designs in a debased Greek Revival style. Illustrations from Ackermann's *Repository of the Arts,* that invaluable guide to so many of the fashionable styles and individuals, and from various important pattern books have been included to demonstrate their significance, and some contemporary interiors are used to show the way in which furniture was arranged.[2] The Regency attitude to interior decoration, which often involved treating each room as a unit with individual furnishings and wall decorations in harmony of theme or colour scheme, is shown at Carlton House where the unifying factor was either colour, as in the Yellow Bow Room, or thematic, as in the Chinese Drawing Room. An example of these unified schemes, in one of the more unusual styles popular at this period, was 'The Plaid or Scotch Room' at Farnborough Hill in 1820 where the walls were 'Painted in Oak, & paper'd with plaid, border of thistles, & 25 views of Scotland pasted on the Walls', the pictures included a portrait of Mary, Queen of Scots and topographical

---

1. J.C Loudon, *A Treatise on Forming, Improving and Managing Country Residences,* 1806, vol. 1, p.70.
2. Mario Praz, *The House of Life,* 1964, p.287, commented on the diligence with which watercolours of interiors 'reproduce every piece of furniture and every household object, every minute detail of carpets and curtains...'

Set of quartetto tables, mahogany c.1820. These were illustrated in Sheraton's *Cabinet Dictionary* 1803 with simulated bamboo legs, and by George Smith, and were intended for use when doing needlework or when taking refreshment.

Movable mahogany bookcase supplied by Gillows c.1801 for Clonbrock, Co. Galway, of the type which was featured in the Gillow Cost Books in 1799 and also in the *Cabinet Dictionary* 1803 as a 'moving library'.

Davenport, rosewood veneer with gilt brass decoration, c.1820. The name is thought to have derived from Captain Davenport for whom Gillows made a desk in the 1790s. Later versions often incorporated writing slopes which extended over the front and were supported by columns.

views of Scotland and the furniture consisted of an oak bedstead with 'canopy of Thistles', 'Royal plaid' bed hangings, plaid window curtains and carpet, a chest of drawers 'painted to suit', a rug with thistles and a pair of plaid slippers.[3] This attitude towards interior decoration was echoed in the carefully conceived schemes for all aspects of upholstery, a particularly important element in the designs for furniture in the rococo or Gothic styles for example, and a feature difficult to appreciate today when so much furniture has lost its original coverings and trimmings. It is therefore necessary to use contemporary inventories, accounts and other written descriptions, pictorial evidence and surviving examples of fabrics to gain an impression of the importance of upholstery in the Regency period.

Although the Prince Regent gave his name to the period, his taste was not necessarily the same as that of his contemporaries, but the styles he favoured were echoed by popular fashion at different times during the Regency, from the beginning when Holland's Anglo-French influence at Carlton House coincided with Sheraton's

3. Inventory of the contents of Farnborough Hill and of the house in Harley Street in the possession of Luke Forman 1820.

Commode, mahogany and gilded wood, c.1810, with the French influence apparent in the peg top feet.

illustrations of current fashions to the preference for a richer, more elaborate style in the 1820s at Windsor, when there were an increasing number of furniture pieces being produced with ormolu mounts and boulle inlay. The importance of the Prince Regent lay in his role as a ruler of taste and artistic perception, in his patronage of such disparate figures as Sir Walter Scott and Jane Austen, or Henry Holland and Jeffry Wyatville, in his preference for exquisite if expensive decoration like the Chinoiserie interiors at Brighton Pavilion which encouraged such craftsmen as the Crace family, and in his acquisition of great works of art like the eighteenth century furniture from the French Royal Collections.

Many aspects of the Regency period appeal to modern taste in their convenience and elegance, for example the development of a certain style of architecture, villas decorated with balconies and other exterior ironwork, and interiors planned for comfort and convenience rather than for display. Rooms were designed for an informal style of living with double doors or rows of pillars dividing areas, windows were large and often used as doors to lead into the garden, while the cultivation of house plants, building of conservatories and addition of verandahs all helped to remove the barriers between house and garden. Francis Goodwin expressed this

Mahogany revolving bookstand, with ebonised turned finial and tiers divided by false book spines, c.1815. A circular and movable bookcase was illustrated by Ackermann's *Repository* March 1810, pl.15, patented by Morgan and Sanders.

Dressing chest, mahogany, c.1810, shown closed and open, an example of space-saving yet elegant furniture popular at the beginning of the nineteenth century. Similar designs were illustrated in the *Cabinet-Makers' London Book of Prices,* 1793, and in the 1863 edition.

Dining table, mahogany, c.1815. One of the extending tables patented by William Pocock of 26 Southampton Street in 1805 and described as a 'Sympathetic' dining table where the twin flap top swivels and opens to allow three more flaps to be inserted, supported on a system of extending brackets.

attitude in his description of a verandah which 'may almost be said to take the room itself out abroad, for when rendered so attractive as it may be made here, it would frequently seduce the work-table or the reading-table into its own neutral ground, between the house and the open air'.[4]

To fit suitably into these new interiors furniture had to be light and small enough to be easily moved about and new types like the whatnot (p.10) (a free standing tier of open shelves first recorded by Margaret Jourdain in 1808), quartetto tables, (p.12) (a nest of four tables of graduated size illustrated in Sheraton's *Cabinet Dictionary* 1803), and other small occasional tables must have been very useful as Fanny Burney observed, 'I think no room looks really comfortable, or even quite furnished without two tables, — one to keep the wall . . . the other to stand here, there and everywhere, and hold letters, and make the agreeable'.[5] The type of bookcase with receding shelves and castors (p.13) epitomises this desire for small elegant and flexible pieces, and was described as a 'moving library' in Gillows Cost Book in 1799 and in Sheraton's *Cabinet Dictionary* in 1803.

The desire for novelty, a prominent feature of the Regency, necessitated the constant production of new types of furniture, a feature commented on by Robert Southey in 1807. 'This is the newest fashion, and fashions change so often in these things, as well as in everything else, that it is easy to know how long it is since a house has been fitted up, by the shape of the furniture. An upholder just now advertises Commodes, Console-tables, Ottomans, Chaiselonges and Chiffoniers; — what are all these? you ask. I asked the same question, and could find no person in the house who could answer me; but they are all articles of the newest fashion, and no doubt all will soon be thought indispensably necessary in every well furnished house.'[6] Commodes (p.15) and chiffoniers both derive from French eighteenth century originals, and the commode, with shaped or straight front, with tapering fluted columns, on plinths, bun or peg top feet, and with ormolu mounts or doors with decorative brass grilles, appeared throughout the Regency period. George Smith in 1808 recommended commodes for drawing rooms, living rooms or ladies' dressing rooms in satinwood, rosewood, mahogany and japanned finishes with marble or japanned tops. Chiffoniers, (p.42) commodes with open shelves instead of cupboards and a superstructure of more open shelves, were recommended by Smith to be made in the same woods or finishes for 'almost every apartment of a house . . . for such books as are in constant use' or in libraries for 'the reception of books taken for present reading',[7] and later examples incorporated cupboards

4. Francis Goodwin, *Domestic Architecture,* 1834, 'Description of a Small Villa in the old English Cottage Style', Design No. 16, p.4.

5. Fanny Burney, letter of 6 September 1801, quoted by Margaret Jourdain, *Regency Furniture,* 1934, p.48.

6. Robert Southey, *Letters from England:* by Don Manuel Espriella, 1807, vol. 1, pp.154-5. Dining tables, supported on pillars with claw feet, were also very fashionable, having been first mentioned by Sheraton in 1793, and remained popular into the 1820s. Rectangular tables, with extending leaves supported by folding flaps or extra legs, were patented by various inventors including Richard Gillow from the 1790s, and circular tables, supported on a pillar and claw structure or pedestals of triangular form popularised by Hope, were also popular, being sometimes called breakfast tables.

7. George Smith, *Collection of Designs for Household Furniture and Interior Decoration,* 1808, p.21.

Plate 2. The ladies' dressing room, Pellwall, from an album of designs by Sir John Soane who was commissioned to design the house for Purney Sillitoe in 1822, and this room shows typical furnishings including a washstand and a cheval glass on the left, a dressing table in the window and fitted cupboards on the right.

'Patent Metamorphic Library chair', combined mahogany chair and library steps, c.1815. This design was patented by Morgan and Sanders and illustrated in the *Repository* July 1811, pl.3.

instead of open shelves underneath and often scroll-shaped supports for the shelves on top. Another low piece, the dwarf bookcase, was deliberately designed so as to leave the wall above free for paintings or for pier glasses, like those designed by Henry Holland for the piers between the windows in the golden drawing room at Carlton House, or in the library at Southill.

Popular interest in novelty and invention also resulted in the production of a specialised group of pieces, known as 'patent' or 'patent metamorphic' furniture, incorporating space-saving devices and other ingenious features. As Thomas Martin pointed out in 1819, 'it is the fashion of the present day, to resort to a number of contrivances for making one piece of furniture serve many purposes, 'a bed by night,

Metamorphic library chair illustrating the alternative use as library steps.

a chest of drawers by day'.[8] The popularity of these pieces is obvious from the number of surviving examples and from the numerous documentary references and although furniture combining two or more functions dates back to the early eighteenth century the 1780s saw the beginning of its greatest period of popularity. The principal types included extending or folding dining tables (pp.16, 24), chairs, tables or cupboards which could be turned into library steps, and chairs or settees which converted into beds. There were two specific functions for patent furniture both of which involved ingenious and inventive solutions. One of these was for

8. Thomas Martin, *The New Circle of the Mechanical Arts*, 1819, p.111.

Mechanical chair, mahogany with brass fittings, c.1830. Similar designs appear in the Gillow records from c.1787, described as 'Gouty' chairs and Ackermann illustrated 'Merlin's Mechanical Chair' in October 1811, pl.21.

furniture designed for travellers including those involved in the many military campaigns of the late eighteenth and early nineteenth centuries, and folding beds, tables, chairs and sets of drawers enclosed in travelling chests all provided practical solutions to the problems. Patent furniture designed for invalid use included reclining chairs with footrests, gouty chairs (early examples of wheelchairs) and couches which could be adjusted to provide more comfort for the back or legs.[9]

9. Brian Austen, 'Morgan & Sanders and the Patent Furniture Makers of Catherine Street', *The Connoisseur*, Vol. 187, No. 753, November 1974, pp.180-191. Phillips of Hitchin (Antiques) Ltd. *Patent Metamorphic*

Croft, mahogany, c.1810. Named after the Rev. Sir Herbert Croft, Bt., for whom the first example was made to house his Mss. for a new edition of Dr. Johnson's *Dictionary*. Examples are known to have been made by the firm of Seddon.

Although Sheraton included designs for this type of furniture, and firms like Gillows who patented the telescopic dining table in 1800, made pieces, most examples were made by specialist firms and it is clear that after c.1790 patent furniture had acquired sufficient market value for many shops to advertise it although not responsible for legally patenting the articles themselves. Among the firms well known for their products are Morgan and Sanders, Thomas Butler, William Pocock

Furniture 1780-1830. Catalogue of the exhibition, 3rd-29th July 1978. E.T. Joy, 'Georgian Patent Furniture', *The Connoisseur Year Book,* 1962, pp.8-15.

'Capstan' mahogany expanding table, c.1835. The circular top expands on an iron frame to allow eight extra leaves to be inserted. Patented by Robert Jupe 1835 and made by Johnstone Jupe & Co. 1835-1840, the firm formed by Robert Jupe and John Johnstone at 67 New Bond Street c.1835. By 1840 the firm at 67 New Bond Street had become Johnstone & Jeanes while Jupe had moved to Welbeck Street.

and Robert Daws, and Ackermann's *Repository* featured many examples of patent furniture including Pitt's globe writing table in 1810, and a metamorphic library chair (pp.20, 21) in 1811 by Morgan and Sanders, and Pocock's Reclining Patent Chair in 1813.[10] Morgan and Sanders seem to have been particularly well known with large premises in Catherine Street (the address of other patent furniture makers like Thomas Butler) and apparently supplied furniture for Lord Nelson, using the publicity value of such a commission to advertise 'Nelson's Patent Sideboard Dining Table'.[11]

In spite of the popularity of trends like patent furniture, such fashions were not universally approved, since, as the *Architectural Magazine* observed, 'this incessant craving... corrupts the taste of the cabinet-maker, by creating an incessant demand for novelty, which no designer, unless he possesses a highly cultivated mind, and an almost unlimited stock of ideas, can long supply without degenerating into absurdity.'[12] The problem of providing cabinet makers with suitable designs for the range of fashionable styles was much discussed, with Ackermann wondering in 1813 'Can we expect the artizans and manufacturers to alter their present mode of

10. R. Ackermann, *Repository of the Arts*, Vol. III, February 1810, pl.8; Vol. VI, July 1811, pl.3; Vol. IX, March 1813, pl.19.

11. Ackermann, Vol. III, April 1810, pl.24.

12. *The Architectural Magazine*, Vol. I, 1834, pp.8-9.

Cellaret, mahogany with stringing of ebony and box and giltwood mounts, with the arms of Leyton-Blenkinsopp and fitted with lead lined compartments for bottles, c.1810.

Label of Farringtons, Newcastle, stuck inside the lid of the cellaret, indicating the range of their stock and the popularity of furniture in the Egyptian taste.

Design for rocking chair from advertising leaflet of John Porter, 81 & 82 Upper Thames Street, c.1840, similar to the chair exhibited at the Great Exhibition in 1851 by R.W. Winfield of Birmingham.

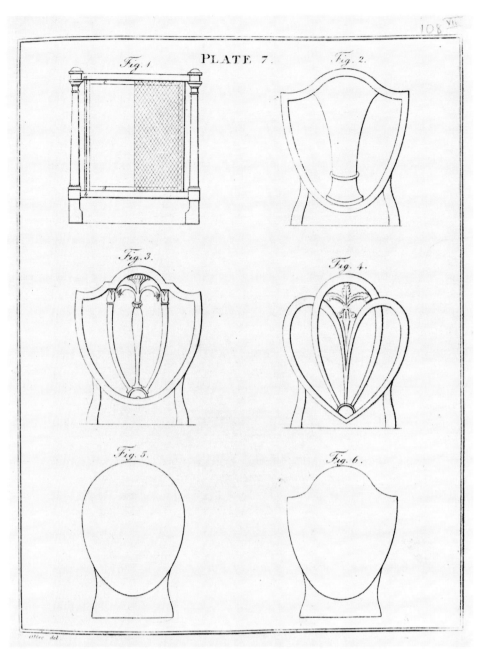

Designs for chair backs from *The London Chair-Makers' and Carvers' Book of Prices,* London 1823, indicating the survival of style popularised by Sheraton.

education, and ascend to the study of those higher and more copious sources of elegance?',[13] and the solution apparently depended on the study of architectural design by cabinet makers. Many of the pattern books referred to the necessity for cabinet makers to study basic principles of perspective and geometry, since designs published by such authors as Richard Brown in 1822 were 'only intended for the purposes of composition and selection' and not to be slavishly copied 'for it is not by copying particulars, but by attending to principles, that lessons become instructive'.[14] The list of over 700 subscribers to the first edition of Sheraton's

---

13. Ackermann, Vol. X, October 1813, p.232.
14. Richard Brown, *The Rudiments of Drawing Cabinet and Upholstery Furniture,* 1822, pp. v-vi.

Interior 1822, showing typical furniture including a games table, stool and bookshelves of the type illustrated by George Smith in 1808.

Drawing Book shows how popular such publications were for introducing new ideas or patterns which could be adapted by cabinet makers for pieces made in their own workshops. The pattern book used by Gillows between 1770 and 1800 illustrates designs published by Hepplewhite and Sheraton, including a Carlton House Table in 1796, and the hundreds of surviving designs included in their records demonstrate the way in which a successful firm, with businesses in London and in Lancaster, collected ideas from printed sources and probably from pieces supplied by their rivals to the same clients.[15] The various books of prices produced for the trade as a guide to the cost of different patterns offered unlimited opportunity for innovation on the part of the craftsmen since there were a number of alteratives included for each design. The popularity of these books can be seen in the number of editions produced of the first, *The Cabinet-Maker's London Book of Prices* in 1788, and the numerous provincial publications produced for tradesmen in centres like Edinburgh, Leeds or Norwich.[16]

There was an innate conservatism among many cabinet makers and their customers and designs first introduced during the late eighteenth century were still being produced thirty or forty years later. The Carlton House Table (p.58) first illustrated in *The Cabinet-Maker's London Book of Prices 1793* appeared in all subsequent editions up to 1866 and some of Sheraton's plates were republished in a volume *Designs for Household Furniture by the late T. Sheraton, cabinet maker* produced

15. Ivan Hall, 'Patterns of Elegance: The Gillows' Furniture Designs — I', *Country Life*, Vol. CLXIII, No. 4222, June 8th 1978, pp.1612-15, 'Models with a choice of leg. The Gillows' Furniture Designs — II', *Country Life*, Vol. CLXIII, No. 4223, June 15 1978, pp.1740-2.

16. See reprint of *The Cabinet-Makers' London Book of Prices*, 1793, with comment and bibliography on the various editions, *Furniture History*, Vol. XVIII, 1982.

Interior at 4 Seamore Place, London, June 1836, showing a sofa table and sofa in use. Watercolour by Emily Prinsep.

by J. Taylor at the Architectural Library, 59 High Holborn, in 1812. Cabinet makers catering for a less sophisticated clientele or workmen of less skill could find in the books of prices a variety of ideas for simple and regular furniture designs originally produced by Hepplewhite, Sheraton or their contemporaries. *The Modern Style of Cabinet Work Exemplified* originally published by Thomas King in 1829, which included designs in the debased classical taste typical of the period, was reissued several times, finally appearing as the trade catalogue of William Smee and Son, one of the largest furniture manufacturers of the later nineteenth century.

The organisation and size of the furniture making trades at the beginning of the nineteenth century working both in London and in the provincial centres, make it very difficult to be certain who made what, as there was a great deal of competition. The complexity of the trade also meant that a London cabinet maker could be a craftsman making and selling his furniture himself, or a dealer or retailer selling the products of others, either directly to the public or to other dealers for sale elsewhere in the country or abroad. Other variations were craftsmen making pieces for dealers or for other craftsmen, or doing repair work, and finally there were always journeymen who worked at home as outworkers on piece-work for craftsmen or for shops, or were employed directly.

One of the interesting developments in the furniture trades was in the number of firms listed in the trade directories with two addresses, indicating a separation between workshop and showroom. For example George Oakley, with an upholsterer's shop in St. Paul's Churchyard, opened a second in Old Bond Street, a far more fashionable address. The first was simply described as a 'Chair and Cabinet Manufactory' while the second was far more grandly entitled 'Magazine of General and Superb Upholstery and Cabinet Furniture'. By 1833 Seddons had built workshops in the Gray's Inn Road, designed for them by J.B. Papworth between 1830 and 1832 with drying sheds added in 1836, as well as their well-known establishment in Aldersgate Street.

Plate 3. The Dinner Locust, a satirical print c.1823, showing the interior of a modest house, with a dining table pulled up to the fire and standing on a cloth to catch the crumbs, dining chairs with a typical curving horizontal back and a small old-fashioned side table.

The main provincial centres of furniture making were Liverpool, Manchester, Lancaster, Bath, Birmingham, Bristol, and York and these had long contained cabinet making and upholstery businesses capable of providing for the needs of the local gentry. Wealthy families who ordered their best furniture from a London firm would often use local sources for less important pieces for bedrooms or servants' rooms. With the tremendous growth in better communications and in prosperity in the nineteenth century the standing of these provincial firms increased, but not noticeably until after 1850. Another group, who had flourished since the eighteenth century, and continued to do well in the early nineteenth, were the dealers in secondhand and antique pieces, sometimes described as brokers, who took advantage of the growing interest in antiquarian furnishings.

View of the Long Library, Woburn, from P.F. Robinson's *Vitruvius
Britannicus* 1827, showing the room as remodelled by Henry
Holland, and among later furniture one of the set of mahogany chairs
with pierced backs supplied by Holland and Dominique Daguerre and
made by Georges Jacob, c.1790.

Bergère of gilded wood from Chatsworth and probably part of the set
of furniture supplied by Francis Hervé in the 1780s for the Private
Apartments.

30

1. Henry Holland, French Taste and Neoclassicism

In 1783 when the Prince of Wales, later George IV, reached his majority he was given Carlton House as a residence of his own and £60,000 was voted for its refurbishing, as the house had been empty since the death in 1772 of its last royal occupant, the Prince's grandmother, Augusta, Dowager Princess of Wales. The house had evolved from its seventeenth century origins into an unco-ordinated complex of buildings, surrounded by other houses, and was ripe for the kind of remodelling with which the Prince of Wales was to occupy himself all his life. Although there was a growing romantic movement in favour of remodelling old houses rather than demolishing and rebuilding, George's reasons for doing so were probably financial. His enthusiastic interest in architecture and interiors was matched by his willingness to spend as much money as possible on settings which he considered suitable to his position. All through his life his expenditure was to outrun his income, which certainly caused difficulties for the architects, designers, artists and craftsmen associated with his projects although the surviving results are of great quality and importance.

The opportunity to remodel Carlton House for the Prince was offered to Henry Holland after Sir William Chambers, as Surveyor General, had initiated some immediate repairs. Holland was to create for the Prince an elegant and restrained architectural setting which gave the Prince the regal background he desired, though small in scale, and which provided Holland with the opportunity to develop his interest in French neoclassicism to the fullest extent.[1] From the beginning the project had a markedly Gallic flavour with Guillaume or William Gaubert's appointment as Clerk of Works in 1783 (although he was replaced two years later) emphasising the Prince's interest in all things French and his close contacts with such influential courtiers as the Duc d'Orléans. However, the Prince was not the first to employ the group of Anglo-French craftsmen like Francis Hervé and Sefferin Nelson who later became prominent through their work with Henry Holland. At Chatsworth, the Duke and Duchess of Devonshire, both francophiles and intimates of the Prince of Wales, remodelled their Private Apartments using Hervé for the furniture, Sefferin Nelson for the carving and William Gaubert for some of the fixed fittings during the period 1782-5.[2] Only Hervé's seat furniture and some tables can now be traced, and the style of the chairs, some of which have rather unfashionable Louis XV backs, is definitely French in inspiration as are the duchesses or angle confidants for the Drawing Room and the chairs with caned backs and seats.

Although the financial crisis for the Prince in 1785 stopped work at Carlton House while a commission investigated the situation, enough work had been done to excite Horace Walpole, who wrote to the Countess of Upper Ossory 'We went to see the

1. See Dorothy Stroud, *Henry Holland: His Life and Architecture*, 1966. F.J.B. Watson, 'Holland and Daguerre: French Undercurrents in English Neo-Classic Furniture Design', *Apollo* Vol. XCVI, No. 128, October 1972, pp.282-7.

2. Ivan Hall, 'A neoclassical episode at Chatsworth', *The Burlington Magazine*, Vol. CXXII, No. 927, June 1980, pp. 400-414. Francis Hervé and Sefferin Nelson also collaborated on a suite of furniture in the French taste at Althorp for Holland in 1791 — see *Henry Holland*, Catalogue of the exhibition at Woburn Abbey, 1971, no.33.

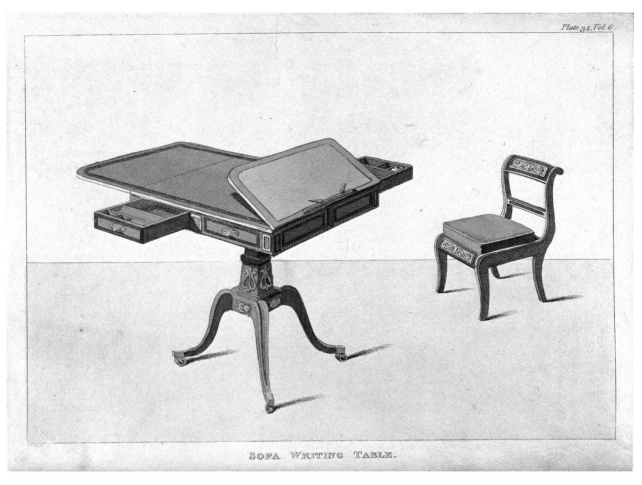

Plate 34. Vol. 6

SOFA WRITING TABLE.

Plate 4. Sofa Writing Table and Trafalgar Chair from Ackermann's *Repository,* Vol. VI, December 1811, pl. 34. The Trafalgar chair was one of the most popular of Regency designs, usually shown with arms resting on curving ends.

Prince's new palace in Pall Mall; and were charmed. It will be the most perfect in Europe. There is an august simplicity that astonished me. You cannot call it magnificent; it is the taste and propriety that strike. Every ornament is at a proper distance, and not one too large, but all delicate and new, with more freedom and variety than Greek ornaments, and though probably borrowed from the Hôtel de Condé and other new palaces, not one that is not rather classic than French... How sick one shall be, after this chaste palace, of Mr. Adam's gingerbread and sippets of embroidery!'[3]

The major phase of the furnishing and decoration did not begin until after the settling of the Prince's debts in 1787 when Parliament agreed to produce £60,000 towards the completion of the interiors. Gaubert had been replaced by another Frenchman, Dominique Daguerre, who acted as intermediary or marchand-mercier between the Prince and his French suppliers, although Gaubert appears as William Gaubert of Panton Street, Maker of Ornamental Furniture, in a list of the Prince's debtors in 1795. Since the new building owed so much of its architectural inspiration

---

3. *The Yale Edition of Horace Walpole's Correspondence,* edited by W.S. Lewis, Vol. 33, pp. 498-500, letter of 17th September 1785.

Chair, painted, gilded and distressed beech, in the Anglo-French style of Henry Holland, c.1790.

Chair, painted and gilded beech, thought to have been designed by Henry Holland for Carlton House, c.1800.

to France it seemed obvious to obtain furniture and fittings from that country, either by obtaining pieces from émigrés since there was an established trade in smuggled goods, or by ordering items to be made specially in the Parisian workshops. Daguerre was to profit by his association with the Prince with the establishment in 1787 of a London branch of his Paris showroom, and with his personal contacts with such major French cabinet makers as Adam Weisweiler and Georges Jacob. These made it possible for him, even after settling in London, to establish a profitable line in supplying French furniture and objects d'art for Carlton House as well as for other Royal houses and for such patrons as Lord Spencer.[4]

Holland apparently visited Paris in 1787 and it is from this point that the decidedly French aspects of the project begin to impress so strongly. Much of the decorative work at Carlton House was to be carried out by Alexandre Louis Delabrière who had worked for the Comte d'Artois at Bagatelle, his pavilion, on the outskirts of the Bois de Boulogne which was designed by François-Joseph Bélanger in 1777. This pavilion probably influenced much of the work in the period between 1787 and 1789 at Carlton House, and through its chinoiserie bath house, pagoda and bridge is an

4. Stroud, pp.75-9, 101.

interesting forerunner of the Prince's later Chinese fantasy at Brighton Pavilion. Holland had in fact already worked at Brighton for the Prince of Wales by 1787, extending the original farmhouse which became known as the Prince's Marine Pavilion, thus echoing the French original, with furnishings in the French style supplied by craftsmen like Seddon and Carrington.[5] Other Frenchmen involved at Carlton House include the painters Jean Jacques Boileau, Dumont le Romani, T.H. Pernotin and Louis Belanger, who may have been related to the designer of the Bagatelle and who exhibited at the Royal Academy in 1790, describing himself as 'painter to the Duke of Orleans'. Biagio Rebecca also worked at Carlton House and submitted an account in 1794 for 'painting and finishing part of a room . . . consisting of Ornaments in the Antique grotesque style'.[6]

Through Daguerre Holland would have been able to transmit designs or specifications to Paris for particular pieces of furniture and from the mid-1780s it is possible to discern a new trend in the style of the products of the Parisian workshops. The arrival of this 'style étrusque' encouraged a move away from the highly decorated pieces ornamented with ormolu, marquetry, pietra dura or Sèvres plaques, towards designs for chairs and commodes à la anglaise which were comparatively plain in design and often of mahogany, a wood more favoured by English rather than French cabinetmakers until this decade. Georges Jacob supplied a set of chairs with mahogany frames and backs pierced in a pattern of lozenges and

5. Stroud, pp.74, 87-90.
6. Quoted by Stroud, p.75.

Library bookcase with reading desk, mahogany, probably designed by Henry Holland for the Library, Woburn, c.1795.

Interior of the Chinese Drawing Room, Carlton House, from Sheraton's *Cabinet-Makers' and Upholsterers' Drawing-Book,* 1793.

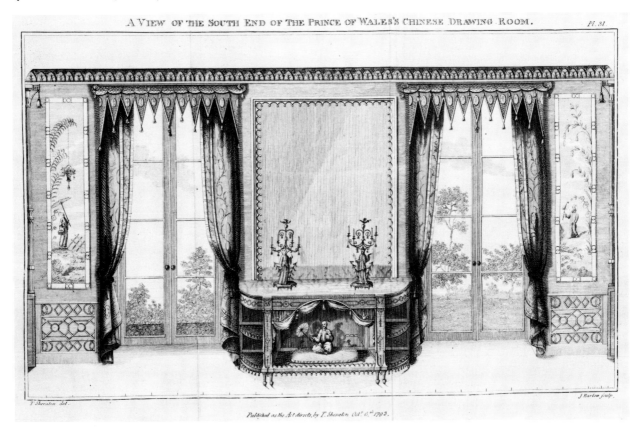

The South End of The Chinese Drawing Room, Carlton House, from the *Drawing Book,* showing the pier table probably made by Adam Weisweiler c.1790.

Chair, gilded wood, with painted panel by Delabrière, in the Louis XVI style, one of a pair originally supplied for the Boudoir at Southilll in the 1790s.

circles for Carlton House, and a similar set was apparently supplied by Holland and Daguerre for Woburn Abbey when Holland was working there for the 5th Duke of Bedford from 1787.[7] One of Holland's assistants, P.F. Robinson, shows the Long Library as remodelled by Holland (p.30) with one of the Jacob chairs in the engraving in his *Vitruvius Britannicus* of 1827.

This understatement of style and materials was reflected in Holland's architecture, and Carlton House epitomised this striking chasteness which was to influence the

7. Stroud, p.79. *Henry Holland* exhibition catalogue, no.33. Geoffrey de Bellaigue, 'George IV and French Furniture', *The Connoisseur*, Vol. CL, No. 784, June 1977, pp.116-125.

Chair, gilded wood, from a set of seat furniture supplied for the Chinese Drawing Room at Carlton House by Francis Hervé, 1790, and originally covered with brocaded satin with a Chinese pattern.

whole field of furniture design through Holland's important position as the Prince's architect. Holland must also be credited with popularising in England the French taste for complete schemes for the interiors of specific rooms, which was reflected at Carlton House in such titles as the Blue Bow Room, Flesh Coloured Room and Yellow Bow Room where the colour of the architectural features and the upholstery clearly provided the unifying factors.[8]

Holland and Daguerre collaborated at other houses besides Carlton House,

8. Geoffrey de Bellaigue, 'The Furnishings of the Chinese Drawing Room, Carlton House', *The Burlington Magazine,* Vol. CIX, No. 774, September 1967, pp.518-528.

China cabinet, rosewood and ebony with ormolu mounts, made by William Marsh and originally in the Boudoir at Southill, c.1795.

principally on additions and alterations to Althorp for Lord Spencer, and at Woburn for the 5th Duke of Bedford. Daguerre supplied Holland with furniture for Althorp, acting as entrepreneur both for existing and commissioned pieces, though not in the same proportion as for Carlton House, and other furniture suppliers are mentioned in the accounts, including John King whose bill amounted to over £1,000. Furniture supplied by Daguerre from 1785 included a set of stools, a fauteuil de Reine, and a tête-à-tête to match from Francis Hervé, and in 1790 items apparently from his showroom in Paris.[9] At Woburn again Daguerre was one of only several craftsmen supplying goods, the others including Ince and Mayhew, Francis Hervé and John Kean apparently making furniture to Holland's designs. 'On the articles of furniture, was anyone to examine the endless number of drawings I have made, and witness the trouble I have had, they would not envy me my charge on that account' he wrote to the Duke on January 12th, 1796.[10]

Since very few of Holland's records survived the wholesale destruction of his papers after his death, it is impossible to discover to what extent he gave Daguerre designs for the large amount of furnishings for Carlton House and the other domestic interiors on which they collaborated. There are however some pieces of furniture at Woburn traditionally associated with Holland himself which exhibit some of the facets of the 'style etrusque', a French fashionable style which appeared from the early 1780s.[11] One of the pieces, a classical mahogany library bookstand (p.34) with desks at either end forming reading stands, can also be seen in P.F. Robinson's view of the Long Library of 1827. This piece is associated with a set of four bronze torchères of antique Roman design on tripodal feet also at Woburn, similar to four torchères shown by Robinson flanking the library bookstand and Jacob chair (p.30). Two designs by Henry Holland for pier tables, one for the boudoir at Carlton House, and the other for the drawing room at his own house in Sloane Place are in the Pierpont Morgan Library, New York.[12]

The amount of refurbishing carried out at Carlton House by Walsh Porter for the Prince, and the alterations made by Nash before the publication of Pyne's plates has resulted in only two surviving views of one of the rooms in its original form in Sheraton's *Drawing Book* of 1793, but at least the Chinese Drawing Room (p.35) illustrates Holland's use of French craftsmen and the French inspired unity of interior designs which must have been echoed throughout the rest of Carlton House. Sheraton's description of the furnishings does not tally with two accounts of November 1789 drawn up by Henry Holland, which lists the furnishings of Carlton House room by room, and the tradesmen with their individual estimates. Geoffrey de Bellaigue has shown that the Accounts were a device for the Prince to obtain more money, an habitual problem, and has identified the set of seat furniture as having

9. Stroud, p.101.

10. Quoted by Stroud, p.111.

11. Watson, p.286. *Henry Holland* exhibition catalogue.

12. John Harris, *Regency Furniture Designs 1803-1826,* 1961, figs. vii, viii. See also Peter Ward-Jackson, *English Furniture Designs of the Eighteenth Century,* 1958, figs. 298-302, and Jill Lever, *Architects' Designs for Furniture,* R.I.B.A. Drawings Series 1982, nos. 19-21 for other Holland designs.

Commode, probably designed by Henry Holland, of rosewood with ebonised borders gilt mouldings and ormolu mounts. From Mrs. Whitbread's Room, Southill.

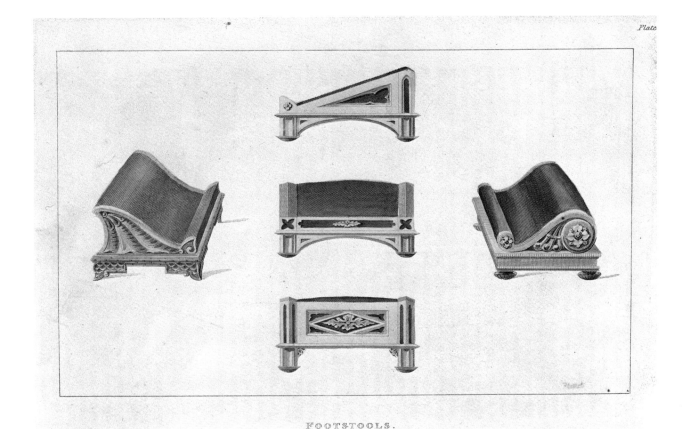

FOOTSTOOLS.

Plate 5. Designs for Footstools in the Chinese, Grecian and Gothic styles from Ackermann's *Repository,* Vol. X, October 1813, pl. 25. The stool on the right based on a Greek console was designed by Matthew Gregson, a Liverpool cabinetmaker and there are a pair of footstools after the design in Brighton Pavilion.

been supplied in 1790 by Francis Hervé, the London cabinet maker of French extraction.[13] The set consisting of four arm chairs (p.37), six chairs, four bergères and a banquette in four parts, illustrates definite French motifs in their straight, tapering legs, cut off corners of the top rail, and bird's head terminals to the arm supports although the pierced motifs of the front and side rails are less obviously Gallic and lighten the whole effect of the pieces. The set today includes two settees which were provided by Thomas Tatham in 1811 to enlarge the set when it had been moved to the Bow Room Principal Floor or Rose Satin Drawing Room where it can be seen in Pyne's engraving of 1817, re-upholstered in crimson damask (Frontispiece). Although the cost of the original upholstery materials, including yellow silk and brocade, accounted for over fifty percent of the total, in fact each chair cost more in real terms than other seat furniture provided by Hervé for Carlton House, probably because of the intricate nature of the pierced back and seat rails.[14]

13. de Bellaigue, *The Burlington,* 1967, pp.519-520.
14. The bills are listed by de Bellaigue, 1967, pp.520, 523.

One of a pair of chiffoniers, en suite with the commode (on page 40), of rosewood with ebonised banding, gilt mouldings and ormolu mounts and japanned open shelves. Probably made by Marsh.

The work of French craftsmen, whether working in London or Paris, can be seen in the two pier tables, one with Chinese caryatid supports echoing the design of the fireplace opposite as seen in Sheraton's engraving, and the other with carved drapery and tassels decoration and open curving shelves on the corners. Again Geoffrey de Bellaigue has shown that with their details of construction and the quality of the chasing of the mounts these tables are definitely of French workmanship, whether from émigré or Parisian makers.[15] Interestingly enough, copies were made of these two tables by the firm of Bailey and Saunders in 1819 for the four to be used in the Music Room Gallery at Brighton Pavilion, where two tables with caryatid supports and one of the others can be seen in Nash's view of 1824.

15. de Bellaigue, p.524. The tables are now in Buckingham Palace.

Tambour desk, rosewood with ormolu mounts, in the French style. Acquired for Southill, c.1811.

The interior decoration of the Chinese Drawing Room, with its Chinese and arabesque painting on the walls, doors and overdoors, was carried out by Jean Jacques Boileau, possibly assisted by his compatriots, L.A. Delabrière and A.J. de Chanlepie, while other furnishings, like the chimney piece, clock and possibly the candelabra were either inspired by French designs or actually of French manufacture. Although the seat furniture was made by Hervé, designs could have been supplied for these by Daguerre as his predecessor, William Gaubert, had done in 1787 and the tables certainly show French influence. It is debatable whether Holland should be credited with the overall design since both Gaubert and Daguerre worked as decorators as well as suppliers of furniture, and the effect of the room in Sheraton's engraving and the surviving pieces of furniture show a rather over-elaborate use of Chinese motifs, quite unlike Holland's usual chaste approach. His

Armchair, carved and gilded wood, one of a set of four similar to designs by Georges Jacob, at Southill. Footstool, rosewood with ormolu mounts, one of a pair formerly in the Boudoir at Southill.

almost simultaneous use of Chinese motifs for the dairy at Woburn and later at Brighton Pavilion illustrate his delicate understanding of this style.

This understated and elegant use of French taste can be seen in Holland's masterpiece, Southill,[16] which still survives today with the integral harmony of its furniture and interiors as designed by Holland for Samuel Whitbread II. Through Holland's work with the Prince of Wales, and members of the Whig opposition like Lord Spencer and the Duke of Bedford, he may have come into contact with Samuel Whitbread I who purchased Southill in 1795 and commissioned Holland to remodel the house. After his death in 1796, his son became Holland's client and it was he who acquired most of the furniture from 1796 until his death in 1815, when an Inventory was taken of the contents of the house which can be used to identify pieces today. Expenditure in the accounts for the period when Holland worked at Southill rose to a peak of over £2,000

16. *Southill A Regency House*, 1951. 'The Furniture and Decoration by F.J.B. Watson', pp.19-41.

Armchair, gilded wood, similar to the Southill type, c.1800.

in 1798 and remained high for several years, reaching a maximum in 1802 of nearly £4,000. Spending on furniture dropped until in 1807 only just over £100 appears in the accounts although in later years slightly larger sums were expended. Although only one design for the commode bookcase and the mirror above it in the library survive in Holland's sketch book in the RIBA, and Holland is only mentioned once in the Southill records, the furniture shows much of his taste and is so obviously influenced by French motifs of the understated effect that he favoured that he must have been personally involved in the design. A considerable amount of the furniture is shown by the accounts to have been supplied by firms that Holland had already used at Carlton House like Morel, Marsh, Lichfield and Tatham.[17]

Probably the most refined surviving example of Holland's adaptation of the Louis XVI style to an English interior is the boudoir at Southill with its white and brightly coloured

---

17. Watson, p.23.

Cabinet, rosewood and gilt with painted Chinese porcelain plaques and feet similar to those on the Southill commode and chiffoniers, c.1800.

Sideboard table, mahogany, c.1800, in the dining room at Southill with lion monopodia similar to those illustrated by Tatham.

Design for a tripod from C.H. Tatham's *Etchings*, 1800. Thomas Hope used very similar designs in *Household Furniture*, 1807.

Mahogany pedestal based on Tatham's drawing of the Barberini candle stand in the Vatican and made for Henry Holland c.1795-9.

Detail of the candle stand.

Pompeian style decoration, grisaille cameos and porphyry coloured roundels on the ceiling, and delicately gilded architectural details. The influence of such examples of the style Artois as the pavilion at Bagatelle, on the outskirts of the Bois de Boulogne, can be seen in this exquisite green and gold setting, with its faded green and white damask wall hangings. Most of the furniture originally made for this room can be identified with the help of the Inventory although some is now in other rooms but the 'rich green & white damask Curtains & Drapery, lined with silk & decorated with silk fringe'[18] have disintegrated although the rosewood gilded cornice survives. The Inventory states that the painted panel over the chimney glass and certain other architectural features were the work of Delabrière, presumably the same Delabrière who worked at Carlton House and probably also at the Bagatelle. He also painted the two adjustable fire screens and the pair of 'Round Seat Chairs with painted Tablet backs' (p.36) with their swan and urn motifs, a theme used in the boudoir at the Bagatelle.[19]

In a long letter written to his sister in April 1800, the Rev. Samuel Johnes, Rector of Welwyn, describes the boudoir and Mrs. Whitbread's sitting room next door, which were both finished by then. He was very much impressed by the rosewood china cabinet with ormolu mounts (p.38) made by Marsh in the boudoir which is perhaps the most French inspired of all the furniture at Southill, and as Sir Francis Watson has pointed out, could have been attributed to the workshop of Weisweiler, a French ébéniste supplying furniture to Holland's specification for Althorp in 1791.[20] The cabinet has the typical Weisweiler fluted and tapering feet while the ormolu mounts representing candelabra are very similar to those on the Louis XVI clock and barometer, now in the dining room, which bear Weisweiler's stamp and came from the French Royal Collection to Southill by 1816. Another piece of furniture of decidedly French taste originally in the sitting room is the shallow rosewood commode, (p.40) partly ebonised, with ormolu mounts and a large brass rosette on the front with a marble relief of a woman's head, probably made by Marsh and almost certainly designed by Holland. En suite are the pair of rosewood commodes (p.42) of a French form with the curving ends containing open shelves, reminiscent of the one in the Chinese Drawing Room at Carlton House, but with an unmistakably English addition of a small bookcase above the marble top. The commodes have ebonised borders and gilt and ormolu details, echoing the black and gold frames of the wall panels which originally contained 'rich chintz calico, bordered with calico border' to match the curtains, the calico being held in position by 'silk Rosettes' and ormolu palmettes.[21] Over the mantel-piece and between the windows opposite are mirrors supplied by Marsh and designed by Holland, each with a panel ornamented in relief with a honeysuckle design, this use of a decorative panel above a mirror being a favourite device of Holland's but going out of fashion soon afterwards.

18. 1816 Inventory quoted by Watson, p.27.
19. Watson, pp.26-7.
20. Watson, pp.27-8.
21. 1816 Inventory quoted by Watson, p.23.

Also in Mrs Whitbread's sitting room originally was the tambour writing desk (p.43) of figured rosewood with ormolu mounts, with a mixture of French and English motifs in its interlacing stretchers and bisected lyre devices, which was acquired slightly later for the house in 1811. It illustrates the Whitbread family's continuing interest in French style furniture after Holland had finished his work. In the drawing room are more pieces of furniture of decidedly French inspiration like the set of smaller sofas, single headed couches and chairs with their bolt-head decoration, the design of which can be traced back through Jacob's work to classical origins. There is a similar set of Louis XVI chairs at Brighton which came originally from Colworth. The large sofa with gilded frame and a tablet on the centre of the back also derives from a classical source, and the tablet and part of the frame were originally painted green as background to the gilt ornament, similar to a sofa at Weston Park. The pair of armchairs in the drawing room were originally in the boudoir where their French details of tapered, carved front legs and palm-leaf decoration would have blended in with the rest of the furniture there, though their design is more square and solid than a French equivalent would have been. The drawing room was entirely furnished after 1800 when the walls were hung with crimson and green material, while the curtains of red sarsnet with green manchester velvet draperies were hung from the gilt cornices with their draperies caught by the great eagles in the centre, a device Holland also used in the Rose Satin Drawing Room at Carlton House, one of the rare survivals of this typical Regency device.

After 1793 the unrest in France caused problems for Holland as his partner Daguerre would not have found it easy to commission pieces directly from the Parisian workshops. Although French furniture could be obtained in London, the pieces were mainly from the pre-Revolutionary period, either being sold by the French government who had seized them from the Royal and aristocratic collections or by émigrés desperate for money.[22] It was at this period that the English passion for collecting examples of French eighteenth century furniture and objects d'art as historical antiques really began. Sir Gilbert Elliot, later 1st Earl of Minto, wrote to his wife in 1790 'The quantity of French goods of all sorts, particularly ornamental furniture and jewels, has sunk the price of such things here.'[23] The Prince of Wales took enthusiastic advantage of this situation, buying through intermediaries at such auction sales as the one organised by the marchand-mercier Dominique Daguerre, in March 1791.[24] Perhaps the seeds of the later Rococo Revival in England can be seen in this wholesale dispersal of some of the best pieces of French eighteenth century furniture. Daguerre's death in 1795 effectively removed Holland's link with the Parisian furniture makers, although Daguerre's partner, Martin Eloi Lignereux, supplied various furnishings to the Prince of Wales and Lord Spencer.[25]

22. F.J.B. Watson, 'George IV as an Art Collector. Some Reflections on the Current Exhibition at the Queen's Gallery', *Apollo*, Vol. LXXXIII, No. 52, June 1966 pp.410-419.

23. *The Life and Letters of Sir Gilbert Elliot, First Earl of Minto, 1751-1806,* ed. the Countess of Minto, 1874, vol. 1 p.359, letter of 27 April 1790.

24.Stroud, p.76. Watson, *Apollo* 1966, pp.111-112.

25. Stroud, p.146.

Designs for friezes from C.H. Tatham's *Etchings of Ancient Ornamental Architecture,* 1800.

Unlike his contemporaries, Holland never studied classical remains in their native setting, and therefore had to rely on published sources of designs for Greek and Roman antiquities like Stuart and Revett's *Antiquities of Athens,* 1762. One of his assistants, Charles Heathcote Tatham, who joined him c.1789 and had a particular interest in French furniture and decoration, was to provide Holland with the means to develop designs for furniture based on classical remains. Holland's heavy commitments with Carlton House, Southill and other commissions resulted in him constantly searching for new inspiration, and the war with France cut him off from his normal sources, which had of course become so unpopular that the Prince of Wales was forced to abandon his Gallic leanings at Brighton for a new style '. . . the Prince says he had it so because at that time there was such a cry against French things &c., and he was afraid of his furniture being accus'd of jacobinism', Lady Bessborough wrote to Lord Granville in 1805.[26]

---

26. *Lord Granville Leveson Gower (First Lord Granville), Private Correspondence 1781 to 1821,* ed. Castalia Countess Granville, 1916, vol. 11, p.120 letter of 9th October 1805.

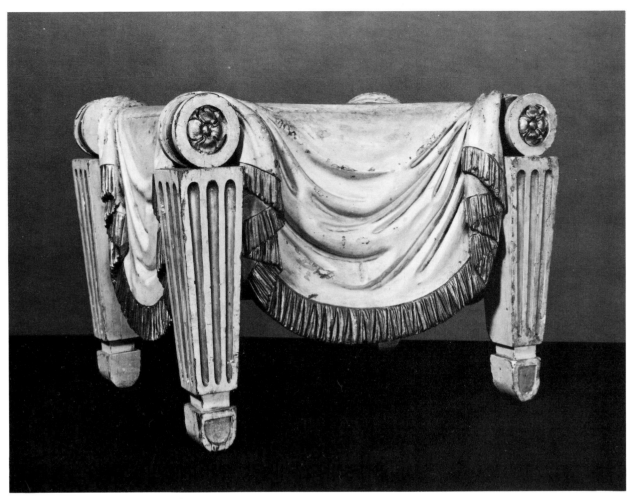

Stool, beechwood painted white and gold with traces of marbling, c.1800.

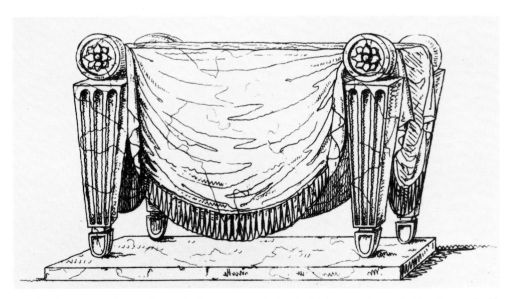

Design for a seat from Tatham's *Etchings,* pl.46, 1799 which was to be copied by George Smith for hall seats.

Design for antique seats of white marble from Tatham's *Etchings, 1799.*

Tatham went to Italy between 1794-7 in order to provide Holland with new ideas about which he wrote to him in a series of illustrated letters,[27] and which he published in his largest single contribution to the development of Regency furniture design, *Etchings of Ancient Ornamental Architecture drawn from the Originals in Rome and Other Parts of Italy during the years 1794, 1795, and 1796* (p.51). Although the title page is dated 1799 many of the plates are dated 1800, and the book achieved tremendous popularity, going through three editions by 1810, and was obviously used by Hope in his *Household Furniture* of 1807, although he does not acknowledge Tatham's invaluable work. Tatham's method of illustrating antique furniture based on the results of the eighteenth century excavations at Pompeii, Herculaneum, Tivoli and Rome in outline engravings followed the technique pioneered by Flaxman which was to be used by Hope and by Percier and Fontaine in their *Receuil de Décorations Intérieures,* 1812. Tatham was to introduce such familiar Regency motifs as the lion-headed monopodia which, translated from their marble, stone or bronze originals were to enhance such pieces as the sideboard tables (p.47) in the dining room at Southill. Sometimes such features were bronzed in imitation of their ancient Roman prototypes as in the supports of the rosewood writing table in Mrs. Whitbread's sitting room, while his lion masks holding rings appear on the kingwood carved and gilt writing table and the large monopodium kingwood table, both in the drawing room. David Udy has identified other features of the furniture at Southill which originate in Tatham's publication.[28]

27. A Collection of original letters and drawings, principally from C.H. Tatham to Henry Holland, 1794-1796. Victoria and Albert Museum, Print Room (D 1479/1551-1898).

28. David Udy, 'The Neo Classicism of Charles Heathcote Tatham', *The Connoisseur,* Vol. 77 No. 714, August 1971, pp.269-276.

Cabinet, pollard yew inlaid with ebony, with ormolu mounts and bronze busts. One of a set supplied for Carlton House in 1806 by Marsh and Tatham and possibly designed by C.H. Tatham.

Tatham also collected architectural and decorative fragments from archaeological sites in the vicinity of Rome which he sent to Holland by the beginning of 1796. These were to provide Holland with inspiration for his work at Southill as can be seen in the lively acanthus and anthemion scrollwork panel over the drawing room chimney piece, and in the panels above the pier glasses in the library where the griffins flanking tripods are based on part of the frieze of the Aldobrandini Palace. The design of the set of four carved tripod stands now at Buckingham Palace, supplied in 1811 for Carlton House by Tatham, Bailey and Saunders, can be traced back through one of Tatham's drawings to an antique candelabra in the Farnese Collection at the Royal Palace in Capodimonte.[29]

Other pieces of furniture that can be proved to be based on Tatham's drawings of antique Roman remains include a mahogany pedestal (p.48) based on the drawing Holland received of the Barberini candelabrum in the Vatican Museum. Holland acquired a cast of the original, and using it as a model ordered a copy half the size

29. Christopher Proudfoot and David Watkin, 'The Furniture of C.H. Tatham', *Country Life*, Vol. CLI, No. 3912, June 8th 1972, pp.1481-1486. Many of Tatham's classical fragments are now in Sir John Soane's Museum, having been acquired by Soane in 1821.

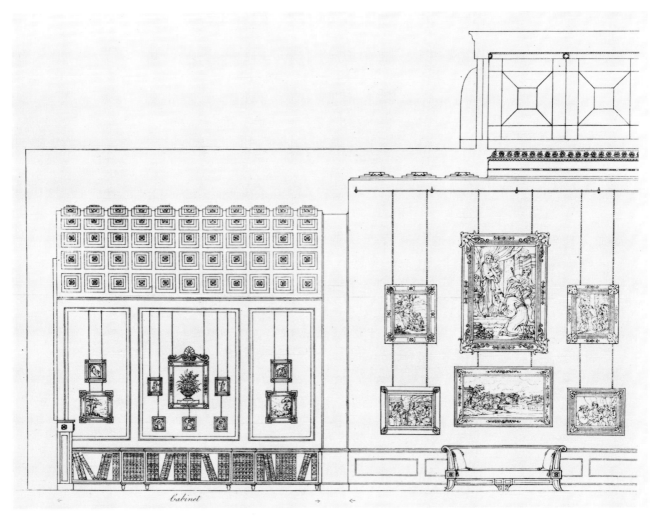

Design for the Gallery, Brocklesby from C.H. Tatham's *The Gallery at Brocklesby,* 1811, showing bookcases and a sofa perhaps designed by Tatham.

of the original, possibly intended for Carlton House.[30] This change of size and material from the original to the copy can be seen in other examples of monumental pieces of furniture based on antique remains, as in the stool (p.52) based on a design on plate 46 of Tatham's publication, where the original carved stone was translated into marbled paintwork on the beechwood Regency copy.

Although nothing definite is known about the cabinet maker responsible for these pieces of furniture, it is very likely that they were made by Marsh and Tatham who were Holland's principal collaborators at Carlton House, Southill and Brighton Pavilion after the disappearance of Daguerre and Jean Pierre Trécourt by death or illness between 1795-6.[31] Thomas Tatham, who founded the partnership with William Marsh in 1802, was Charles Heathcote Tatham's brother, and presumably would have profited from his brother's professional association with the most successful and influential architect of the time. There is in fact some furniture which might be associated with C.H. Tatham himself and this includes a pair of console

30. Udy, pp.271-274. The pedestal is now at Kenwood.
31. Stroud, p.84.

tables supported on gilded dolphins from the gallery at Cleveland House, and an antique marble seat in the orangery at Brocklesby Park where Tatham is known to have worked.[32] Tatham's publications of antique Roman remains were popular enough to introduce Regency furniture designers to the more strictly archaeological theories about furniture and interior design which were to be elaborated by Thomas Hope, and the importance of Tatham's contribution to this development was recognised by later commentators.[33]

Holland's responsibility for the use of characteristic French motifs and designs in English interiors and furniture of this period of the early Regency, and his development of the classically French harmony of interior decoration have all survived in his small masterpiece at Southill, but Carlton House, the palace he built for his most important and probably most demanding patron, has been demolished. Holland withdrew from royal service after 1802 and was replaced at Carlton House by the decorator, Walsh Porter, about whom Farington commented in his Diary in May 1806. 'Lysons said the Prince of Wales is incurring vast expenses. Although Carlton House as finished by Holland was in a complete and new state, he has ordered the whole to be done again under the direction of Walsh Porter who has destroyed all that Holland has done & is substituting a finishing in a most extensive and motley taste.'[34]

---

32. Proudfoot and Watkin, p.1484.

33. *The Dictionary of Architecture,* Architectural Publication Society 1853-92, Vol. III, p.104.

34. Joseph Farington, R.A., *The Farington Diary,* ed. by James Greig 1924, vol. III, p.214. Walsh Porter was not a professional architect or designer but an enthusiastic collector with some talent as an interior decorator, particularly expressed in his house at Fulham.

2. Thomas Sheraton and the Pattern Books of the Early Regency

Designers like Henry Holland and C.H. Tatham worked for a relatively small clientèle who demanded furniture of high quality and exclusive design. These designs were copied for use by more ordinary cabinet makers through the medium of the books of patterns for furniture produced by authors such as George Hepplewhite, Thomas Sheraton and George Smith. Generally these interpreters of fashionable taste were not cabinet makers themselves but simply publicisers of furniture designs suitable for the vast number of ordinary cabinet makers, '. . . .to be useful to the mechanic and serviceable to the gentleman. With this view, after having fixed upon such articles as were necessary to a complete suit of furniture, our judgement was called forth in selecting such patterns as were most likely to be of general use — in choosing such points of view as would shew them most distinctly — and in exhibiting such fashions as were necessary to answer the end proposed, and convey a just idea of English taste in furniture for houses'[1] as Hepplewhite said. His publication, *The Cabinet Maker and Upholsterer's Guide,* was the pioneer of these popularising handbooks, first appearing in 1788 with subsequent editions in 1789 and 1794. There were, however, changes in the last edition, probably due to criticism by Sheraton in 1791, and rococo designs, particularly those for cabriole legs, were replaced by patterns for more fashionable square backed chairs (p.59). Generally Hepplewhite's illustrations were designs in the Adam style already in fashion, but he was responsible for the motif of the three Prince of Wales' feathers as a decorative feature for the back splats of chairs and as a device for inlay at the tops of table legs. Although he claimed that one of his chair designs had been made for the Prince of Wales there is no trace of his name in the Royal Accounts.[2]

However, Hepplewhite may have been responsible for one of the most familiar Regency designs which appeared in the second edition of *The Cabinet Makers' London Book of Prices, and Designs of Cabinet Work,* published in 1793 as a practical guide for regulating and calculating labour charges or piecework rates when making specific pieces of cabinet furniture.[3] This pattern book includes a plate signed Hepplewhite and dated October 1792, entitled 'A Gentleman's Writing Table', which in fact shows a Carlton House table (p.58), with tapering square legs and alternative patterns for the top of three tiers of drawers on the left and a writing slope with one drawer on the right. This and the other plates signed Hepplewhite were presumably supplied by his widow, Alice, who carried on the business after her husband's death in 1786. Sheraton was to copy this design in 1793 with his Lady's Drawing and Writing Table, plate 60 in his *Cabinet-Maker and Upholsterer's Drawing Book,* which shows the table with supports linked by an unbecoming tier. Gillows also featured the Carlton House table in their Cost Books in 1796-8 and the

---

1. A Hepplewhite and Co., Cabinet-Makers, *The Cabinet-Maker and Upholsterer's Guide,* 3rd edition 1794, Preface.

2. See Clifford Musgrave, *Adam and Hepplewhite and other Neo-Classical Furniture,* 1966.

3. This was reprinted in *Furniture History,* Vol. XVIII, 1982. See also Ralph Fastnedge, *Shearer Furniture Designs,* 1962.

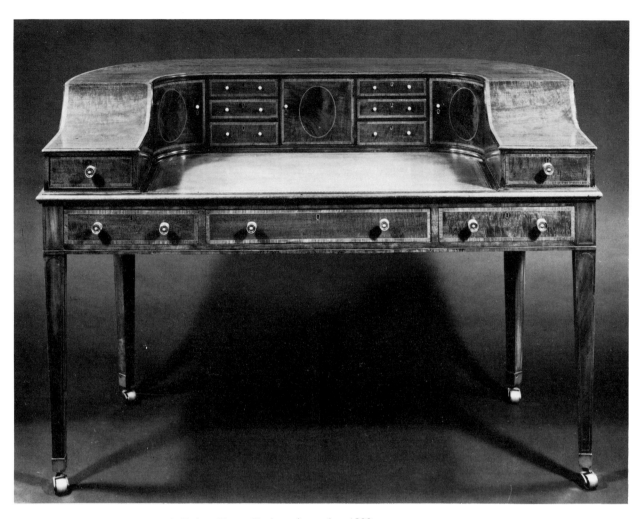

A Carlton House Desk, satinwood, c.1800.

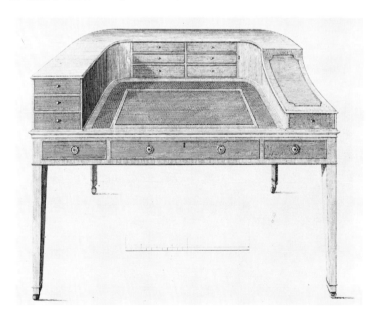

A Gentleman's Writing Table from *The Cabinet-Makers' London Book of Prices,* 1793, signed by Hepplewhite, showing alternative designs for drawers.

Chair, mahogany, c.1795, similar to a design published by Hepplewhite, 1794, with a square back copied from Sheraton.

Plate 6. The Library, Frogmore, from W.H. Pyne's *History of the Royal Residences,* Vol. I, 1817, showing a chair and library steps combination on the left, furniture with loose covers concealing their shapes and a davenport positioned in front of an armchair on the right.

pattern was still being produced twenty years later, though with turned legs ornamented with fluting or reeding.[4]

The Cabinet-Maker's London Book of Prices also included, besides six rather progressive ideas by Hepplewhite, designs by Thomas Shearer and William Casement, both presumably cabinet makers, the latter in fact being one of Sheraton's subscribers in 1793. Shearer reissued many of the plates under his own name in *Designs for Household Furniture* in 1788, which suggests some kind of professional connection between him and Alice Hepplewhite, particularly since designs for a Rudd's Table (p.62) appear both in Hepplewhite's *Guide,* dated 1787, and in the 1793 edition of the *Book of Prices,* signed by Shearer and dated 1788. The *Book of Prices* however only included cabinet furniture as seat furniture, carving, upholstery

4. Geoffrey Wills, 'The Carlton House Writing-Table', *Apollo,* Vol. LXXXIII, No. 50, April 1966, pp.256-261.

Harlequin Writing and Dressing Table, mahogany veneered with harewood, tulipwood, box, and oak, c.1790. Based on two slightly different designs in *The Cabinet-Makers' London Book of Prices,* 1788, pls. 10 and 19.

and small fancy articles were produced by separate branches of the trade. Generally the designs, although not very sophisticated, represent the popular trend in furniture and there are a large number of extant pieces which can be identified with the plates in the *Book of Prices.* Christopher Gilbert has pointed out that careful study of the text and plates can elucidate certain interesting points about cabinet furniture, such as the function of the glass bowl as a container for sugar in teapoys, and that decorative marquetry shells were provided ready made for cabinet makers from specific suppliers.[5]

In his introduction to *The Cabinet-Maker and Upholsterer's Drawing Book,* published in parts between 1791-4, Thomas Sheraton reviewed earlier pattern books, including Thomas Chippendale's *The Gentleman and Cabinet-Maker's Director* and

---

5. Christopher Gilbert, 'London and Provincial Books of Prices: Comment and Bibliography', *Furniture History,* Vol. XVIII, 1982, p.14.

Dressing table, mahogany with inlay, after a Rudd's Table design by Shearer 1788 included by Hepplewhite 1794.

Ince and Mayhew's *Universal System of Household Furniture,* and referred disparagingly to the old fashioned nature of Hepplewhite's designs, though he admitted the *Guide* was useful as a reminder of the taste of former times.[6] Sheraton actually praised the *Book of Prices* as illustrating prices for cabinet furniture but qualifies this by pointing out that it could not pretend to be a Book of Designs. His publication was intended to remedy this by including new designs in Part III 'intended to exhibit the present taste of furniture, and at the same time to give the workmen some assistance in the manufacturing part of it.'[7] The importance of Perspective and Geometry for cabinet makers and others in the furniture trades was emphasised by their inclusion in Parts I and II as Sheraton considered these subjects had been neglected by furniture makers, 'Books of various designs in cabinet work, ornamented according to the taste of the times in which they were published, have already appeared. But none of these, as far as I know, profess to give any instructions relative to the art of making perspective drawings, or to treat of such geometrical lines as ought to be known by persons of both professions, especially such of them as have a number of men under their directions.'[8] Sheraton in fact advertised

6. Sheraton had obviously forgotten that Hepplewhite had contributed designs to both his own book and to *The Cabinet-Makers' London Book of Prices.*

7. *Drawing Book,* 1802 edition, Part III, p.289.

8. *Drawing Book,* 1802 edition, p.17.

Table, rosewood with boxwood inlay, after a more elaborate design for a Lady's Writing Table dated 1792 from the *Drawing Book,* pl. XXXVII.

Table, satinwood, similar to the design for a French Work Table, pl. LIV in the *Drawing Book*.

himself as a teacher of Perspective, Architecture and Ornament and a seller of Drawing Books on his trade card and, although he is believed only to have worked as a journeyman cabinet maker in his early years in the North, the title page of the *Drawing Book* describes him as 'Cabinet-Maker'.

The *Drawing Book* was to be the most influential pattern book of the period up to the publication of Thomas Hope's *Household Furniture and Decoration* in 1807, a second edition appearing in 1794 with additional plates, and a third in 1802 with further illustrations. Perhaps the most important feature of his designs was their popularisation of the French style, particularly in the illustrations of the Chinese Drawing Room at Carlton House (p.35) with furniture now attributed to Henry Holland and Francis Hervé, indicating Sheraton's awareness of the fashionable francophile movement which was just emerging under the encouragement of the

Plate 7. Armchair, painted satinwood, part of a set of furniture supplied by Seddon, Sons and Shackleton to D. Tupper of Hauteville House, Guernsey, in 1790, each chair costing £66. 3s.

Cabinet, satinwood with gilded brass decoration, taken from a design for a Lady's Cabinet, pl. 16 *Drawing Book*, where the marble shelves at either end were intended for 'a tea equipage' and the fall front was supported on a drawer below or on brass arms inside.

Pair of mahogany chairs, taken from the design for Parlour Chairs, pl. 33 in the *Drawing Book*.

Backs for Painted Chairs, pl. 25 in the *Drawing Book*.

Plate 8. Secretaire-bookcase, satinwood painted in various colours and inlaid with different woods, some stained, c.1785. The hinged front of the top drawer lets down on metal quadrants, released by press-buttons, to form a writing surface.

Table, mahogany, from Southill copied from the design for a Lady's Work Table, pl. 54 *Drawing Book*.

Prince of Wales and his circle. Other features of French influence can be seen in the designs for Duchesse and French State Beds, Chaise Longues, chairs for dining rooms, and in references to French taste in furnishing drawing rooms and in upholstery. Sheraton admitted that he had obtained ideas from various sources and some of them are acknowledged in the text, like the anonymous originator of the Harlequin Pembroke Table and Mr. Thompson, groom of the household furniture to the Duke of York, but it is likely that he was responsible for the development of many ideas since he refers to the views of his subscribers who 'say many of the designs are rather calculated to shew what may be done, than to exhibit what is or has been done in the trade'.[9] Among the 700 or so subscribers listed in the first edition were cabinet makers, upholsterers, joiners, carvers and gilders, chair makers and makers of musical instruments, all of whom would have been interested as members of the trade, but also included are engravers, painters and drawing masters, indicating Sheraton's professional circle. However there are no wealthy patrons, either Royalty or nobility, included in the list, a sign of Sheraton's position as an interpreter of fashionable taste to the trade rather than as a supplier of fine furniture

9. Ibid., Part III, p.292.

A LADY'S DRESSING COMMODE.

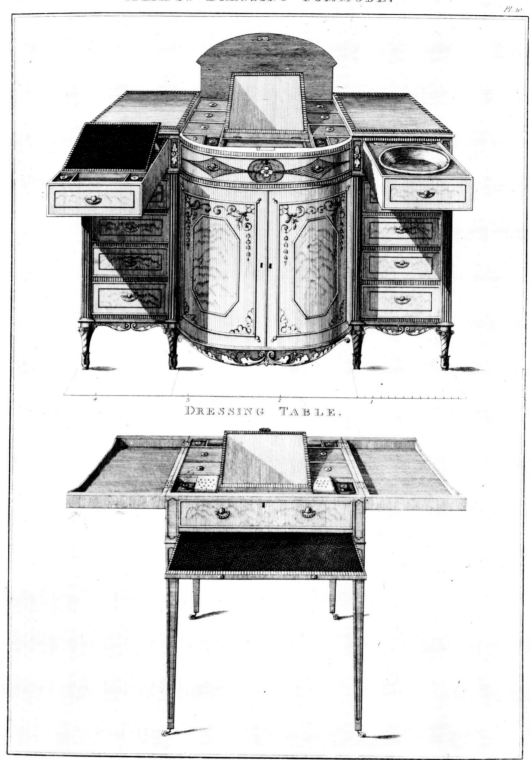

DRESSING TABLE.

Designs for a Lady's Dressing Commode and a Dressing Table, pl. 20 *Drawing Book.*

Dressing table, mahogany veneered with harewood, satinwood and tulipwood, similar to designs published by Hepplewhite, pl.72, and Sheraton, pl. XX Appendix.

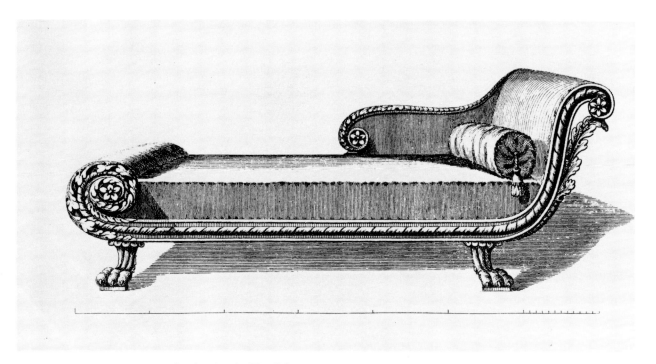

Grecian Squab, *The Cabinet Dictionary*, 1802, pl. 50.

to the rich. Two-thirds of the subscribers were based in London and a third in the provinces, mainly from the north-east, Sheraton's old home, although Scotland was also well represented.

Sheraton was responsible for popularising a number of features which were to appear in furniture until the early years of the nineteenth century and perhaps the most familiar aspect of these were those for painted decoration in the Italian style, echoing the designs of Angelica Kauffmann and others, with floral garlands and sprays, nymphs and vases all appearing in the back splats of chairs, on table tops and on the fronts of commodes (pp.67, 70). He recommended using inlay of contrasting woods, especially of sycamore or mahogany on satinwood, frequently in the form of a shell in the centre of a table top or tray, or in a fan-like shape in the corners of a table or box (pp.71, 78). Interestingly the *Book of Prices* included a design by Shearer dated 1788 which showed a kneehole desk and a sideboard, both with the same fan-like motif in the angle of the top and the supports. Sheraton showed slender, square tapered legs and fluted legs with decorative carved plumes at the tops for tables, cabinet furniture and chairs. The backs of chairs had vertical designs (p.67), usually incorporating motifs like plumes, ribbons and drapery while the arms were set high, with either a right angle join, a flattened scroll or a continuous downward curve. Various decorative motifs like swags, guilloches and urns showed Sheraton's use of Adam designs. Although most of these designs were to disappear within a few years, their use by cabinet makers was to be revived in the later nineteenth century.

However, Sheraton was also innovative and some of his ideas survived well into the nineteenth century, including the lyre form on splayed feet as a support for such items as writing tables and work tables (p.69). Again he used a design from the *Book of Prices*, that of the kidney-shaped Social Table by Hepplewhite dated 1792, and presents it as a refined piece of dining room furniture which was to remain popular for some years. He referred to the current fashion in dining tables, 'a large range of dining tables, standing on pillars with four claws each, which is now the

Chair, painted beech, c.1795. Backs with a raised centre section in the top-rail were featured by Hepplewhite, 1788, pls. 6 and 11 and also in Sheraton, 1791-4, pls. 32-6.

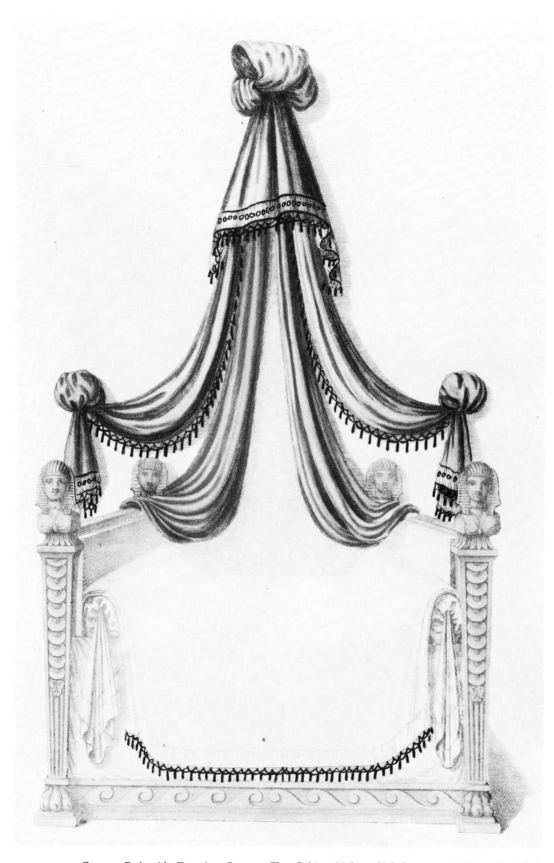

Canopy Bed with Egyptian figures, *The Cabinet-Maker, Upholsterer and General Artist's Encyclopaedia*, 1805, pl. 2.

Occasional table, rosewood veneer on oak and mahogany carcase with gilt bronze border and gallery and boxwood stringing, c.1805. Similar to the design for Pouch Tables, pl. 65 in *The Cabinet Dictionary*, said to have been supplied by John McLean, Marylebone Lane, Tottenham Court Road.

fashionable way of making these tables',[10] again a design which was to survive into the nineteenth century. Other features advocated in the *Drawing Book* which survived after 1800, included bow or concave fronted chests of drawers and commodes, horizontal designs for chair backs, the use of reeding for the legs of tables and chairs and as an edging for shelves, splayed claw feet for tripod and table supports and splayed bracket feet for commodes and chests, and the use of stringing lines of inlay in wood, and later in brass.

---

10. Ibid., Part III, p.359.

Bookcase, mahogany with bronzed composition busts of Charles James Fox, William Pitt, Admiral Nelson and Admiral Duncan and gilt bronze mounts, c.1810. Design taken from *The Encyclopaedia*, dated June 1806.

Table, rosewood, c.1810, similar to a design for a sideboard and pedestals, pl. 32, *The Encyclopaedia*. Margaret Jourdain illustrated an almost identical writing table from Heveningham Hall in *Regency Furniture* 1949, fig. 139.

Sheraton illustrated in the *Drawing Book* suggestions for different types of ornament, figurative, floral and architectural, with instructions on japanning, carving and gilding for these and for furniture. He advocated the use of mahogany for dining rooms, libraries and more masculine pieces like library desks and washstands, while satinwood was recommended for drawing room furniture, with decoration like fluting for the mahogany pieces, while satinwood was combined with japanning and sometimes with crossbanding as in the lady's writing table. Painting and gilding was considered suitable for the drawing room and for feminine pieces like the sofa bed. Brass mouldings could be used with satinwood, for edgings around

Clothes press, mahogany inlaid with various woods, c.1795, with the label of 'Mant, Upholder &
Cabinet Maker, High Street, Winchester'. John Mant was also an appraiser, auctioneer and may
have sold furniture from London. His label has also been found on a cylinder front desk, c.1795.

Label from inside the clothes press.

marble shelves and table tops, and for pieces made of black rosewood with tulip crossbanding, while Wedgwood plaques were considered suitable for ornamenting commodes in the drawing room. His designs are distinctive in their use of drapery for beds, naturally, but also for curtains behind the doors of carcase furniture and around the bottom of such dissimilar pieces as chaise longues, ladies' worktables and ladies' cabinet dressing tables, sometimes giving a rather incongruous effect.

Sheraton's second book of designs, the *Cabinet Dictionary,* was published in 1803 and was less successful than the *Drawing Book,* although it was to introduce the Greek style with a collection of typically Regency features such as animal monopodia and lion's heads and paws, and was to further develop the French influence originally seen in the work of the Anglo-French group of craftsmen who worked with Holland. Again there is very little claim to originality in his designs but his sensitivity to the changing moods of taste, and his refined treatment of existing prototypes illustrate his importance as a forecaster of future styles. He also suggested principles for tasteful interior decoration for every room and included a Treatise on Painting as a response to the demand for fancy furniture, with specific instructions on techniques for decorating furniture, walls and panels. The *Dictionary* covered a wide range of subjects, including botany, allegorical symbols and metals, besides the expected topics of furniture, construction and techniques. Also included was a list of Master Cabinet Makers, Upholsterers, and Chair Makers in and around London.

Included in the *Dictionary* was the first illustration of that typical Regency piece, the couch with a scroll end and lion's paw feet (p.72), epitomising the adaptation of Greek ideas which Sheraton and, later, George Smith were to popularise. In fact Sheraton showed both types of this idea, one being the sofa with ends of similar height and design and with an upholstered back, and the other the couch with one low end and a short scrolled arm. In his description of the plates Sheraton speaks of having some of the later French chairs which 'follow the antique taste and introduce into their arms and legs various heads of animals.'[11] From this point animal motifs are increasingly to be found in furniture, echoing the designs of

---

11. Thomas Sheraton, *The Cabinet Dictionary,* 1803, p.146.

C.H. Tatham, with the use of lion masks and heads as the capitals of legs, lion paw feet, and animal monopodia, lions, griffins and other classical beasts, forming supports for tables. Designs incorporating dolphin and eagle motifs, reminiscent of the furniture designs of William Kent in the early eighteenth century, also appear though with a greater delicacy and on a smaller scale than their Kentian counterparts. Other designs based on the Antique included one for a 'Grecian Dining Table' which was made in several sections to be joined together, and chairs called 'Herculaniums' which featured arms ending in small scrolls on concave supports curving to the front legs and decorated with female heads. Chair legs followed a number of styles including inward curving back legs, later to be refined into the scimitar or sabre leg, and crossing double curved supports, paired back and front, which were sometimes of circular section and sometimes of square. The latter type are also to be seen as supports for writing and work tables.

The French influence can be seen in the turned legs with raised rings representing lengths of bamboo, shown as supports for 'Supper Canterburies' or for sets of 'Quartetto Tables' (p.12), which are very similar to designs for guéridons made by French masters like Jacob and Weisweiler. Other distinct Louis XIV features can be seen in the delicate colonnettes which form the angles at the corners of bookcases, cabinets and sideboards, reminiscent of the china cabinet (p.38) at Southill by Marsh, and in the curricle shaped chairs, similar to bergères. Sheraton recommended brass borders, beading and stringing for decoration on dark woods, such as rosewood or coromandel, and mentions French superiority in this technique, 'In the brass work adapted for cabinet work, the French far exceed this country; as well as in their manner of gilding, stiled or-molu. The elegance of their furniture chiefly depends upon their superior brass work: I am informed, however, that there are one or two English brass founders in London, not much inferior to the French.'[12]

Mahogany was still fashionable though Sheraton considered the Spanish or Cuban type more suitable than the Honduras because of the former's clean, straight grain which would give a brighter and cleaner finish when polished. Carving and gilding and painting were again proposed, with painted black rosewood with gilding, and such deceptions as turned and painted beech in imitation of bamboo being particularly recommended. Woods were stained for use with inlaying, red and black stains being 'most in use', for example holly wood, dyed black, as a suggestion for corner lines. The introduction of caning, particularly for the backs and seats of chairs, and for bed heads and steps, was linked with the revival of japanning, both echoes of the seventeenth century. 'About 30 years since, it was gone quite out of fashion, partly owing to the imperfect manner in which it was executed.'[13] Silk curtains were again shown behind brass trellis in the doors of commodes with green, white or pink silk being considered the most suitable.

---

12. *Cabinet Dictionary*, p.95.
13. Ibid., p.126. Thomas Martin in *The New Circle of the Mechanical Arts*, 1819, p.117, also referred to the revival of cane work in connection with japanned furniture and new uses for it, including panels set in mahogany for the ends of beds.

Pair of torchères, gilded wood, perhaps supplied by George Seddon and Sons and J. Shackleton in 1790 for D. Tupper of Hauteville House, St. Peter Port, Guernsey.

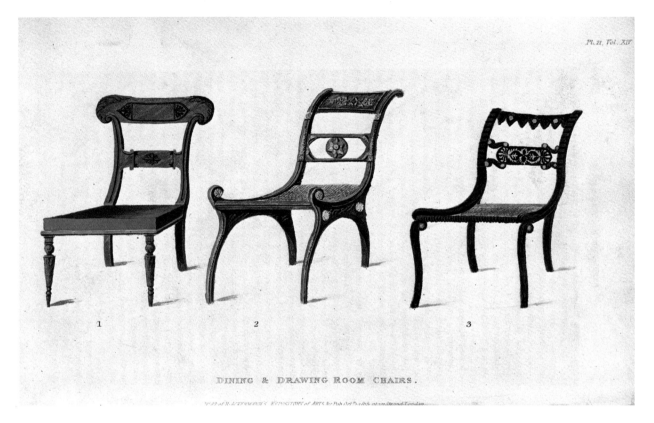

Plate 9. Dining and Drawing Room Chairs from Ackermann's *Repository,* Vol. XIV, October 1815, pl.21. The dining chair on the left in mahogany with ebony inlay and leather upholstery contrasts with the more elaborate designs for drawing rooms for which rosewood or coromandel, silver or ormolu mounts, and silk or chintz upholstery were recommended.

Sheraton's last book, *The Cabinet-Maker, Upholsterer and General Artist's Encyclopaedia* was published in parts between 1804-6, but only 30 of the projected 125 parts appeared before his mental illness and death in 1806. Some of the designs illustrate Sheraton's disturbed mental state, like the chair with shaggy lion legs and camels forming the back decorated with drapery, or the pier table with more elaborate drapery and pairs of hairy animal paw feet. However Sheraton was still capable of capitalising on current fashions and illustrated for the first time designs in the Egyptian taste, including terminal figures with sphinxes' heads forming bed heads (p.74), or capitals and bases for cabinets, bookcases, or sideboards. Although rather elementary in form his illustrations of such motifs were revolutionary and were to be copied by others after his death. He also showed designs in the Gothic taste, including a bookcase with ogee panels and a pier table with clustered legs, and designs for 'Nelson's Chairs' festooned with ropes, anchors, dolphins and other

Commode, rosewood with gilded decoration. Supplied by Gillows, c.1800 for Clonbrock, Co. Galway.

suitable naval detail.

Sheraton's publications, particularly the *Drawing Book,* epitomise in their decorative elegance the style of the early Regency which he interpreted for the use of cabinet makers and other craftsmen. Peter Ward Jackson has described his originality, 'Though he borrowed some of his ideas from others and worked in the fashionable style of the day, each of his books displays throughout a firm consistency of style which indicates that most of the designs were his own inventions; and his skill in handling new ideas suggests that he was among those who led rather than followed the fashion.'[14] In response to the claim made by Ralph Fastnedge,[15] that

14. Peter Ward-Jackson, *Victoria and Albert Museum English Furniture Designs of the Eighteenth Century,* 1958, p.66.
15. Ralph Fastnedge, *Sheraton Furniture,* 1963.

Writing table, mahogany, c.1810. Similar to designs in the Gillow *Estimate Sketch Books,* 1806 and typical of their restrained and elegant pieces.

Sheraton simply illustrated ideas already current, Ralph Edwards wrote 'There is much too big a gap between the rather dull Adamitic vernacular of Hepplewhite's *Guide* (1788) and the fin de siècle feminine elegance of the *Drawing Book* plates to be accounted for by what Mr. Fastnedge calls the "overall stylistic development of the decade". An overwhelming proportion of the plates witness to a single creative mind gifted with a remarkable faculty for decorative design'.[16] Since Sheraton himself referred to his intention to illustrate 'the present taste of furniture' and to give craftsmen assistance in construction and techniques, his role might appear to be more of an interpreter than an innovator, though the influence of his ideas can be seen in the large number of pieces of furniture which exhibit features first published by Sheraton, and in the popular revival of his style which took place in the later nineteenth century.

Among cabinet making firms prominent during the 1790s were two particularly well-known firms, Gillows and Seddons, both of whom flourished right through the Regency period and well into the nineteenth century. Gillows, originally founded in Lancaster in the early eighteenth century, opened a London branch at 176 Oxford Road in 1769. In spite of this they remained essentially a provincial firm but a very important one, since Lancaster as a flourishing port had good connections not only with the rest of Britain but with the West Indies, bringing in readily available raw materials and providing good export routes. As Catholics the Gillow family could

16. Ralph Edwards, 'Review of *Sheraton Furniture'*, *The Burlington Magazine*, Vol. CV, No. 718, January 1963, p.36.

expect to be patronised by many of the prominent families in the north-west and they were also in a position to take advantage of cheaper labour than in the capital. They had a high reputation at the end of the eighteenth and beginning of the nineteenth century and produced several pieces after designs by Sheraton (including his Alcove Bed), and Hepplewhite.[17] Through their records which survive it is possible to trace their innovations including designs for dining tables, one of ten sections, measuring up to 24 feet being recorded in 1795. In 1800 Richard Gillow took out a patent for an Imperial extending dining table with a system of slides which supported the flaps and thus reduced the number of legs, pillars and claws. They are also known to have featured designs for revolving bookshelves, a small tiered set of book shelves of circular form (p.16) where each shelf could be moved separately, and davenports (p.14), first noted in their records in 1816 as 'library cabinet of drawers' and featured as davenports in 1819. In 1807 the firm, then run by George and Richard Gillow, was described as among the 'first grade manufacturers in London; their work is good, and solid though not of the first class in inventiveness and style.'

The firm of Seddon was founded by George Seddon in the early 1750s at London House, Aldersgate Street and in spite of three fires at the workshops in 1768, 1783 and 1790 the business flourished with different branches being established by members of the family in Charterhouse Street, Dover Street and Lower Grosvenor Street. Thomas, grandson of the founder, stood as surety for his brother George when he and Nicholas Morel joined up to provide furniture and furnishings for the new interiors created by George IV at Windsor Castle, and the large Seddon workshops were used to make many of the pieces required. Seddons are also known to have been associated with some patent furniture designs including the croft (p.23), an early form of filing cabinet thought to have been invented by the Rev. Sir Herbert Croft, and some other pieces of dual-purpose furniture patented in 1798 by Day Gunby, carpenter of Hatton Garden, including a patent pembroke table with an elevating section of drawers and pigeon holes. A detailed description of the workshops in 1786 by Sophie von la Roche[18] included the information that Seddon 'employs four hundred apprentices on any work connected with the making of household furniture — joiners, carvers, gilders, mirror-workers, upholsterers girdlers — who mould the bronze into graceful patterns — and locksmiths. All these are housed in a building with six wings.' The establishment also contained showrooms full of furniture and upholstery workshops, in fact 'anything one might desire to furnish a house' and the 'entire story of the wood, as used for both inexpensive and costly furniture and the method of treating it, can be traced in this establishment.'

---

17. Ivan Hall, 'Patterns of Elegance. The Gillows' Furniture Designs I', *Country Life,* Vol. CLXIII, No. 4222, June 8th 1978, pp.1612-15, 'Models with a choice of leg. The Gillows' Furniture Designs. II', *Country Life,* Vol. CLXIII, No. 4223, June 15 1978, pp.1740-2.
18. *Sophie in London* 1786 being the Diary of Sophie v. la Roche, trans. by Clare Williams, 1933, pp.173-5.

3. Thomas Hope and Greek Revival

The most important figure in the development of the taste for the antique as formulated by Henry Holland and Charles Tatham was Thomas Hope the banker, collector and theorist, who in the designs he published of the furniture and interiors of his house, in his collections of classical objects, and in his patronage of craftsmen, was to prove the most influential authority on the next phase of Regency design.[1] Hope was a member of a rich and cultivated Amsterdam family, who fled to England in 1795 to escape the French invasion of Holland, and who had some architectural training and personal knowledge of archaeological remains through his tour of Greece, Turkey, Asia Minor, Syria and Egypt. He was to use such experience and the knowledge gained from his distinguished collection of classical antiquities, Greek vases, contemporary neoclassical sculpture, and Italian and Dutch paintings to develop his theories on the Classical Revival in its most severe form.

Hope's characteristics included a partiality for ostentation, although expense was carefully planned, and a conviction that France was the centre of European civilisation. He visited France regularly and through his friendship with the royal French designers, Percier and Fontaine, who had been appointed in 1799 to refurbish the royal palaces plundered during the Revolution, was to be influenced by the Empire style as advocated by them in their *Recueil de Décorations Intérieures,* some designs of which were available in 1801, although it was not published in its complete form until 1812. Although Percier, Fontaine and Hope used an outline form of illustration in their publications which showed a common familiar grasp of the Classical styles of furniture the elaborate detail and sumptuous upholstery of the Empire style was quite a contrast to Hope's clean lines and refined decoration, as interpreted in his authorative *Household Furniture and Interior Decoration,* 1807.

It was in this book that Hope published the results of his research and interest into neoclassical interiors and furniture as illustrated in settings in his London home in Duchess Street, built by Robert Adam 1768-71, bought by Hope in 1799 and remodelled by 1804. The house was deliberately planned by Hope to show off his acquisitions in the most appropriate setting to the public, whether invited or by ticket, with the first floor arranged in a series of reception rooms, each devoted to a different aspect of his collections, while Hope and his wife, a far more sociable and popular figure than her husband, lived on the second floor. The rooms included three devoted to Hope's discriminating group of antique vases, some of which he had bought from Sir William Hamilton in 1801, galleries for his collections of sculpture and paintings, and drawing rooms devoted to the Egyptian and 'Saracenic or Moorish' tastes.[2] The drawing rooms were each furnished appropriately with the Egyptian Room being decorated with a frieze based on papyrus rolls, a colour scheme of pale yellow, bluish green, black and gold, furniture in a severe uncompromising style decorated with suitable Egyptian gods, goddesses, scorpions and scarabs, antiquities and exotic materials like granite, serpentine, porphyry and basalt.

1. For a comprehensive survey of Hope's life and influence, see David Watkin, *Thomas Hope 1769-1831 and the Neo-Classical Idea,* 1968.
2. *Household Furniture and Interior Decoration,* p.24.

The Egyptian Room, Duchess Street, from Thomas Hope's *Household Furniture,* 1807.

In the Indian Room paintings by William Daniell of suitable scenes of mosques and temples were combined with a classical view by Pannini, and exotic decoration in the 'Saracenic or Moorish' taste including Persian carpets and receptacles for incense and perfumes. Furniture in this room showed classical influences, with winged lions forming the arms of the ottomans and decorating the sides of the armchairs, while the fire screens were formed of javelins supporting shields, and the wall lights of a combination of Greek and Roman motifs in carved, ebonised and gilded wood. The Flaxman Room was designed around the sculpture of Aurora and Cephalus, commissioned by Hope from Flaxman in the early 1790s, and exhibited Hope's preoccupation with symbolic ornament, as the theme of the decoration echoed the motifs of night and day with appropriate details like the table with front legs formed by pairs of the Horae, the four goddesses of the seasons (Plate 10). However, Hope's eclectic tastes were illustrated by the ceiling in the Indian Room, based on a Turkish original, by the decorative drapery in the Egyptian Room, a popular Empire motif, and by the miscellany of 'Egyptian, Hindoo, and Chinese idols, and curiosities'[3] arranged on the chimney piece in the Closet or Boudoir,

---

3. *Household Furniture,* p.28.

The Indian Room, Duchess Street, from Hope's *Household Furniture*, 1807.

taken from an Egyptian portico, which stands under an arch of Empire fringed drapery on bamboo laths.

As well as the illustrations of the rooms in Duchess Street, Hope's book included plates showing pieces of furniture in detail which he designed and published to prevent 'extravagant caricatures such as of late have begun to start up in every corner of this capital',[4] a reference presumably to George Smith's plates, some of which are dated 1804 and 1805.[5] Hope's mission was to present designs in the classical taste which he praised for 'that breadth and repose of surface, that distinctness and contrast of outline, that exposition of plain and enriched parts, that harmony and significance of accessories, and that apt accord between the peculiar meaning of each imitative or significant detail, and the peculiar destination of the main object, to which these accessories belonged, which are calculated to afford to the eye and mind the most lively, most permanent and most unfading enjoyment.'[6] He found it difficult to discover craftsmen with the necessary skill and talent to execute his

4. *Household Furniture,* p.11.

5. However examples of the new style had also appeared in *The London Chair Maker's and Carver's Book of Prices* 1803, where 'Grecian' designs for backs and legs are illustrated, and by the time the 1808 Supplement was published, a far greater range of illustrations for furniture in the Greek and Egyptian styles was included.

6. *Household Furniture,* p.2.

The Flaxman Room, Duchess Street, from Hope's *Household Furniture*, 1807.

Nos. 1 and 2, end and front of a table from the Boudoir or Lararium. No. 3 table from the Flaxman Room dedicated to Aurora with front legs composed of figures of the Horae, the four goddesses of the seasons with four medallions in the frieze above their heads representative of the gods of night and sleep.

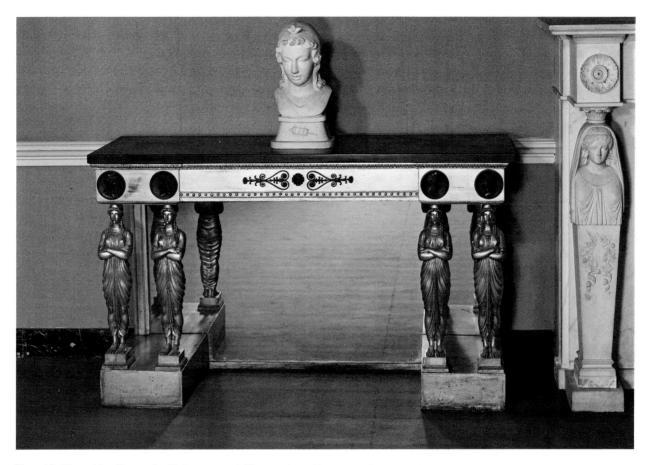

Plate 10. Pier-table gilt wood with bronze medallions and marble top, designed by Thomas Hope for the Flaxman Room in his house in Duchess Street, c.1800. The table is supported by figures representing the Horae, goddesses of the day, while the medallions portray gods of night and sleep, all appropriate symbolism for the room which contained John Flaxman's sculpture of Aurora and Cephalus.

designs and mentions two, both Continental, Decaix, a French bronzist, and Bogaert, a Flemish carver. His comment that furniture makers 'are rarely initiated even in the simplest rudiments of designs, whence it has happened that immense expense has been employed in producing furniture without character, beauty or appropriate meaning'[7] summarised his reaction to contemporary furniture and justified his attempts to show purer and less debased designs for furniture.

Hope's furniture designs are distinguished by their close relationship to classical models and he gave sources for his ideas, including some of the best architectural authorities, although not C.H. Tatham's influential publications. He also referred to

---

7. *Literary Gazette,* 12th February 1831, p.107.

The Picture Gallery, Duchess Street, from the *Magazine of Fine Arts,* 1821, showing some of the lion monopodia tables from *Household Furniture* and other interesting pieces including couches with armrests of crouching dogs.

the original antique remains that he studied in museums and private collections which provided him with inspiration, like the table in plate 12 of *Household Furniture,* which is based on part of a throne in the Vatican, a design also copied by Tatham, and by Percier and Fontaine. The influence of his compositions can be seen in the furniture styles fashionable for two decades after the publication of *Household Furniture,* where winged chimeras formed leg or arm supports, backs were based on the 'Klismos' concave designs or were variations on horizontal styles; chairs and stools were formed of x-framed supports with some of crossed swords, and couches followed the classical design with one or both ends scrolling, and outwards curving feet. Supports for side tables were formed of caryatids, singly or in pairs, with either classical or Egyptian figures, of lion monopodia, lyres or even swans. Circular tables, a common Regency type, appear with triple chimera monopodia supports, or with central pedestals, several versions of which exist with different decoration, while smaller tripod tables are shown, some with monopodia supports and others with folding supports.

Hope's use of the range of classical ornament, including the anthemion, palmette and acanthus, was detailed and precise and he illustrated a variety of lotus forms, particularly the device of the double lotus as part of vertical supports or at the intersection of cross members of stools, an example of the influence of Percier and Fontaine. Other examples of ornament, like the use of the round flower or star

Design for a table from *Household Furniture*, pl. 19, No. 5.

shaped bolt head which runs along the front rail of couches or chairs or decorates the frieze of side tables, can be linked with surviving pieces like the settee in the drawing room at Southill. Inlaid star patterns appear in the tops of round tables and decorate, appropriately, the cradle with other classical devices of night, sleep and hope. The contemporary fashion for flat areas of veneered dark woods like mahogany or rosewood set off by metal inlay was followed by Hope, who advocated metal inlay instead of raised ornaments on chairs as the latter collected dirt and dust. However, he did recommend ornaments in cast bronze since they were cheap to reproduce, could be easily removed and reapplied and were very durable.

The difficulty with the outline technique that Hope employed for the plates in *Household Furniture* was the impression that they gave of cold formality, and although Hope was aware of this disadvantage of his approach he believed that the 'strong contrast of the light and of the shaded parts... the harmonious blending, or the gay opposition of the various colours'[8] could only have been achieved by making the book so expensive as to defeat its principal purpose. However it is possible to gather some impression of how the furniture and furnishings were intended to be used in the plates engraved for Hope by Henry Moses in 1812 entitled *Designs of Modern Costume,* which were later reprinted, with additional plates, in

8. *Household Furniture*, p.15.

Pair of candelabra, bronzed and painted wood, after the design in *Household Furniture,* pl. 22. no. 4.

Table, mahogany with inlay, after the design in *Household Furniture* for a round monopodium in mahogany inlaid in ebony and silver, pl.39. Other versions of this table are known, including one at the Victoria and Albert Museum with both the stem and the top inlaid as in the Hope design.

Library table, rosewood with gilt gesso, c.1810, based on Hope's design, pl.2.

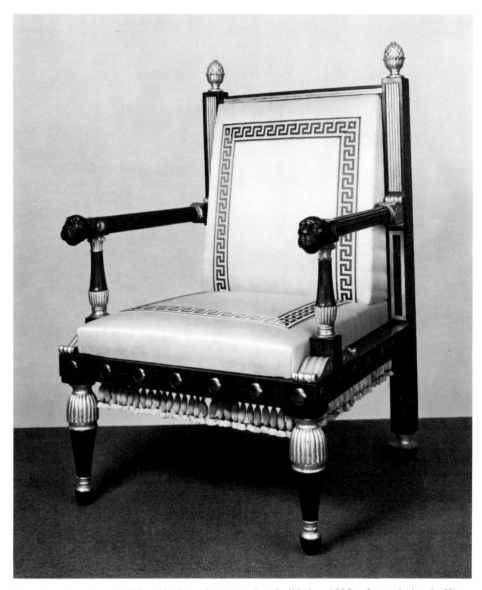

Chair, beechwood painted in imitation of rosewood and gilded, c.1805, after a design in Hope, pl. 11, Nos. 5 and 6.

1823 as *A Series of twenty-nine designs of Modern Costume*. These plates show actual pieces of furniture from the Duchess Street house in informal use, making it possible to imagine how the Hope style could be adapted for more relaxed surroundings.

One of the most famous criticisms of Hope's publication was that by Sydney Smith in *The Edinburgh Review* [9] who disapproved of such preoccupations with 'paltry and fantastical luxuries' during a period of national emergency. He considered that such designs, although 'unquestionably beautiful' in themselves, were quite unsuitable for household furniture, partly because of their bulky and massive

9. *The Edinburgh Review,* Vol. X, 1807, pp. 478-486. *The Gentleman's Magazine,* Vol. LXXXVIII, July 1808, pp.624-6, was however much less disapproving and recommended Hope's book to 'possessors of every magnificent library... a testimony of the abilities of Mr. Hope in invention and design'.

Bookcase, mahogany with female Egyptian heads and lion monopodia in bronzed and carved wood. Acquired from the Deepdene Sale in 1917 by Edward Knoblock, sold from his estate in 1946 to James Watson-Gandy-Brandreth who was encouraged to collect Regency furniture by Margaret Jourdain; the bookcase is now in the Bowes Museum.

construction copied from marble monuments which resulted in lack of mobility, a convenience much favoured in more relaxed attitudes to room arrangement. Smith also poked fun at Hope's advocacy of appropriate ornament derived from classical mythology which results in 'a chaos of symbols and effigies which no man can interpret who has not the whole Pantheon at his finger ends!'[10] thus destroying Hope's principle of symbolic decoration. The idea that the decoration should be relevant to the use of the object was also mocked by Smith who asked why should 'a chair be in the shape of a lyre, — or of two antique swords — or have a ram's head on the arm, and a bronze pine on the top of the corner?'[11] thus emphasising the incongruity and inconsistency of the designs with Hope's statements.

---

10. *Edinburgh Review*, p.484.
11. *Edinburgh Review*, p.486.

Chair, mahogany, based on a design 'after the manner of the ancient curule chairs', Plate 20 no. 3, *Household Furniture*.

Stool, ebonised and gilded frame, the design copied from *Household Furniture,* pl. 29, no. 1 folding stool.

Illustration from *A series of twenty-nine designs of Modern Costume,* 1823, by Henry Moses, showing the way in which Hope's furniture could be absorbed into contemporary interiors.

Table, mahogany with ebony inlay, based on Hope's design in *Household Furniture,* pl. 12. Other versions exist with the anthemion decoration carved rather than inlaid.

Armchair, painted black with gilded decoration, c.1805. Design taken from a plate in George Smith's *Household Furniture*, pl. 56 dated 1804. From the collection of Edward Knoblock.

Dressing table, mahogany with ebony inlay, c.1805, the design based on pl. 72 of George Smith's *Household Furniture and Interior Decoration*, 1808. From the collection of Edward Knoblock.

In spite of these witty and authoritative comments, other critics were more favourable, and by 1827 John Britton pointed out that 'To Mr. Hope we are indebted, in an eminent degree, for the classical and appropriate style, which now generally characterizes our furniture and ornamental utensils. Like most other innovations, his was decried as whimsical and puerile by some persons... *Household Furniture and Interior Decoration* has not only improved the taste of cabinet-makers and upholsterers, but also that of their employers.'[12] Hope's influence had an immediate effect on the house of Samuel Rogers, the poet, which he had remodelled during 1803-4. Apparently Rogers 'had made notes of household arrangements he had seen in houses in which he had visited; had given much study to questions of decoration and ornament; and had designed the furniture himself, with the assistance of Hope's work on the subject... The furniture and decoration followed the Greek models, and one of the striking features of the house was its large and beautiful collection of Greek vases.'[13] Rogers had studied in the Louvre and this experience combined with the knowledge of Hope's

12. John Britton, *The Union of Architecture, Sculpture and Painting*, 1827, pp.22-3.
13. P.W. Clayden, *The Early Life of Samuel Rogers*, 1887, pp.448-449.

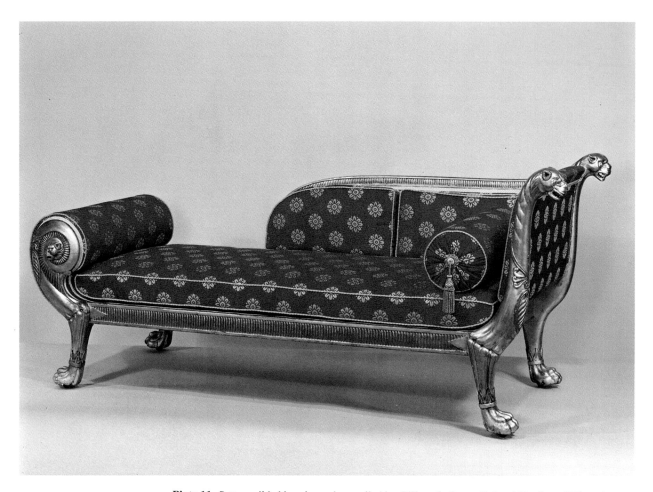

Plate 11. Settee, gilded beechwood, supplied by Gillow & Co. to Colonel Hughes of Kinmel Park, Denbighshire, in 1805 as part of a suite of 12 armchairs and 2 settees in the refined Greek Revival taste, illustrating the Gillow firm's knowledge of fashionable styles.

designs, before *Household Furniture* was published, helped to create the stylish interiors at 22 St. James's Place. The idea of combining a museum and a home was to be followed by Sir John Soane in his house in Lincoln's Inn Fields which was remodelled in 1812 and 1824, using similar details to those of the interior arrangement at Duchess Street, including the room formed to take Soane's collection of vases. However, it was the architectural sculpture and casts that Soane acquired which formed the distinctive element of his house, rather than the decorative furniture and furnishings of Duchess Street.

Chaise longue, ebonised and gilded wood, c.1810, after a design by Smith, pl.63.

Chair, beech painted in terracotta on black ground, in the Greek klismos style, c.1800. The painted design depicts the gathering of the apples of the Hesperides from a plate in d'Harcanville's *Collection of... the Hon. William Hamilton*, 1776-7. Similar curving broad backs appear in French and Italian Empire furniture.

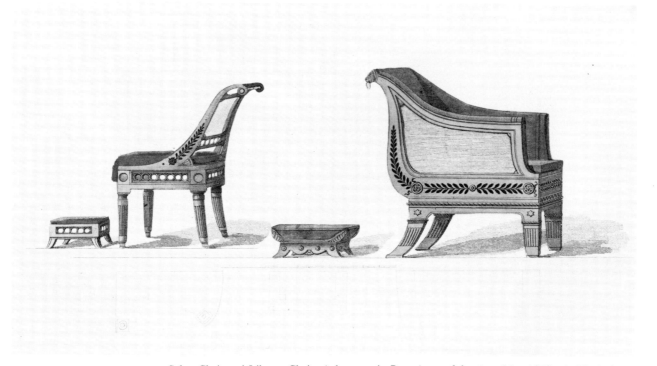

Salon Chair and Library Chair, Ackermann's *Repository of the Arts,* May 1810, pl. 30, designs said to be Roman and intended to be carved and gilded, japanned to match other pieces, or made of mahogany, with red leather cushions.

Hope's designs were to have a powerful influence on designers, not least through the medium of the pattern books as exemplified by George Smith's *A Collection of Designs for Household Furniture and Interior Decoration,* published in 1808 with 158 coloured plates dated between 1804 and 1807. Smith popularised Hope's designs so that 'the beauty and elegance displayed in the fittings-up of modern houses may not be confined to the stately mansions of our Nobility in the metropolis, but be published for the use of the country at large, as a guide to foreign nations, and as an evidence of the superior taste and skill exhibited in the manufactures of this country.'[14] Although not a great deal is known about Smith, and his claims to have worked for the Prince of Wales have not yet been corroborated, his publication was important in its adaptation of classical motifs and several pieces of furniture survive after his designs. Smith notes in his Preface that a 'propitious change' has taken place 'in our national taste of Furniture: this has arisen from a more close investigation and imitation of the beautiful remains of ancient sculpture and painting' and points out that in France artists do not think it degrading to provide designs for cabinet makers and upholsterers whereas in England 'our higher class of artists do not give their attention, in some degree, to providing our manufacturers with patterns of tasteful outline for this species of furniture: their previous course of study, aided by a reference to books of antiquities, would enable them to supply Designs, which in execution would produce a pleasing effect, and merit the just praises of true

14. George Smith, *A Collection of Designs for Household Furniture and Interior Decoration,* 1808, p.v Preface.

Armchair, japanned dark green and gilded on gesso ground, c.1810. Similar designs were illustrated by Smith, pl.55.

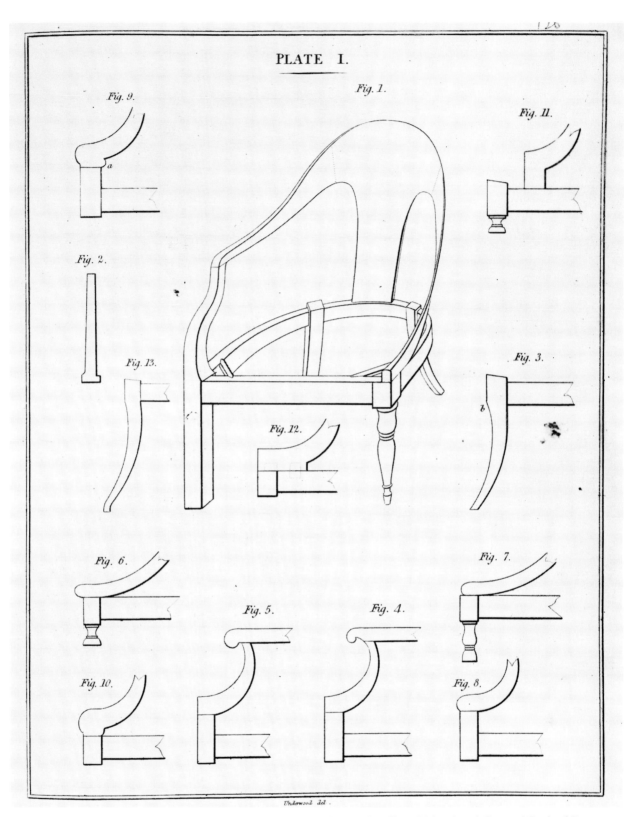

Roman chair from the *Supplement to the London Chair-Makers' and Carvers' Book of Prices*, 1808, with various designs for arms and legs.

Bookcase, mahogany with ebony, supplied by George Oakley for the library at Papworth Hall, Cambridgeshire, in 1810. The bookcase, which cost £47.5s, originally had two bronzed plaster busts and a plaster urn on the top.

Chair, rosewood inlaid with brass, c.1820.

Chair, japanned black and gilded, c.1815, with the typical anthemion and twisted rope rail of the Greek style.

Bergère, with cane back, sides and seat, c.1815. Other variations had straight fluted front legs with arm rests rising vertically from them.

Grecian furniture, *Repository of the Arts,* 2nd Series Vol. I, May 1816, pl. 26. The furniture intended for a library was designed by George Bullock.

Stand, ebonised and inlaid wood, made by George Bullock in 1816 for Abbotsford. The silver neoclassical urn of 'Attic' bones presented by Lord Byron to Sir Walter Scott in 1815 was placed on this in the library.

taste.'[15] However, Smith was not deterred by this lack of interest and was quite capable of learning from such authorities as Tatham whose illustration of an antique seat he copied in the console of his dressing table in plate 72 of his *A Collection of Designs*...

Smith expanded and elaborated Hope's ideas for furniture construction and motifs, particularly in his use of animal monopodia, that familiar Regency motif, which he used singly or in pairs as supports for sofa tables, sideboards and library tables or

15. Smith, p. xiii.

Plate 12. Bergère chair, aburra wood with carved and gilt decoration, supplied by Morel and Hughes for the Ante Room to the Crimson Drawing Room, Northumberland House, in 1823, the original upholstery being striped pink-grey silk with rosettes. This is a fine example of the rich late neoclassical style of the 1820s.

Cabinet, oak with ebony inlay, c.1815, probably by George Bullock.

for the legs of chairs and sofas. Chair designs generally follow rather rigid outlines, emphasised by solid supports for the arms decorated with anthemions or open arms supported on winged animals. In spite of the klismos and other types of curved backed chairs illustrated by Hope, Smith did not develop this theme, apart from some bergère designs, and his chairs with horizontal backs, as in plate 39 of his book, are too stiff and angular to follow the popular type with its design of contrasted curves. The use of the lion paw for the feet of table, chair, sofa and cabinet furniture legs was interpreted by Smith in a number of ways ranging from those arranged pointing forwards to others facing sideways, from naturalistic depictions of paw and part of the leg, to panelled square section legs which suddenly end in paws. Hope's double lotus ornament, and bolt head and star sequence were all used by Smith as were the classical forms of the anthemion, palmette and acanthus, the shield shaped screens on javelins, and small tables with more exotic central supports formed of palm tree trunks of or large leaves curving outwards at top and bottom.

While Smith's designs were not as elegant and precise as Hope's, probably partly due to the latter's original use of the outline drawing technique, and sometimes overloaded by elaborate decoration, they were nonetheless to give a new impetus to

Writing cabinet, rosewood veneer with inlay, in the manner of George Bullock, similar to a design illustrated in the *Repository of Arts,* January 1810, which incorporates the same locking device which simultaneously fastens the front panel and writing slide.

furniture design with their detailed range of rather robust designs. Their importance can be further underlined by the number of surviving pieces which can be traced to Smith's book, including the armchair after plate 56 with its typical lion monopodia legs, of which there are several versions, the dressing table after plate 72 and the sideboard at Brighton after plates 83 and 87.[16] Smith was also to be acknowledged by Ackermann's *Repository,* who featured Greek designs in their first number in January 1809, observing that his 'classic taste in this line is evinced in his splendid work on furniture and decoration.'[17] By August of that year Ackermann commented that 'It cannot but be highly gratifying to every person of genuine taste, to observe the revolution which has, within these few years, taken place in the furniture and decorations of the apartments of people of fashion. In consequence of this revolution, effected principally by the study of the antique, and the refined notions of beauty derived from that source, that barbarous Egyptian style, which a few years since prevailed, is succeeded by the classic elegance which characterized the most polished

16. See Nancy McClelland, *Duncan Phyfe and the English Regency 1795-1830,* 1939, pls. 5, 6.
17. *The Repository of Arts,* Vol. 1, March 1809, p.189.

Designs for ornament in the Greek style from Ackermann's *Selection of Ornaments* 1817-1819.

ages of Greece and Rome.'[18] Ackermann continued to publish plates for Fashionable Furniture of Grecian design, including in May 1810 'elegant antique furniture for salon and library' and in December 1812 a bookcase with persic pillars, the colonnette introduced by Hope with the double lotus form in the middle and with similar base and capital. This decorative detail was to be very common in cabinets and secretaires, sometimes made of carved wood and sometimes of cast brass or bronze. In August 1813 Ackermann illustrated an 'antique sofa and table', observing that it 'is not sufficient, that the ornaments and the colours of the furniture should correspond, but a harmony of this principle must pervade the whole' and using a corner cupboard to illustrate that 'the quantity of horizontal and of vertical lines' were not similarly proportioned since 'the upright lines predominate' in this piece without linking the furniture with the architectural detail as successfully as candelabra and tripods.[19]

The problem of providing more appropriate and acceptable designs for furniture

18. Vol. 11, August 1809, p.132.
19. Vol. X, August 1813, pp.115-116.

Sideboard, mahogany, c.1825, very similar to designs published in the *Repository of Arts* for a sideboard and cellaret in October 1822, Pl.13, p.121.

Cabinet, oak veneer with ebonised inlay and brass decoration, c.1825, similar to designs by Bullock and Brown with the same distinctive pattern of brasswork in the doors.

Lady's Book-case, with Cabinet, from *The Rudiments of Drawing Cabinet and Upholstery Furniture* by Richard Brown, 1822, pl. XVIII.

Cabinet, rosewood veneer with ormolu mounts and brass grillwork, c.1825, based on the plate in Brown's book.

Games table, rosewood, the interior with chess and backgammon boards, c.1830. Similar designs were published by Gillow in 1823.

Design for a pier table, *Designs of Cabinet and Upholstery Furniture* by Henry Whitaker, 1825.

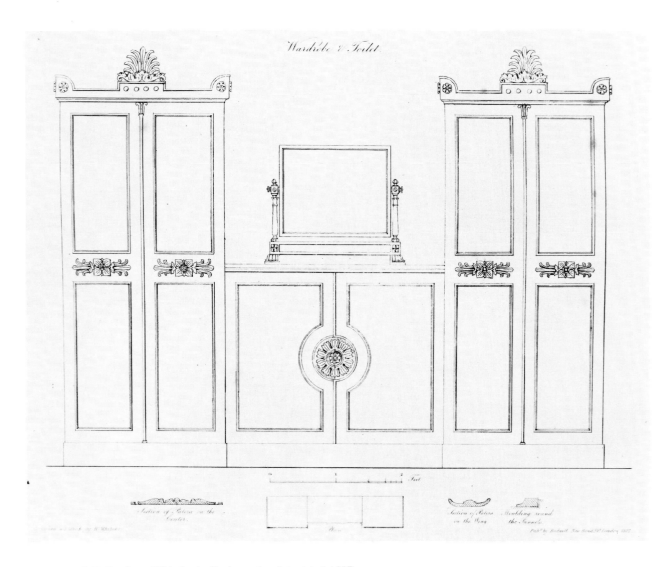

Wardrobe & Toilet from Whitaker's *Designs,* the plate dated 1827.

was commented on in *The Repository* in October 1813 when referring to Hope's *Household Furniture,* 'But how, we will ask, is so great a change in household furniture to be effected? Can we expect the artizans and manufacturers to alter their present mode of education, and ascend to the study of those higher and more copious sources of elegance? or are our artists and architects to descend, in making it their business to point out and correct the designs suitable for carpets, or the manner of making up window-curtains, articles which will be ever used and adopted in these more northern climates? When that takes place, then alone can we expect to find our furniture in unison with our mansions, and the whole in a style truly classical.'[20] The illustration of a footstool (pl. 5) from a design by Mr. Gregson was however considered to be both chaste of design and practical to use. However by May 1816 Ackermann was able to offer comfort in such a depressing situation by publishing designs by Mr. G. Bullock described as 'Art indeed it may properly be called, when the designs of this species of embellishment embrace the combinations of form, composition, light, shade, and colour, and are as classically united agreeably to the

20. Vol. X, October 1813, p.232.

Design for a bookcase from John Taylor's *The Upholsterer's and Cabinet Maker's Assistant,* c.1825.

laws of fitness and truth, as they are found to be in the works of masters eminent in the walks of pictorial beauty.'[21] The pieces intended to form part of the furnishings of a library (p.109) included a sofa, cabinets decorated with boulle and ormolu, supporting urns, a footstool and a pedestal, some of the details of the ornament echoing Bullock's introduction of native floral designs, and others, like the decoration of the pedestal the influence of Hope.

Sources for Greek ornament and decoration suitable for furniture were provided by a series of publications including George Smith's *A Collection of Ornamental Designs, after the Manner of the Antique,* 1812, Henry Moses's book, *A Collection of Vases, Altars, Paterae, Tripods, candelabra, sarcophagi &c.,* 1814, dedicated to his patron Thomas Hope, and Ackermann's *Selection of Ornaments* 1817-1819. Later pattern books also showed a grasp of Greek design and pattern, of which the

21. Vol. 1, Series 2, May 1816, p.308.

Plate 13. Design for Sideboard and Cellaret from Rudolf Ackermann's *Repository of the Arts,* Vol. XIV, 2nd Series, October 1822, pl. 21, an example of the debased classical style popular in the later Regency.

Drawing-Room Table, Chairs, & Footstools, *Repository of the Arts,* 3rd Series Vol. III, June 1824, pl. 28, described as being in the character and style of Bullock which was being continued by the leading upholsterers.

Design for clothes press by John Taylor, c.1825.

Drawing Room Chairs, *The Practical Cabinet Maker* by P. and M.A. Nicholson, 1826.

first was *The Rudiments of Drawing Cabinet and Upholstery Furniture* by Richard Brown, 1822, who acknowledged in his Preliminary Discourse, the 'new character, bold in the outline, rich and chaste in the ornaments, and durable from the rejection of little parts. This style, although in too many instances resembling the Greek tombs, has evidently arisen in a great measure from Mr. Hope's mythological work on Household Furniture, Mr. Smith's excellent book of Unique Designs, and Percier's splendid French work on Interior Decoration.'[22] Hope's influence can be seen in the elaborate detail that Brown suggests for the symbolism of his ornament, for example a loo table used for breakfast and for games should have the 'tea tree and coffee plant for its ornaments, with the masks of Ceres and Bacchus... perhaps the mask of Comus, the god of festivals and mirth, will be found to accord.'[23] However, Brown also criticises one of Hope's ideas, 'a very absurd misapplication of ornaments; namely, that of inserting stars of brass on the tops of tables; when it is clear, that they can only with propriety be introduced into beds, girandoles,

22. Brown, p.x.
23. Brown, pp.32-3. Elaborate symbolism for decorative ornament suitable for different types of furniture was also included in *The Complete Cabinet Maker and Upholsterer's Guide* by J. Stokes, 1827.

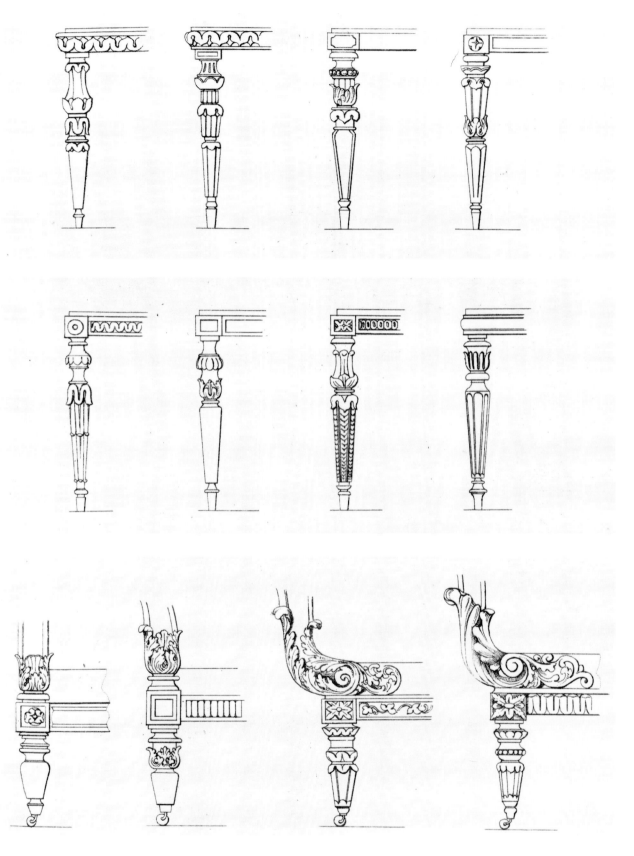

Chair Legs and Rails, Sofa Feet and Rails from George Smith's *Cabinet-Maker's & Upholsterer's Guide*, 1826.

Teapoy, mahogany, c.1830, taken from a design by Nicholson.

Dining chair, carved mahogany, designed by Philip Hardwick and made by W. & C. Wilkinson for Goldsmiths' Hall, 1834.

chandeliers, &c.'[24] The plate for an Ottoman, 'chiefly intended for music rooms and picture galleries' had a striking resemblance to Bullock's design published in Ackermann 1816 (p.109), using the same idea of a couch with commodes with applied or inlaid classical winged figures supporting amphorae. Brown in fact acknowledged the excellence of Bullock's progressive designs 'The late Mr. Bullock was the only person who ventured into a new path: though some of his designs were certainly too massy and ponderous, nevertheless grandeur cannot be obtained without it; such are the standards to his octagon tables... He appears to have been peculiarly happy in his mouldings, which were of true Grecian taste, sharp, bold,

24. Brown, p.33.

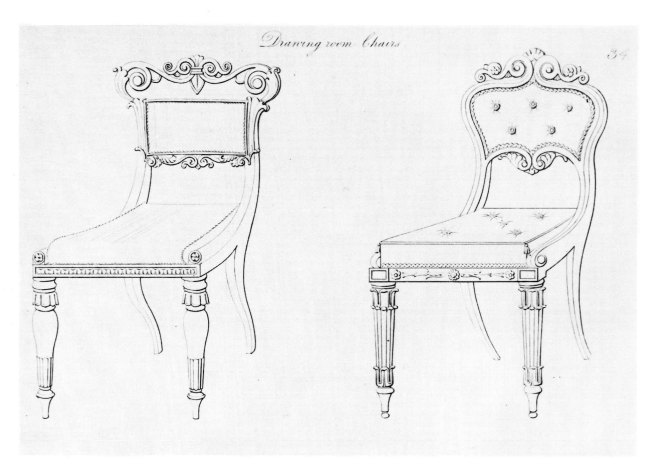

Design for Drawing room Chairs by Thomas King, 1839.

Design for washstand from *The Modern Style of Cabinet Work Exemplified* by Thomas King, 2nd edition 1839.

126

Designs for screens by Thomas King, *The Modern Style of Cabinet Work Exemplified*, 1839.

and well relieved. . .'[25] However, in spite of this evidence of classical taste, many of Brown's designs show more ordinary forms of Regency furniture with the Grecian symplicity of line being replaced by heavier, more obvious proportions with a noticeable increase in the amount of turning and the introduction of stump feet for sofas and bun-shaped feet for tables and cabinets.

After Brown's book the development of the Greek style in later furniture designs is illustrated in *The Practical Cabinet Maker, Upholsterer and Complete Decorator* by Peter and Michael Angelo Nicholson, published in 1826 with plates by the latter, a talented draughtsman. This pattern book includes plates showing a sophisticated

25. Brown, p.55.

Design for Grecian furniture by J.B. Papworth from *The Social Day* by Peter Coxe, 1823.

use of typical Greek motifs like anthemion in a variety of forms on the backs of chairs, ends of sofas and cornices of beds. Paterae are shown in lines as ornament for chair and sofa rails and table frames, while large scale leaf forms are used for the backs of chairs and sofas and for front supports of sofas. Henry Whitaker's *Designs of Cabinet and Upholstery Furniture in the Most Modern Style,* 1825, with plates dating 1825-7, also included the same naturalistic forms, particularly in the use of acanthus and honeysuckle motifs, for the tops of legs, colonnettes and other supports, while chair backs are formed of scrolls with leaf forms filling the interstices. John Taylor, whose designs in various styles were illustrated in *The Repository,* in the 1820s,[26] published two volumes of plates of furniture and curtains about 1825, *The Upholsterer's and Cabinet Maker's Pocket Assistant,* which included among a wide range scrolled pediments for carcase furniture and console shaped supports with acanthus or other foliage decoration at the top for cabinets. The floridity of his designs was echoed in George Smith's *The Cabinet Maker's and Upholsterer's Guide,* 1826, the plates dated 1826-8, where the author acknowledged that his earlier work of 1808 had 'become wholly obsolete and inapplicable to its intended purpose, by the change of taste and rapid improvements which a period of twenty years has introduced.'[27] However, Smith included designs in the Gothic, French and Greek styles as well as schemes for interior decoration in the Egyptian, Greek, Etruscan, Gothic and Louis XIV styles in order to meet the demand for new forms. His furniture designs have become coarser and clumsy, with the front legs of chairs being straight and usually turned, while shafts for bed posts or the legs of cabinets and tables are divided into sections by leaf shaped cups. Heavily ornamented pediments appear on wardrobes and chimney glasses but the use of animal motifs, so marked in his earlier publication, has almost disappeared and the bun and scroll shape for the feet of cabinet furniture is very popular.

By 1833 the myriad of styles prevalent in the earlier years of the Regency had been reduced by Loudon to four, the Grecian or modern style, the Gothic, the Elizabethan and the Louis XIV.[28] His preference and in fact probably that of most of his readers was for the Grecian, 'which is by far the most prevalent' but he observed that one of the greatest faults in the designs for furniture in the Grecian taste was the 'deviation from simplicity' caused by demand for cabinet furniture and for novelty.[29] However, the designs he published for a wide selection of furniture for the Grecian villa resembled those by Brown, the Nicholsons and George Smith, and Thomas Hope's chair designs are used to point out that such a style 'would be prized for its expression, for its suitableness as a seat, for its simplicity, and for the greater effect produced in it by a very few lines. This effect of the Grecian chair being independent of all historical associations, since it is, in fact, merely an imaginary composition, results wholly from the beauty of the design.'[30] Later commentators considered that C.H. Tatham's designs had been most influential, since to him 'perhaps more than to any other person, may be attributed the rise of the Anglo-Greek style which still prevails, as shown in LOUDON, Encyclopaedia of Cottage, etc., Arch.'[31] The importance of J.B. Papworth as a talented exponent of the

---

26. The Repository including a Dress Sofa, Vol. XI February 1821, pl. 9; Gothic side table and cellaret, Vol. XII, July 1821, pl. 6; Drawing Room Sofa, Vol. IV 3rd Series, September 1824, pl. 16; Library and Drawing Room Chairs, Vol. IV November 1824, pl. 28.

27. Smith, 1828, Introduction p.vi.

28. J.C. Loudon, *An Encyclopaedia of Cottage, Farm and Villa Architecture,* 1835, Of the Furniture of Villas, p.1039.

29. Loudon, Grecian and Modern Villa Furniture, p.1083.

30. Loudon, Elizabethan Furniture for Villas, p.1098.

31. *The Dictionary of Architecture,* Architectural Publication Society 1853-92, Vol. III, p.104.

Design for Grecian Furniture by J.B. Papworth, 1823.

Anglo-Greek style was also acknowledged and his ability to 'exhibit a simplicity of which it was said in 1822, "the English is more chaste than the French-Greek, and has advanced so rapidly during the last ten years that the French have adopted much of it" '.[32] Papworth's illustrations for Peter Coxe's poem, *The Social Day,* which were drawn in 1814 although not published until 1823, are perhaps the best record of how Tatham and Hope's designs were translated for more conventional settings.

32. *The Dictionary of Architecture,* op. cit. See also Edward T. Joy, 'A Versatile Victorian Designer J.B. Papworth', *Country Life,* Vol. CXLVII, No. 3802 January 15th 1980, pp.130-1.

Secretaire bookcase, *Repository of Arts*, 2nd Series Vol. XIII, April 1822, pl. 21, after designs by Percier and Fontaine.

4. French Influence in the Later Regency

English interest in French styles and designs continued to flourish throughout the period of the Napoleonic Wars, in spite of the natural difficulties of access, as Ackermann pointed out in 1815, 'The interchange of feelings between this country and France, as it relates to matters of taste, has not been wholly suspended . . . . . the taste of both has been improved . . .'[1] and anglicised versions of the Percier and Fontaine Empire style began to appear after the publication of their designs in 1812, some shown in Ackermann's plates of that year. However, after the restoration of the Bourbon monarchy in 1814, this vogue for the Napoleonic style was matched by interest in the period of Louis XIV, the most famous monarch of the ancient regime, and was deliberately encouraged by the Bourbons to foster nationalist and royalist opinion in post-revolutionary France. English visitors began to visit Paris again, influential collectors led by the Prince Regent, enlarged their collections of furniture and other works of art, and English cabinet makers began to produce furniture both in the Empire and the Louis Quatorze idiom. The Duke of Wellington took advantage of the situation in France to acquire fine pieces of furniture, including an important group of boulle examples from the dealer Bonnemaison with four stamped by Etienne Levasseur, and some from the ébéniste Jacob Desmalter.[2] There were also sales in London of collections of French furniture including pieces from the Royal Collections, as shown in a sale catalogue of June 1816 where Mr. H. Phillips was offering items from Versailles, Compiègne and Malmaison, and commodes made by Daguerre, Lignereux and Jacob.[3]

As usual with historic revivals during the Regency there was some confusion about appropriate designs arising from ignorance about the correct style and pieces considered to be in the Louis Quatorze manner were in fact Louis Quinze, a name sometimes given to the revival which was also known as the Rococo, Old French, or 'florid Italian, which is characterised by curved lines and excess of curvilinear ornaments.'[4] Such florid ornament was to be combined with an increasing use of boulle inlay and metal mounts in pieces which reflected typical Louis Quatorze forms like commodes on plinths or on ball or bun feet, with console supports replacing animal or human monopodia. In spite of the influence of the Rococo Revival the popularity of Empire forms continued with Ackermann responding to public demand by publishing a secretaire bookcase (p.131) after Percier's design in 1822, and a sofa or French bed illustrating their influence in its use of antique ornament in 1822, pointing out that the 'taste for French furniture is carried to such an extent, that most elegantly furnished mansions, particularly the sleeping-rooms, are fitted up in the French style'.[5]

---

1. Ackermann, *Repository of the Arts,* Vol. XIII 1st Series, February 1815, p.120.

2. Geoffrey de Bellaigue, 'George IV and French Furniture', *The Connoisseur,* Vol. 195, No. 784, June 1977, pp.116-125; F.J.B. Watson, 'The Great Duke's Taste for French Furniture', *Apollo,* Vol. CII, No. 161, July 1975, pp.44-9.

3. 'A Catalogue of a Magnificent and Superlatively Elegant Assemblage of Parisian Furniture . . . which will be sold by Auction by Mr. H. Phillips, at His Great Rooms, No. 73 New Bond Street', 8th to 17th June 1816.

4. Loudon, *Encyclopaedia,* The Furniture of Villas, p.1039.

5. Ackermann, Vol. XIII 2nd Series, April 1822, pl. 21; Vol. XIV 2nd Series, November 1822, pl.27.

Rosewood and boulle cabinet, c.1820, the boulle dating from the late seventeenth century.

Table, rosewood with boulle top, c.1820.

The Alcove, The Golden Drawing Room, Carlton House, from W.H. Pyne's *Royal Residences,*
1819, showing boulle tables of rosewood, tortoiseshell and ormolu.

Opposite, above: Cabinet, larch with brass inlay on ebony ground, brass mounts and Glen Tilt
marble top, the interior fitted with drawers on runners. Possibly the one supplied by George
Bullock for Blair Atholl, Perthshire, in 1817, and very similar to a pair of cabinets supplied by
him in 1819 and still in situ.

Opposite, below: Cabinet, rosewood with brass inlay, mounts and grilles, Mona marble top,
attributed to George Bullock, c.1815.

Loo table, frame veneered with ebony and brass and top of ancient classical marbles and hardstone. Frame thought to have been made by George Bullock, c.1817, to support the Italian top.

Detail of the pedestal of the table, showing Bullock's use of oak leaves and acorns rather than classical motifs on the stem, and the thyrsus on the base entwined with hops rather than grapevines.

Chair, ebonised with gilt mounts, c.1825. Very similar to the black and gold seat furniture from the Saloon, Devonshire House, after the 6th Duke of Devonshire's redecoration in the 1820s, which is now at Chatsworth. Morel and Seddon made similar pieces for George IV.

Design for furniture and furnishings of a drawing room by Gillow and Co., dated 1819, showing two cabinets with boulle panels and a chair marked 'This chair chosen' with distinctive neo-rococo carving.

George IV was to play an important role in the development of the Rococo Revival in England as he had been acquiring French furniture from both London and Parisian sources, since he built Carlton House, but his taste had changed from the classically inspired designs of C.H. Tatham and Henry Holland into the more elaborate grandeur epitomised in the interiors designed by Walsh Porter at Carlton House. Some of the finest pieces acquired for Carlton House, for the final phase of furnishing at Brighton Pavilion, and for Windsor, were of boulle, inlaid with brass, ebony and tortoiseshell.[6] Just before the Revolution there was a revival of the fashion for boulle in France itself, and the popularity of certain Louis XIV motifs like the spirally fluted peg top feet appeared on Louis XVI commodes. There was some confusion between the work of earlier craftsmen and that in the Louis XIV mode by later ébénistes, and the popularity of boulle with such individuals as the Prince Regent and Lord Yarmouth increased demand for both original Louis XIV pieces and later examples in the same style. The Prince Regent acquired an early

6. Bellaigue, *Connoisseur,* 1967, op. cit.

AN ENGLISH BED.

An English Bed designed by George Bullock, *Repository of the Arts,* 2nd Series Vol. II, November 1816, pl. 26.

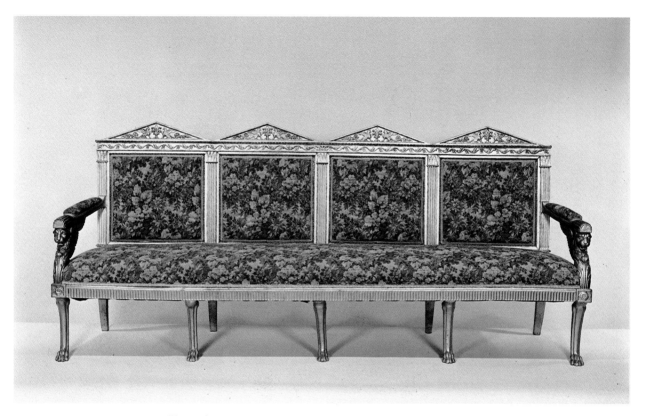

Plate 14. Sofa, gilded and distressed wood, c.1820. A similar suite in the Grand Drawing Room at Fonthill and illustrated in J. Rutter's *Delineation of Fonthill and its Abbey* in 1823 express an even more marked Empire influence and some pieces from this suite survive in Malmesbury House, Salisbury.

Bookcase, rosewood with brass inlay in the manner of George Bullock, carved and gilded ornament, marble top, c.1825.

Stool, 'X' frame, rosewood with gilded ornament, c.1825.

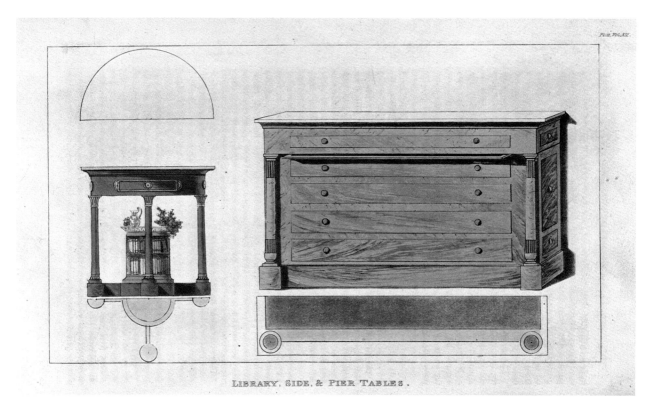

LIBRARY, SIDE, & PIER TABLES.

Plate 15. Design for Library, Side and Pier Tables from Ackermann's *Repository of the Arts,* Vol. XIII, October 1821, pl. 21. These designs which illustrate a definite French influence were intended to be carried out in fashionable woods and the pier table could also be made in marble or bronze for a conservatory or dairy.

anglicised version in 1810 when George Oakley supplied him with 'A capital Mahogany pedestal library Table, inlaid with Bhull bordering...' for £84.[7] Beau Brummell, the arbiter of taste and intimate of the Prince Regent, was one of his friends who shared his love of boulle, and the sale of his furniture after his flight from his debtors to France in 1816 included several articles of boulle among which were a 'pier table of Buhl manufacture, the drawer and legs of tortoiseshell inlaid with arabesques of brass work, and enriched with masks and mouldings of or-molu, a statuary slab at top' and a 'small armoire of Buhl manufacture, the doors, pilasters and frieze richly inlaid with brass and ornamented with masks of or-molu, and griotta slab at top.'[8]

Collecting of boulle furniture in England became fashionable enough to enable specialist shops to be opened like that of Louis Le Gaigneur who established his Buhl Manufactory at 19 Queen Street, Edgware Road, c.1815, and supplied the Prince

7. George Oakley Bill November 10 1810, Royal Archives 25318.
8. Christie's Catalogue of the contents of No. 12 Chapel Street, Park Lane, May 22-3, 1816, Lots 45, 46.

Armchair, walnut carved and gilded, originally upholstered in geranium silk velvet trimmed with gimp and lace. Supplied by Morel and Seddon, c.1828, for the Great Drawing Room, Windsor Castle.

Regent with a number of boulle pieces including a library table in 1815. The only piece of furniture signed by him that has been identified so far is a fairly accurate copy of an eighteenth century boulle piece in the Wallace Collection, an example of the interest in reproductions of earlier boulle designs. Other craftsmen who provided furniture with boulle inlay included Thomas Parker of Air Street and George Bullock of 4 Tenterden Street, Hanover Square. Bullock was to be particularly praised by Richard Brown for his mastery although Brown considered that his 'articles were considerably overcharged with buhl; sometimes the buhl-work was sunk in brass, and on other occasions the counterpart was of the same wood as the furniture itself, and the whole surface presented a brazen front.'[9] George Bullock had originally

9. Richard Brown, *The Rudiments of Drawing Cabinet and Upholstery Furniture,* 1822, p.55.

Table, chair and window seat, *Repository of Arts*, 3rd Series, Vol. V, May 1825, pl. 29, described as examples of modern French Furniture incorporating the introduction of metalwork to achieve a lighter effect.

One of four tables of oak, veneered and partly gilded, the top inlaid with ebony, mahogany, and purplewood on a ground of satinwood. From the Crimson Drawing Room, Carlton House, probably made by Tatham and Bailey, and altered by Morel and Seddon for the Great Drawing Room, Windsor Castle, c.1828.

Cabinet, rosewood, part gilded, with brass shelves and trellis, in the manner of John McLean,
c.1810.

Cylinder desk, rosewood with gilded brass mounts, by John McLean, c.1815.

Bonheur-du-jour, rosewood with gilded brass mounts, in the manner of John McLean, c.1820.

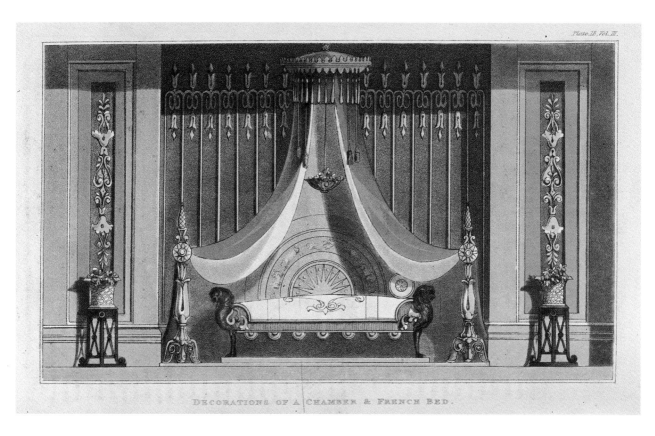

DECORATIONS OF A CHAMBER & FRENCH BED.

Plate 16. Decorations of A Chamber and French Bed from Ackermann's *Repository,* Vol. III, 3rd Series, March 1824, pl. 15. The bed was on rollers to allow it to move forward and the draperies were designed to enclose the bed fully when drawn. The tripods contained artificial flowers.

worked in Liverpool as a sculptor, marble worker, upholsterer and cabinet-maker at various addresses, including Church Street, in partnership with Joseph Gandy, and had moved to London. Bullock was particularly noted for his use of brass inlay combined with native plants like hops, heartsease and oak leaves rather than designs based on classical prototypes and he also used native timbers like oak and larch as well as more exotic ones like rosewood, mahogany and zebra wood. He also used inlay of wood, for example holly with double fillets of ebony and oak. As Richard Brown pointed out 'He has shewn that we need not roam to foreign climes for beautiful ornaments, but that we have abundance of plants and flowers equal to the Grecian, which, if adopted, would be found as pleasing as the antique.'[10] His furniture is also distinguished by the use of marble for the tops, a revival of an earlier fashion, with Mona, Glen Tilt or other marbles from British quarries used extensively for tables and cabinet furniture, either in whole slabs or in chequered patterns of various examples. Bullock was in fact proprietor of the Mona Marble Works in Anglesey, and produced designs for chimney pieces in Mona marble for the *Repository* which acknowledged the importance of this marble in interiors because of its varied richness of colour. Ackermann in fact published many of

10. Brown, op. cit.

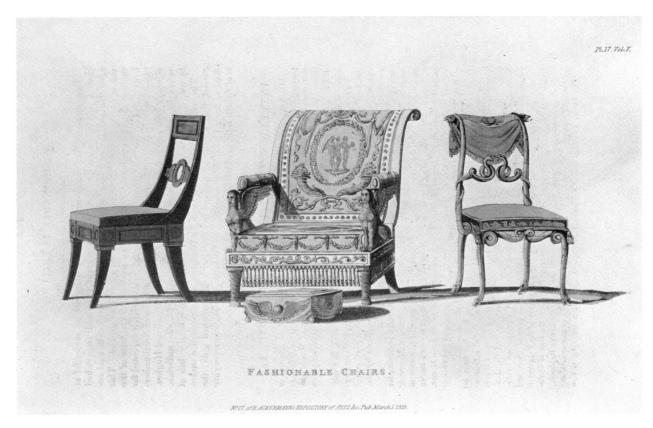

N°27. of R. ACKERMANNS REPOSITORY of ARTS &c. Pub. March 1. 1825.

Plate 17. Fashionable Chairs from Ackermann's *Repository,* Vol. V, 3rd Series, March 1825, pl. 17, including in the centre a chair comparable to pieces produced by Morel and Hughes for the Duke of Northumberland. Although of undoubtedly French inspiration these chairs were intended to have upholstery of British manufacture.

Bullock's designs, mentioning in February 1816 that the illustration of a cabinet was 'designed for execution in our native woods, relieved by inlaid metal ornaments'[11] and presenting Bullock's designs as alternatives to the Empire style with a design for an English bed (p.139) in November 1816 selected 'for the tasteful simplicity that pervades it' as a contrast to the French Sofa Bed with its heavy gilt decoration and elaborate drapery shown in November 1822.[12]

One of the earliest examples of the Rococo Revival in English interiors was at Belvoir where the Duke and Duchess of Rutland employed Benjamin Dean and Matthew Cotes Wyatt, sons of James Wyatt, to decorate the principal rooms in the 1820s. There was a great deal of French furniture at Belvoir, some of which was probably acquired by the Duke and Duchess on their trip to Paris in 1814, and the Elizabeth Saloon, named after the Duchess, incorporated genuine Louis XV boiseries, pier glass frames and other carvings said to have come from a château belonging to Madame de Maintenon.[13] Matthew Cotes Wyatt had acquired the carvings in Paris as a job lot for 1,450 guineas and the rest of the decoration was

---

11. Ackermann, 2nd Series Vol. 1 February 1816, p.123.
12. Ackermann, 2nd Series Vol. II, November 1816.
13. John Martin Robinson, *The Wyatts: An Architectural Dynasty,* 1979, p.13.

Designs for chairs from Henry Whitaker's *Designs of Cabinet and Upholstery Furniture in the Most Modern Style*, 1825, showing typical slightly coarse carving of foliage.

Cabinet from Henry Whitaker's *Designs of Cabinet and Upholstery Furniture*, 1825.

Design for Interior Decoration, Age of Louis XIV from George Smith's *Cabinet-Maker's and Upholsterer's Guide,* 1826.

Design for a French chair, after the taste of the age of Louis XIV, from George Smith's *Cabinet-Maker's and Upholsterer's Guide,* 1826, pl. CXLVI.

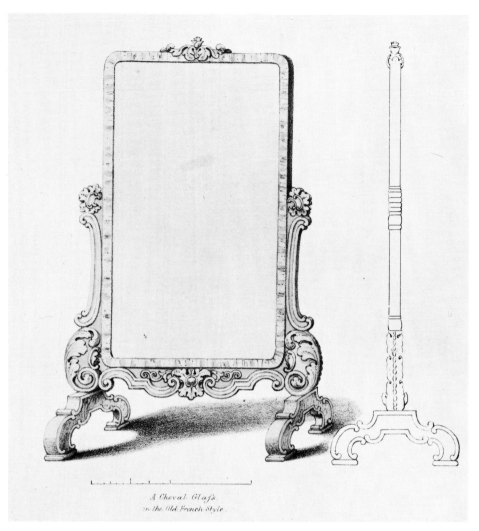

A Cheval Glass in the Old French Style from Thomas King's *Designs for Carving and Gilding,* c.1830.

made up to match either on site or in London. Both the Wyatts were involved at different times in buying French furniture and decorations for English customers, an interest encouraged by the Duchess of Rutland who produced designs for the house of her friend, the Duke of York which were never executed. Lewis Wyatt was also designing in the French style for the Egerton family at Tatton Park where opulent seat furniture was supplied in the 1820s.[14] Benjamin Dean Wyatt and his younger brother, Philip, designed four London interiors in the new style including the gaming house, Crockfords, begun in 1824 which Prince Pückler-Muskau described as 'a gaming palace on the plan of the ''salons'' at Paris, but with a truly Asiatic splendour almost surpassing that of royalty. Everything is in the now revived taste of the time of Louis the Fourteenth; decorated with tasteless excrescences, excess of gilding, confused mixture of stucco painting, &c., — a turn of fashion very consistent in a country where the nobility grows more and more like that of the time of Louis the Fourteenth.'[15] Wyatt's other commissions were for more aristocratic clients like the

14. Lewis Wyatt supplied the pier glasses and swan console tables in 1817 and the seat furniture made by Gillow's in a full-blown rococo style was probably supplied soon afterwards.

15. Prince Pückler-Muskau, *Tour in Germany, Holland and England,* in the Years 1826, 1827, 1828, 1832, Vol. IV, pp.338-9.

(The old French Style)

Design for console table and mirror in the old French Style from Thomas King's *Designs for Carving and Gilding*, c.1830.

Cabinet, mahogany, showing the French influence in its shape, c.1815.

Duke of York at York House, 1825-7, for the Duke of Wellington at Apsley House, 1828, and from 1827 for the Marquis of Stafford (later Duke of Sutherland) at Stafford House as York House was renamed, now called Lancaster House. The Rococo Revival became extremely fashionable for drawing rooms, particularly for those patrons who were taking advantage of the large quantities of French furniture and porcelain becoming available.

Another member of the prolific and talented Wyatt family, Jeffry, later Sir Jeffry Wyatville, carried out alterations for George IV at Windsor in the 1820s.[16] The King employed various French craftsmen including Jean-Jacques Boileau and F.H.G. Jacob-Desmalter, the son of the menuisier, Georges Jacob, and sent Nicholas Morel, of the firm of furnishers Morel and Seddon, to France in 1826 to find designs and patterns. George IV also bought works of art for Windsor from France including panelling, Gobelins tapestries and boulle furniture and was closely involved in the decoration of the Ball Room, now called the Grand Reception Room, in the Louis XV revival style. Other rooms contained French furniture, both contemporary and antique, and Morel and Seddon designed pieces to complement these, including a set of upholstered seat furniture with elaborate gilded carving and

16. Geoffrey de Bellaigue and Pat Kirkham, 'George IV and the Furnishing of Windsor Castle', *Furniture History,* Vol. VIII 1972, pp.1-34.

Plate 18. Cabinet, veneered with maple, including bird's eye maple, and ebony, probably made by George Bullock, c.1815. The raised section on the top was probably intended for a piece of sculpture or silver and the interior is fitted with shallow drawers, probably for botanical specimens. The motif on the base also appears on a documented Bullock cabinet at Blair Castle and a similar design to that on the doors is illustrated in a collection of designs associated with the Bullock workshop in Birmingham Museum.

Design for Candelabra and a Flower Stand in the old French Style from Thomas King's *Designs for Carving and Gilding,* c.1830.

tables with inlaid tops of amboyna wood, ebony, brass and tortoiseshell with gilt bronze mounts. The interiors and furnishings at Windsor however indicated George IV's lifelong interest in the French decorative arts with pieces in the Louis XVI and Empire styles from his earlier schemes as well as examples of the Louis XV revival.

Various English cabinet makers produced furniture in the French taste to meet the demand fostered by the Rococo Revival, some like John McClean of Marylebone Street with pieces of undoubtedly English form but with the influence of the French showing in his use of cast and chased metal mounts. His designs include cabinets (pp.145-7) with sets of open shelves above, the earlier type with ribbed colonnettes and peg feet similar to Weisweiler's designs, while later pieces are more elaborate with boulle inlay and engraved brass strips.[17] William and Edward Snell, of 15 Hanover Street, Long Acre, and later of Albemarle Street, are known to have

17. Simon Redburn, 'John McLean and Son', *Furniture History*, Vol. XIV 1978, pp.31-7.

Design for a Fancy Table in the Old French Style from Thomas King's *Designs for Carving and Gilding,* c.1830.

specialised in the Empire style and Ackermann illustrated one of their pieces, a secretaire cabinet (p.131) after the designs of Percier, in 1822, observing that the 'English style for such furniture is, however, more simply chaste, and thence perhaps less liable to be effected by changes of fashion.'[18] J.B. Papworth designed workshops and showrooms for this firm and may have also worked for them on the furniture side since he designed in both the Empire and Louis Quatorze styles.[19]

From 1825 the authors of the various pattern books began to show French influences in response to fashion, with John Taylor including colonnettes for commodes and pier tables, console shaped supports with foliage at the knee and dolphin supports for tables. Henry Whitaker showed chairs with elaborate rails

18. Ackermann, Vol. XIII 2nd Series April 1822 p.237.
19. Wyatt Papworth, *John B. Papworth, Architect to the King of Wurtemburg: A Brief Record of His Life and Works,* 1879.

Plate 19. Fly-chair, carved, painted and gilt beech, c.1834. Designed by Philip Hardwick in the neo-Rococo style and made by W. & C. Wilkinson for the Court Drawing Room, Goldsmiths' Hall.

Armchair from Lancaster House, mahogany with carved and gilded decoration, c.1835. Benjamin Dean Wyatt and his brother Philip designed the interiors at Lancaster House, 1825-40, in the Louis XIV style although this chair is more in the style of Louis XV.

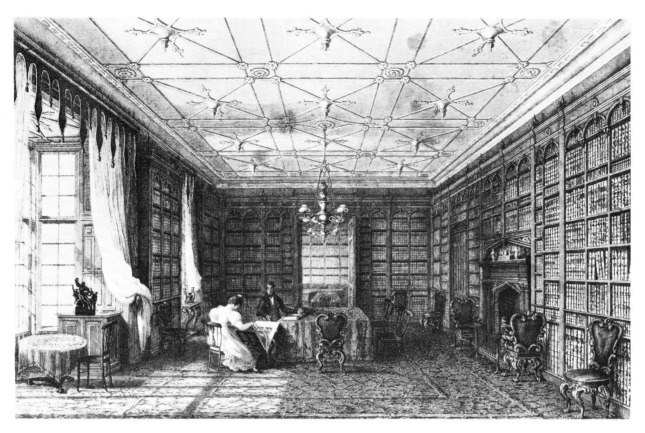

The Library, Eshton Hall, Craven, Yorks, from *Reminiscences of A Literary Life,* by T.F. Dibdin, 1836, showing furniture apparently made of oak in neo-rococo style.

composed of scrolls and foliage and a chiffonier covered with shells, scrollwork, various leaf and bud forms and lion masks and paws. In 1826 George Smith included designs for the decoration of the age of Louis XIV in his *Cabinet-Maker's Guide* referring to the expense of such a style. He also included designs for furniture in this style but commented that they were examples of 'magnificence, but not taste; an elaborate display of ornament, but no beauty in general outline. . .'[20] By 1833 reprints of eighteenth century books of designs, like Locke, Johnson and Copland's *Ornamental Designs,* had begun to appear, bought out by enterprising publishers like John Weale to satisfy the 'demand for the grotesque fanciful ornaments commonly said to be in the style of Louis XIV.'[21]

   The antique furniture market was not slow to respond to a popular trend and the Duke of Devonshire commented that after 'the peace in 1814 there came a rage for collecting and repairing the old furniture called Buhl: cabinets, tables, and pedestals were sold at enormous prices, and some fortunate people found their garrets full of the commodity, rejected by the changes of fashion in decoration. One of these tables was found here, another in a lumber-room at Chiswick, and another was bought for me by a lady as a wonderful bargain at £140.'[22] In 1824 James Morrison wrote to J.B. Papworth, his adviser on the furnishing and decoration of his house in Balham Hill 'If you should see anything (Clocks and Old China) at Paris which you would

20. George Smith, *The Cabinet-Maker's Guide,* 1826, p.187.

21. *The Architectural Magazine,* Vol. I 1834, p.313.

22. The Sixth Duke of Devonshire, *Handbook of Chatsworth* 1844, quoted in The Duchess of Devonshire, *The House A Portrait of Chatsworth,* 1982, p.134.

Design by Philip Hardwick, c.1830 for the Court Drawing Room, Goldsmiths' Hall, showing neo-rococo mirrors, tables, window seats and curtain drapery. The window seats are still in existence.

approve of for us, I should be obliged by your getting M.P*** to purchase it . . . The dealers from London are now purchasing freely old carved frames and clocks of the age of Louis XV.'[23] By 1833 dealers were offering a wide selection of Louis XIV furniture since 'the charm of their being really French is all powerful. Such is the effect of this charm, that many articles of Louis XIV's time are purchased, admired, and imitated, for no other reason than their antiquity.[24]

Although by 1833 Loudon was aware of the popularity of the Louis XIV or XV revival he did not consider it worthwhile to include many designs in the style for furniture because 'of the great expense of carrying them into execution, and because we think a style distinguished more by its gorgeous gilding and elaborate carving than by anything else, unsuitable to the present advancing state of the public taste.'[25] Thomas Hope also considered the style degenerate since some people were not content 'with ransacking every pawnbroker's shop in London and in Paris, for old buhl, old porcelain, old plate, old tapestry, and old frames, they even set every manufacture at work, and corrupted the taste of every modern artist by the renovation of this wretched style.'[26] The kind of designs which Hope criticised were those which appeared in the series of pattern books produced by Thomas King in the 1830s, of which the first, *The Modern Style of Cabinet Work Exemplified . . .*

23. Wyatt Papworth, p.57.
24. *The Architectural Magazine*, Vol. I 1834, p.244, which particularly recommended John Nixon's Show room in Great Portland Street.
25. Loudon, *Encyclopaedia*, p.1039.
26. Thomas Hope, *An Historical Essay on Architecture*, 1835, p.561.

was published in 1829, reprinted several times including an improved edition in 1835, and was to be incorporated into a trade catalogue by W. Smee and Son, one of the largest furniture manufacturers of the mid-nineteenth century. The collection of designs was intended to introduce cabinet makers to the range of styles available since as 'far as possible, the English style is carefully blended with Parisian taste' while the technical problems were minimised since in 'the gilded parts, carving will only be required in the boldest scrolls, or in the massive foliage' and the introduction of composition ornaments facilitated the production of 'rosettes, enriched mouldings, ornamental borders, and generally in the minute detail.'[27]

King's designs for the Old French style, as it was inevitably called, showed the predictable confusion between rococo light elegance and baroque solid scrolls but his furniture is typical of that being produced by many of the cabinet makers in the 1830s. His drawing room chairs have either crest rails with elaborate scrollwork or rounded backs with carving on the crest rail and splat. Chairs with upholstered backs surrounded by carving and with cabriole legs occasionally were painted white with the detail picked out in gold, as in the fly chairs (pl.19) designed for the Court Drawing Room of the Goldsmith's Company by Philip Hardwick and made by W.C. Wilkinson & Co. in 1834. In fact the Old French style was eminently suitable for drawing rooms and other more feminine rooms like boudoirs with consoles of elaborate curves shown for pier tables, teapoys and firescreens standing on plinths with feet composed of scrolls or foliage, and sofas or couches with arm rests composed of stylised honeysuckle or other stiff floral forms. Carcase furniture like commodes, sideboards and bookcases incorporate carved detail on their pediments and in the decoration of the pilasters while a design for a wardrobe has bun feet, anthemion decoration on the pediment and small motifs in the corners of the door panels in a form of furniture that is typical of the early Victorian period with its combination of drawers and cupboards.

In spite of the popularity of furniture in the Rococo Revival style and the general confusion about Louis XIV and XV motifs, certain influential individuals were critical of the examples being produced. J.B. Papworth, in his evidence to the Committee on Arts and Manufactures in 1835, criticised copying of ornament 'executed with facility by workmen unpossessed of theoretical knowledge and of practical accuracy.... erroneously termed that of Louis XIV, but which in fact is the debased manner of the reign of his successor Louis XV, in which grotesque varieties are substituted for Classic Design...'[28] But it was possible to adapt it successfully for furniture, as the *Architectural Magazine* observed in 1834, 'when confined within its proper limits, as applied to various articles of furniture, it is at once characteristic and elegant. It is so, because the flexibility of its prevailing lines renders it easy of adaptation to the forms of common objects....'[29]

---

27. Thomas King, *The Modern Style of Cabinet Work Exemplified,* 2nd Edition 1839.
28. Wyatt Papworth, p.108.
29. *The Architectural Magazine,* Vol. II 1835, p.7.

5. Historic Revivals

In the early nineteenth century the antiquarian movement developed in quite a different form from its eighteenth century counterparts, particularly as epitomised by Horace Walpole and his Committee of Taste who had created at Strawberry Hill and other houses domestic interiors containing copies of Gothic detail taken from monuments with little attempt at scale or architectural harmony.[1] However this Gothic taste could be refined by architects such as James Wyatt in his designs for Lee Priory,[2] and then elaborated by the same hand into such fantastical results as Fonthill (designed for the wealthy eccentric recluse, William Beckford) which collapsed in 1807.[3] This romantic attitude to the medieval period was to be elaborated by nineteenth century enthusiasts with the help of illustrated authoritative publications on medieval architecture, interiors and furniture, by the emergence of knowledgeable collectors and antiquaries, by the growth of specialist dealers and sales, and by developing popular interest, fostered by novels like those of Sir Walter Scott. The resurgence of interest in medieval remains was commented on by Rev. F.V.J. Arundell, 'It is comparatively but a short time ago, when mansion after mansion, possessing even the interest of Cothele, was suffered to crumble disregarded into ruin, or taken down to make way for modern erections. Happily, that vandal spirit is arrested, and there is now as eager a search for buildings that have the smallest pretensions to antiquity, and as anxious a desire to save them from further destruction, as there is for every article of furniture, and for every fragment of ancient carved work, which may be supposed to have existed in these mansions of early days.'[4]

The range of styles available included Norman, Tudor, Elizabethan and Jacobean, but because of the scarcity of genuine Gothic furniture and the relatively large number of pieces from the sixteenth and seventeenth centuries stylistic judgements were often muddled or simply wrong. In the domestic context a suitable mixture of Gothic, Tudor or Jacobean was probably the most popular, particularly Gothic since it was believed that this style was essentially native, '... the English have learnt better than to treat the Gothic with contempt; they have now discovered in it so much elegance and beauty, that they are endeavouring to change the barbarous name, and, with feeling partiality to themselves claim the invention for their own countrymen; it is therefore become here an established article of Antiquarian faith to believe that this architecture is of native growth, and accordingly it is denominated English architecture in all the publications of the Antiquarian Society.'[5] Although the

1. W.S. Lewis, 'The Genesis of Strawberry Hill', *Metropolitan Museum Studies* v (i) 1934; J. Mordaunt Crook, 'Strawberry Hill Revisited I and II', *Country Life*, Vol. CLIII, No. 3963, June 7th 1973, pp.1598-1602, No.3964 June 14 1973, pp.1726-1730; *Horace Walpole and Strawberry Hill*, catalogue of the exhibition at the Orleans House Gallery, Twickenham, 1980.

2. Hugh Honour, 'A House of the Gothic Revival', *Country Life*, Vol. CXI, No. 2889, May 30 1952, pp.1665-6.

3. John Harris, 'Fonthill, Wiltshire - I', *Country Life*, Vol. CXL, No. 3638, November 24 1966, pp.1370-1374; Boyd Alexander, 'Fonthill, Wiltshire - II', *Country Life*, Vol. CXL, No. 3639, December 1 1966, pp.1430-1434.

4. *Cotehele...* by Nicholas Condy. With a descriptive account written expressly for the work by the Rev. F.V.J. Arundell, c.1840, p.1.

5. Robert Southey, *Letters from England* by Don Manuel Espriella, 1807, Vol. 1, p.265.

Side table, ebony, mahogany and ivory, c.1805. Part of a suite consisting of a pair of side tables, an octagonal library table and two chairs, designed for the Gothic library at Stowe, probably by Sir John Soane.

interest in medieval antiquities had an aristocratic bias the popular appeal of Gothic furniture was to include the middle classes, who were to develop into eager patrons. However the popular periodical *The Repository of Arts* pointed out that 'no person of a genuine taste will introduce articles in this style into his apartments, unless there be a general correspondence in the appearance of his house', thus warning potential admirers of the Gothic style of the dangers of 'the grotesque and ridiculous.'[6]

T.F. Hunt in his *Exemplars of Tudor Architecture,* 1830 was aware of the problems as he pointed out in his Preface, 'The attempt at tracing a history of the furniture of the Tudor period is, I fear, very feeble, and the illustrative examples few and unimportant..'[7] but he indicated how, using surviving examples, Tudor furniture might be adapted to modern use. Hunt quoted many archival references for furniture but the surviving pieces he illustrated are far fewer, presumably because there were few suitable subjects, and come from four main sources, Penshurst, Cotehele, Haddon and Conishead Priory. Other scholarly publications which provided information on the medieval period, using surviving or recreated examples,

6. Ackermann's *Repository of the Arts,* Vol. III, June 1810, p.392.
7. T.F. Hunt, *Exemplars of Tudor Architecture,* Adapted to Modern Habitations, 1830, p.vii.

Armchair, oak, with the Windsor Castle inventory mark. Probably designed by James Wyatt, c.1805, as part of his schemes of Gothic revival decoration at Windsor Castle for George III.

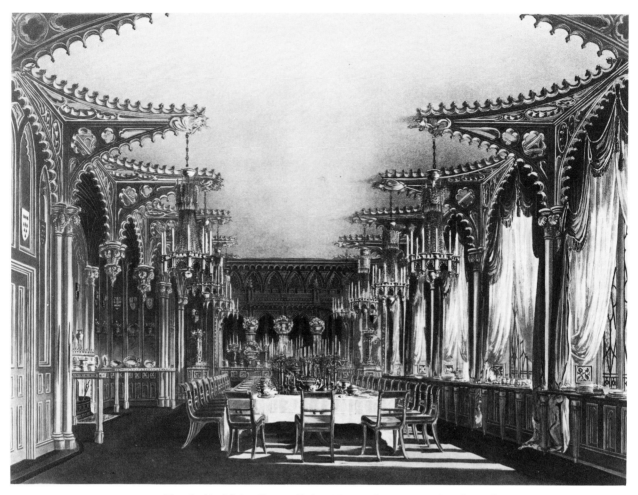

The Gothic Dining Room, Carlton House, from Pyne's *Royal Residences,* Vol. III, 1819, with Gothic carpentry by Jeffry Wyatt and gilding by Edward Wyatt in an interior designed by John Nash.

were those by John Britton, a very prolific publisher of antiquarian works, by P.F. Robinson on Hardwick and Hatfield,[8] and in his *Designs for Ornamental Villas,* 1827, and *Specimens of Ancient Furniture* by Henry Shaw and Sir Samuel Meyrick, 1836.

The problem with Shaw and Meyrick's book was that although there were many more illustrations than in Hunt's work quite a few pieces depicted were of dubious authenticity.[9] Various pieces, for example, Fig. III Cabinet of the time of Elizabeth or James I, are obviously confections and it is interesting to note how many of these belonged to dealers like John Webb or John Swaby. By the early 1820s collectors interested in Elizabethan or Jacobean furniture had a wide range of pieces from which to choose, including a few genuine ones, some with restorations, pieces made up of old fragments of woodwork, and modern pieces in the appropriate style. As Loudon observed 'there are abundant remains of every kind of Elizabethan furniture to be purchased of collectors. These, when in fragments, are put together, and made

8. P.F. Robinson, *Vitruvius Britannicus* London 1833, 1835.

9. For a discussion of some of these illustrations see Clive Wainwright, 'Specimens of Ancient Furniture', *The Connoisseur,* Vol. 184, No. 740, October 1973, pp.105-113.

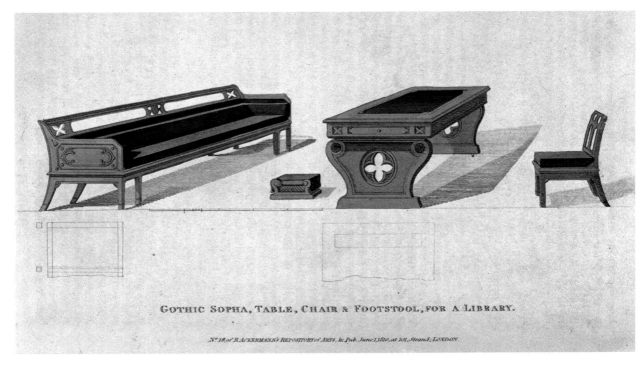

GOTHIC SOPHA, TABLE, CHAIR & FOOTSTOOL, FOR A LIBRARY.

Nº 16 of R. ACKERMANN's REPOSITORY of ARTS, &c Pub. June 1 1810, at 101, Strand, LONDON.

Plate 20. Design for Gothic Furniture for a Library from Ackermann's *Repository of the Arts,* Vol. III, June 1810, pl. 36, with purple leather upholstery. The gothic style was considered particularly suitable for libraries.

up into every article of furniture now in use. . . .'[10] Dealers, like John Webb, catered specifically for such demand, 'Hence it is that we have now upholsterers in London who collect, both in foreign countries and in England, whatever they can find of curious and ancient furniture, including fragments of fittings up of rooms, altars, and religious houses; and rearrange these curious specimens, and adapt them to modern uses.'[11] The publications of Hunt, Shaw and Robinson were all recommended by Loudon for those wishing to study the Elizabethan and Jacobean periods. Surviving original pieces were prized as Pückler-Muskau observed, 'In the apartments there was a quantity of old furniture, preserved with great care to prevent its falling to pieces, in its frail condition. This fashion is now general in England. Things which we should throw-away as old-fashioned and worm-eaten, here fetch high prices, and new ones are often made after the old patterns. In venerable mansions, when not destructive of convenience, they have a very good effect.'[12]

---

10. J.C. Loudon, *Encyclopaedia of Cottage, Farm and Villa Architecture,* 1835, Elizabethan Villa Furniture, p.1102.

11. Loudon, 1835, The Principal Styles of Design in Furniture, p.1039.

12. Prince Pückler-Muskau, *Tour in Germany, Holland and England* in the Years 1826, 1827, 1828, 1832, Vol. IV, p.224 (Arundel).

'Table of the time of Henry VIII, from the Hill Hall, Essex.' Pl. XIX, one of the more dubious pieces in *Specimens of Ancient Furniture*, 1836.

The demand for such pieces was fostered by the collectors with antiquarian interests who wished to furnish their homes with appropriate medieval furnishings and artefacts, like T.L. Parker of Browsholme who made extensive alterations to his basically sixteenth century house from 1804, using Jeffry Wyatt as architect. Parker collected panelling, woodwork, fire surrounds and other architectural material from other houses in the area and incorporated them in interiors decorated with objects which he then described in his *Description of Browsholme Hall*, 1815, 'the hall was ornamented with the armour and other curious things found in the house.'[13] Other enthusiasts for this kind of interior decoration included Thomas Baylis the antiquary and collector, of the Pryor'sbank, Fulham,[14] and the Ladies of Llangollen, Lady Eleanor Butler and Miss Sarah Ponsonby,[15] who embellished their cottage with oak carvings and mementoes of their visitors, 'There is scarcely a remarkable person of the last half century who has not sent them a portrait or some curiosity or antique.'[16] At Charlecote Park, George and Mary Elizabeth Lucy created one of the

13. Thomas Lister Parker, *Description of Browsholme Hall*, 1815. Parker owned a large collection of watercolours and drawings by J.C. Buckler, the topographical and antiquarian artist, who drew the plates for Parker's book and for *Specimens of Ancient Furniture*.

14. Simon Jervis, 'The Pryor'sbank Fulham', *Furniture History*, Vol. X 1974, pp.87-98.

15. Their peculiarly individual approach to interior decoration carried out from 1814 is described in Elizabeth Mavor, *The Ladies of Llangollen*, 1971.

16. Pückler-Muskau, Vol. 1, pp.22-3.

The Entrance Hall, Abbotsford, a photograph taken in 1870 showing the elaborately arranged armour, woodwork and other relics collected by Scott.

Interiors of the Pryor'sbank, Fulham, from *A Walk from London to Fulham* by T.C. Croker, 1860.

Watercolour design c.1817 attributed to Richard Bridgens for one of the dining room chairs at Abbotsford.

most outstanding examples of the Elizabethan Revival, from 1823-1867, with the help of Thomas Willement, author, heraldic expert, medievalist, antiquary and interior decorator, who was one of a distinguished group who combined their medieval interests with professional skills, like Edward Blore, Anthony Salvin, Richard Bridgens and George Bullock.[17]

The popularity of Elizabethan or Jacobean architecture, interiors and furniture was encouraged by the success of romantic novels with medieval themes, like those of Sir Walter Scott. He also incorporated into the rooms at his home, Abbotsford, from 1818, much ancient stonework and woodwork, festooned the walls of the Hall (p.169) and Armoury with a miscellany of weapons, armour and other objects, and collected 'gabions', his term for curiosities of historic value, particularly Scottish.[18] His furniture included pieces made up of fragments of earlier woodwork, like the reading desk in the Library, and earlier furniture, like the two Italian carved chairs in the style of Andrea Brustolon, acquired from John Swaby of Wardour Street who sold two others to Lord Byron for Newstead. Newstead was, in fact, another centre of medieval and literary interest for the visitor, where Byron, having furnished part

17. Clive Wainwright, 'Charlecote Park, Warwickshire', I & II, *Country Life*, Vol. CLXXVII, No. 4566, February 21 1985, pp.446-50; No. 4567, February 28 1985, pp.506-10.

18. For information about Scott's interiors and collections, see Clive Wainwright, 'Myth and Reality', *Country Life*, Vol. CLXXII, No. 4439, September 16 1982, pp.804-6; 'Object of Natural Curiosity', *Country Life*, Vol. CLXXII, No. 4430, September 23 1982, pp.886-8.

Bookcase, mahogany, c.1810, similar to designs illustrated by George Smith in *Household Furniture*, 1808.

The Drawing Room, Eaton Hall, from J.C. Buckler's *Views of Eaton Hall,* 1826.

of the Abbey for his use, finally had to sell the house to his school contemporary and admirer Colonel Wildman, in 1817. Byron's taste in furnishing was however unusual, as a visitor pointed out in 1811, '. . . as the house itself is literally a mansion of the dead, for the monkish cemetery was in the cloisters, it may account for the noble owner's taste in decorating it with the relics of the dead, instead of the more tasty ornaments of bow pots and flower vases'.[19] The restorations and alterations made by the Wildmans in 'a style of classical and appropriate magnificence' to a 'heterogeneous mixture of spendour and ruin'[20] included fitting up the Private Apartments in the south east wing 'in the most exquisite style, and in the best taste, with carved and polished black oak; . . . old carved oak panels being filled in with mirrors; and there is a wealth of similar material in the bedroom and dressing

19. Description of Byron's study written in 1811 from David Laird, *Beauties of England and Wales,* 1815, p.404.
20. *The Mirror of Literature, Amusement and Instruction,* January 24 1824, pp.50-1.

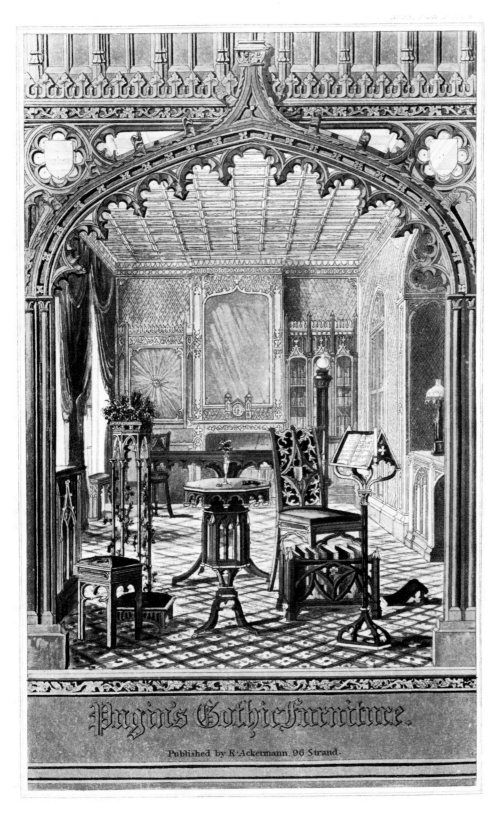

Title page of Pugin's *Gothic Furniture*, 1827, from Ackermann's *Repository of the Arts*, Vol. X, pl. 23.

Design for a Gothic Library, Ackermann's *Repository of the Arts,* Vol. X, July 1813, pl. 2.

room.'[21] This use of earlier woodwork in interiors and in furniture was to be much facilitated by the publication of Hunt's and Shaw's books after Daniel Terry, Sir Walter Scott's friend, had discussed with Scott in 1822 the lack of any publication on furnishing a house like Abbotsford, since only Thomas Hope's *Household Furniture and Interior Decoration,* 1807 and Percier and Fontaine's *Recueil de Décorations Intérieurs,* 1812 existed. However, the contents of various brokers' shops in London and the advice of Scott's friends, who included the cabinet-maker George Bullock and the antiquary Edward Blore, were considered sufficient for the creation of the interiors at Abbotsford.[22]

The problem for the designers of Regency furniture was to translate the illustrations shown in the various scholarly publications into suitable pieces for the commercial market, as Hunt pointed out, 'But the revivers appear to be more deficient in discernment... Their common fault is, in not distinguishing what was

21. Colonel Wildman, who made a fortune in the West Indies, spent almost as much on the restoration as the £94,000 he had paid for the Newstead estate. His architect was John Shaw who worked at Newstead from 1818 to c.1830.

22. Clive Wainwright, 'Walter Scott and the Furnishing of Abbotsford', *The Connoisseur,* Vol. 194, No. 779, January 1977, pp.3-15. The important relationship between George Bullock, the cabinetmaker, and Richard Bridgens, the designer, has not yet been fully studied but they presumably worked closely together judging from the evidence at Abbotsford where furniture supplied by Bullock is almost identical to designs in Bridgens' *Furniture with Candelabra.*

Armchair, carved and gilded mahogany, c.1823. One of a set made for the Drawing Room, Eaton Hall, probably to the design of William Porden and shown in the illustration in the foreground with decorative drapery over the back.

Chair, carved and gilded frame, c.1825, very similar to those shown in Buckler's view of the Drawing Room, Eaton Hall.

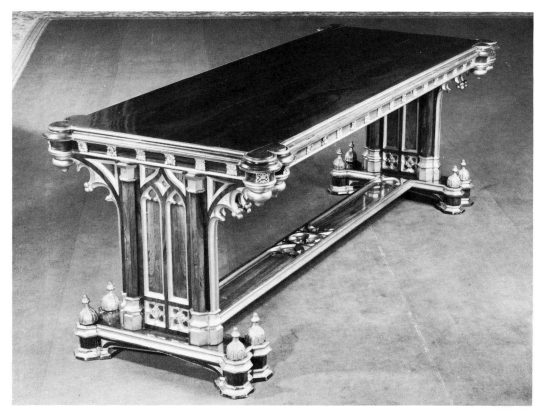

Table, rosewood, partly gilded, with gilt bronze mounts, probably designed by A.W.N. Pugin and made by Morel and Seddon in 1827 for the Dining Room, Windsor Castle.

Two from a set of dining chairs, rosewood, partly gilded, with gilt bronze mounts, probably designed by Pugin and made by Morel and Seddon, 1827, for Windsor Castle.

A GOTHIC BED.

Plate 21. Design for a Gothic Bed from Ackermann's *Repository of the Arts,* Vol. IX, February 1827 (plate dated 1826), pl. 9. The design, intended to be carried out in rosewood and ormolu, indicates some confusion with the mixture of gothic and classical motifs.

Gothic Chair and Sideboard, pl. 58, from Richard Bridgens' *Furniture with Candelabra*, 1838.

Armchair, carved and gilded frame, c.1820-30, with the Windsor Castle inventory mark, in the Gothic style associated with Pugin.

Plate 22. Gothic whist-table from Ackermann's *Repository of the Arts,* Vol. X, July 1827, pl. 41, probably designed by A.W.N. Pugin as a very young man and described as being based on the style of the 15th century as Great Britain was the only country at that time where "this beautiful style of architecture is understood".

devoted to the service of God from that which was devised for the accommodation of man. Church and house architecture were not so dissimilar in character as church and house furniture. Making, therefore, dining-room seats diminutives of cathedral stalls, crenellating footstools, and machicolating bedsteads, as is now the practice, are still more glaring incongruities than mingling ecclesiastical with domestic features in the construction of one edifice.'[23] Loudon also pointed out the lack of understanding of the Gothic style among furniture makers, 'The Designs for Gothic Furniture which we shall submit are few; because such designs are, in general, more expensive to execute than those for modern furniture; partly from the greater quantity of work in them, but chiefly because modern workmen are unaccustomed to this kind of workmanship. What passes for Gothic furniture among cabinet makers and upholsterers is, generally, a very different thing from the correct Gothic designs supplied by Architects who have imbued their minds with this style of art.'[24]

23. T.F. Hunt, *Exemplars of Tudor Architecture,* 1830, p.105.
24. Loudon, *Encyclopaedia,* Gothic Furniture for Villas, p.1088.

180

Design for a Drawing Room from P.F. Robinson's *Designs for Ornamental Villas,* 1836, showing some standard pieces of Gothic furniture, including a table similar to that designed by Soane for Stowe.

Joiners accustomed to working on Gothic domestic or ecclesiastic interiors were recommended by Loudon for making 'Tudor Gothic' bookcases as they would have the correct tools for the mouldings and a greater understanding of the style than cabinet makers experienced in the Grecian or modern style.[25]

The Cabinet Makers' London Book of Prices, 1788, had included some Gothic designs for glazing bars and Sheraton showed some in his *Cabinet Dictionary, 1803* and *Encyclopaedia, 1804-6,* but George Smith was the first designer to show a comprehensive range of designs in *A Collection of Designs for Household Furniture* of 1808. Some of his illustrations echo Hunt's criticism, particularly in pieces which have no medieval counterpart like the quartetto tables (pl.79) or the double chest of drawers (pl.131) but the majority of plates show perfectly acceptable designs for Gothic motifs applied to fashionable furniture. Some of Smith's more successful Gothic compositions were for furnishing halls and libraries and it was in fact the latter that became the epitome of the Gothic interior, particularly as far as

25. Loudon, op. cit., p.1095.

Ackermann's *Repository* was concerned. This fashionable periodical began publishing plates of Gothic furniture in 1810 with a sofa, table, chair and footstool for a library, and in 1813 began a series of Gothic interiors after designs by J.B. Papworth, including a Gothic Book-Room and a Library (p.174) where it was observed 'The application of oak to the Gothic style of architecture, has always been considered as affording great beauty, both by colour and by contrast. ...The manufacture of oak into furniture and other articles of taste and usefulness, has undergone an extraordinary improvement in point of workmanship...'[26] Oak was also a very suitable wood for hall furniture in the Gothic style which often echoed the architectural decoration of the hall itself, as in Benjamin Dean Wyatt's designs for a hall settle for Ashridge Park, designed in the Gothic castellated style by James Wyatt.[27]

However, Gothic designs could be applied to more elaborate and expensive furniture, as in those pieces designed for Eaton Hall,[28] the Grosvenor family home, where work started under the architect William Porden, in 1803, culminating in what Mrs. Arbuthnot described in 1826 as 'the most gaudy concern I ever saw. It looks like the new bought and new built place of a rich manufacturer... the house decorated with a degree of gorgeousness that is quite fatiguing & takes away all appearance of real grandeur. There is something much more imposing in the solemn dignity of Lowther, where nothing appears parvenu & all is oak & stone work.'[29] The furniture probably designed by Porden was made by Gillows in a variety of Gothic forms as can be seen in the illustration of the Drawing Room (p.172), some like the couch in the foreground, which is now at Brighton Museum, as relatively successful adaptations of Gothic motifs to Regency styles, while the sofa at the far end of the room is a far more fantastical piece. However, some contemporary opinion considered that the pieces were the 'truly consistent modern ancient furniture of the most costly kind in earlier days'[30] thus emphasising popular confusion about medieval forms.

By the 1820s the *Repository* was publishing designs for Gothic furniture regularly in spite of the lack of interest shown by other pattern books of the decade, and this run of Gothicism ended with a plate of an interior in 1827 in which all the pieces previously illustrated are shown. The designs were also published separately by Ackermann in *Gothic Furniture* in 1827 (p.173), and it is now believed that the author of the designs was A.W.N. Pugin who, at the age of fifteen, was already producing designs for furniture to be made by Morel and Seddon for Windsor

26. Ackermann, *Repository,* Vol. IX June 1813, p.338.

27. Jill Lever, *Architects' Designs for Furniture,* R.I.B.A. Drawings Series, 1982, pl. 24, p.55.

28. See J. and J.C. Buckler, *Views of Eaton Hall* 1826. Guy Acloque and John Cornforth, 'The Eternal Gothic of Eaton', *Country Life,* Vol. CXLIX, Part I No. 3844 11 February, pp.304-7; Part II No. 3845, 11 February 1971 pp.360-4.

29. *The Journal of Mrs. Arbuthnot,* ed. by Francis Bamford and The Duke of Wellington, London 1950, entry for September 1st 1826.

30. *The Eaton Tourist,* published by J. Seacombe, Chester 1825, p.83. Pückler-Muskau also described this 'chaos of modern gothic excrescences', Vol. III, pp.237-8.

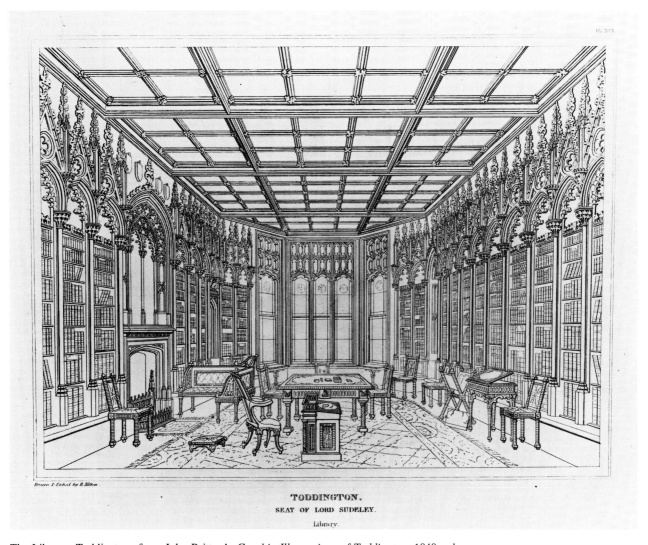

TODDINGTON.
SEAT OF LORD SUDELEY.
Library.

The Library, Toddington, from John Britton's *Graphic Illustrations of Toddington,* 1840, where an elaborate Gothic interior contains furniture in indeterminate style decorated with 'Elizabethan' bobbin turning.

Castle.[31] Pugin was later to deride his work at Windsor 'although the parts were correct and exceedingly well executed, collectively they appeared a complete burlesque of pointed design',[32] but the surviving pieces are examples of more successful attempts to adapt Gothic forms to contemporary furniture than many other Regency designers. Pugin specified different woods and decoration for the different rooms so that in the Beaufette Room and Gallery the pieces are of carved oak with burr walnut panels, in the Dining Room they are of rosewood with some gilding and gilt bronze mounts, and in the Coffee Room oak with some gilding, thus covering the range of suitable materials and decoration for Gothic furniture.[33]

31. de Bellaigue and Kirkham, *Furniture History,* Vol. VIII 1972.

32. A.W.N. Pugin, *The True Principles of Pointed or Christian Architecture . . .* 1841, pp.40-2.

33. Another interesting scheme of redecoration at Windsor, the Royal Library suite, under the direction of Sir Jeffry Wyatville in the 1830s included the adaptation of ebony and ivory furniture originally made for Carlton House by Marsh and Tatham into pieces more suitable for 'Elizabethan' interiors. See Clive Wainwright, 'The Furnishing of the Royal Library, Windsor', *The Connoisseur,* Vol. 195, No. 784, June 1977, pp.104-9.

Seat, oak with incised decoration, c.1838, part of a bedroom suite designed by Anthony Salvin for Queen Adelaide's Bedroom, Mamhead, Devon, in the Elizabethan style.

The Regency interest in the Picturesque, fostered by the writings of Richard Payne Knight, Humphrey Repton and others, recognised the Elizabethan style as an essential part of the landscape and Loudon considered the 'old English style, and in that ornate manner of it called the Elizabethan, as being most adapted to the habits of refined and peaceable times'.[34] He also praised the picturesque aspect and the irregularity of form, which suited the designers of the Regency Elizabethan revival since they could combine several elements of a suitable Old English style, usually a mixture of late Tudor and Jacobean motifs. Ackermann illustrated a chair 'for a book-room in a mansion built in the seventeenth century' in 1817 (p.185) which shows a typical eclectic mixture, with spiral turned uprights either side of a upholstered panel and ball turned legs and stretchers, a design which became a nineteenth century standard for the Elizabethan style.[35] Richard Bridgens, one of the most interesting designers of the Regency, designed the chair which was made in the workshop of George Bullock for Battle Abbey where Sir Godfrey Vassal Webster had decorated the interiors in a deliberate reincarnation of the Battle of Hastings in 1066.

---

34. Loudon, *Encyclopaedia,* Beau Ideal of an English Villa, p.792.

35. Ackermann, *Repository,* Vol. IV N.S. September 1817 pl. 14, p.183. The chair was also illustrated in Richard Bridgens, *Furniture and Candelabra,* 1838, and in an album in the collection of Birmingham Museum, *Tracings by Thomas Wilkinson from the Designs of the Late Mr. George Bullock 1820.* See Virginia Glen, George Bullock, Richard Bridgens and James Watt's Regency Furnishing Schemes, *Furniture History,* Vol. XV, 1979, pp.54-67. Another house where extensive remodelling in the antiquarian spirit was carried out between 1825 and 1835 was Audley End and Lord Braybrooke described his alterations and additions in his *History of Audley End* 1836, having consulted Henry Shaw, author of *Specimens of Ancient Furniture,* over the Library.

Fashionable Chairs, Ackermann's *Repository of the Arts,* 2nd Series Vol. IV, 1817 pl. 14, with the design for the chair from Battle Abbey on the right. Chairs after this design are now in the Victoria and Albert Museum, and the Birmingham Museum.

'X' frame chair from Adare Manor, Co. Limerick, oak, English or Irish, c.1840. Possibly designed by L.N. Cottingham and closely based on a plate in Hunt's *Exemplars of Tudor Architecture,* 1830.

Table, oak, stamped A. Pugin, c.1830. This table, in the 'Jacobean' style, is similar to surviving designs by Pugin for furniture for Mrs. Gough of Perry Hall, Handsworth, Birmingham. Pugin's furniture-making business was located at 12 Hart Street, Covent Garden.

Table, oak with carved and fretted decoration, c.1838. Part of the bedroom suite from Mamhead designed by Anthony Salvin. Very similar designs were published by Richard Bridgens in *Furniture and Candelabra*, 1838.

The Drawing Room from Nicholas Condy's *Cotehele,* c.1840, showing some of the ebony furniture thought to be medieval but in fact Indo-Portuguese, seventeenth century, and a sixteenth century Italian cabinet.

However, there were serious designers and architects who undertook research to ensure that their designs were historically accurate, and among these was the architect Anthony Salvin whose first major commission between 1827-33 was for Mamhead, Devonshire, which he designed in a Tudorbethan style with Jacobean and Stuart elements. The bedroom suite designed for Queen Adelaide's Bedroom incorporates typical Elizabethan motifs of decorative turned uprights and incised surface decoration of a strapwork pattern, similar to that of blackwork embroidery of the seventeenth century, all in oak. The furniture may in fact have been designed by Thomas Willement, since he was responsible for the main decorative schemes at Charlecote where there is a similar pair of tables in the dining room, and is known to have worked at Mamhead.[36] A.W.N. Pugin also designed in the Jacobean style, having made drawings of Hatfield House in 1829 and compiled a collection of designs for furniture for his short-lived cabinet making firm which survived from 1829 to 1831.[37] These original creations in the style of Pugin described as 'James the 1st' compare very favourably with his earlier immature designs for Windsor.[38]

36. Thomas Willement was a serious medievalist and designer of stained glass and wallpaper as well as of furniture. Wallpapers designed by him have been found at Charlecote and at Newstead where he is known to have helped Colonel Wildman with his antiquarian schemes.

37. Clive Wainwright, 'A.W.N. Pugin's Early Furniture', *The Connoisseur,* Vol. CXCI, No. 767, January 1976, pp.3-11.

38. Bellaigue and Kirkham, op. cit.

Elizabethan Table, pl. 39 in *Furniture with Candelabra,* 1838.

Table, walnut, in the Jacobean style, c.1840. This table is very similar to the one from Mamhead on p.186, but the central panel on the support is closer to designs by Bridgens.

ENGRAVED by M.DUBOURG from A DRAWING by G.CATTERMOLE for BRITTON'S ACCOUNT of F.A.

Plate 23. The Southern end of St. Michael's Gallery from John Britton's *Graphical and Literary Illustrations of Fonthill Abbey,* 1823, showing the set of ebony furniture thought by its owner William Beckford to be Tudor which is in fact Indo-Portuguese and dates from 1680. One of the chairs is now in the Victoria and Albert Museum.

Chair, oak, in the Norman style, c.1810, after a design by George Smith, *Household Furniture*, 1808, pl. 37.

Again Hunt's *Exemplars of Tudor Architecture* was recommended as a source for those interested in Elizabethan designs, as was Shaw's *Specimens of Ancient Furniture*, but it was in a review of the former that a writer in the *Quarterly Review* in 1831 approved of the growing taste 'for the rich and elegant designs of the Elizabethan age. Already there is a great and constant demand for its carved cabinets, scrolled chairs, tapestried hangings, and figured velvet cushions; and France and Germany are ransacked for these articles in order to restore to our ancient manor-houses and Tudor mansions their appropriate internal fashion of attire.'[39] However this popular demand was considered by the architect C.R. Cockerell to be based on a 'want of enlightened information' since the Elizabethan style, although occasionally excellent in execution, 'is undoubtedly of spurious origin'.[40] Loudon was also critical about the difference between Elizabethan or Jacobean furniture and its classical counterpart, 'We may here observe that the pleasure derived from seeing or possessing curious ancient furniture, is of a kind often quite distinct from that derived from seeing or possessing furniture in correct style, or in elegant forms... the present taste for Elizabethan furniture is more that of an antiquary, or of a collector of curiosities, than that of a man of cultivated mind.'[41] In spite of this

39. *The Quarterly Review*, Vol. XLV, 1831, p.503.
40. *Report from the Select Committee on Arts and Manufacturers,* 1835-6, Vol. II, p.193.
41. Loudon, *Encyclopaedia*, Elizabethan Furniture for Villas, pp.1098-9.

Wardrobe, oak, c.1835. Designed by Thomas Hopper for Penrhyn, Caernarvonshire, and possibly made by carpenters on the estate.

Furniture in the Norman style designed by E.B. Lamb *The Architectural Magazine,* Vol. I, 1834, fig. 166.

disapproving attitude Loudon was able to recommend the Elizabethan style since 'it is seldom necessary to manufacture objects in this manner, farther than by putting together ancient fragments which may be purchased at the sale of old buildings. Whoever in the present time (1833) wishes to furnish and fit up a house in such a manner as to produce a new and strange effect on the spectator, cannot attain his end at less expense than by having recourse to Elizabethan fragments.'[42] This use of the antique dealers and the interchangeable aspects of the Elizabethan style with other historical styles can be seen in another of Loudon's observations, 'During the past year, and for two or three years preceding, it has become fashionable to import, for fitting up English mansions, the furniture, chimneypieces, wainscoting, and carved wooden ornaments of dismantled French chateaux; and particularly to employ them in houses built in the Elizabethan manner: but this taste is on the decline.'[43]

An example of the type of furniture considered suitable for Elizabethan interiors was the carved ebony chair, illustrated by Shaw and captioned 'Ebony Chair, formerly belonging to Horace Walpole at Strawberry Hill. Now in the possession of Mr. Webb, Old Bond Street.' Although it was well known that Walpole liked such pieces since he had furnished Strawberry Hill with a set of 18 chairs and two tables the auction of his furniture and collections did not take place until 1842, six years

42. Loudon, op. cit., The Principal Styles of Design in Furniture, p.1039.
43. *The Architectural Magazine,* Vol. III, 1836, p.543.

A drawing room in the style of the thirteenth century designed by E.B. Lamb, *The Architectural Magazine*, 1835, Vol. II, fig. 132.

after Shaw's work was published, indicating the popularity of Walpole items for collectors.[44] A similar set of carved ebony furniture acquired for Charlecote in the 1820s was thought to be Elizabethan, although in fact East Indian and dates from the seventeenth century, and the Lucys acquired at the Fonthill Sale in 1822 a bedhead made from another seventeenth century East Indian settee for which ebonized washstands, tables and bedsteps were made in the 1830s.[45] Cotehele was well furnished with this evocative furniture (p.187) and the link between such interiors and the dealers was made by Rev. F.V.J. Arundell 'Twelve beautiful Ebony chairs and sofa-yes, an ebony sofa, notwithstanding Mr. Cowper's determination to modernise that luxury immediately attract the eye, as they would the heart of many a curiosity dealer in Wardour Street, where now and then an ebony chair of much inferior workmanship may be seen at the prohibitory price of from fifteen to twenty pounds. ...Ebony seems to have been in very high esteem with our ancestors, and why should it now be obliged to yield to mahogany and rosewood?... Our chairs and sofa retain their primitive appropriation.'[46] Ebony furniture was also recommended by Loudon for the Saloon and Gallery in interiors of the 'Old English style'. Furniture of ebony and ivory, described as 'Buhl', was also considered suitable for Tudorbethan interiors, particularly libraries, as can be seen in the pieces originally designed for Carlton House which were later altered for use at Windsor.[47]

Furniture with Candelabra and Interior Decoration by Richard Bridgens, published in two editions in 1832 and 1838, illustrated the command that Bridgens had of the Elizabethan style in his designs, particularly for the furniture at Aston Hall, near Birmingham, where Bridgens worked for James Watt from 1819.[48] Some of the plates show the same fretwork patterns based on sixteenth century strapwork and scrollwork as Salvin had used in his furniture for Mamhead, particularly in the plate of the Elizabethan side table (p.188), which indicates the close relationship of this talented group of designers and architects. Another example is Bridgen's professional association with George Bullock, the cabinet maker, which resulted in an interesting collection of furniture, including the chair at Battle Abbey, designed and illustrated by Bridgens and made by Bullock. The complicated nature of this professional relationship also included Abbotsford where Bullock made furniture for the Dining Room after designs by the architect William Atkinson in 1818 and very similar designs were published by Bridgens.[49]

It was natural that the revival of Gothic taste should result in renewed interest in the Norman, or as it was termed at first, the Saxon style. The Neo-Norman revival

44. See *Horace Walpole and Strawberry Hill,* exhibition catalogue 1980.
45. Wainwright, *Country Life,* February 1985.
46. Arundell, *Cotehele,* p.33. Hunt in his *Exemplars of Tudor Architecture* illustrated an ebony seat from Cotehele pl.XXXII. Sir Walter Scott also collected examples of ebony furniture including a rolltop desk acquired from the dealer Edward Holmes Baldock.
47. Wainwright, *Connoisseur,* June 1977.
48. Glenn, *Furniture History,* 1979.
49. Wainwright, *Connoisseur,* January 1977, p.7.

did not achieve the popularity of the Gothic or Tudorbethan styles but George Smith, the interpreter of the popular Regency style, illustrated Designs for Parlour Chairs for 'mansions professedly Gothic' in the Norman Revival style in 1808 (p.190) with a warning 'mahogany is not to be recommended for this kind of work, which requires wood of a close and tough grain, being in places greatly undercut.'[50] Certain contemporary books on domestic architecture, including Robert Lugar's *Architectural Sketches,* 1805, and P.F. Robinson's *Designs for Ornamental Villas,* 1827, refer to the revival and Robinson mentions 'some prejudice may be in existence in opposition to its introduction' which might be considered to be 'a novelty'.[51] The epitome of the Neo-Norman revival is Penrhyn, the vast castle built by Thomas Hopper in North Wales for G.H. Dawkins Pennant, the wealthy owner of the Bethesda slate quarries.[52] Hopper, whose career flourished after he built the Gothic Conservatory for the Prince Regent at Carlton House between 1807 and 1812, was given a great deal of freedom by his patron in the design and choice of much of the furniture which is in a bold Norman style (p.191) and is thought to have been made by estate carpenters. Other examples of furniture in this style are rare, although E.B. Lamb in *The Architectural Magazine* in 1834 advocated designs based on chessmen's chairs in the British Museum, resulting in a rather confusing mixture of Neo-Gothic and Neo-Norman motifs.[53]

The antiquarian revival which covered a wide range of interests, including the romantic medievalism encouraged by the novels of Sir Walter Scott and others, the influential publications of authorities like T.F. Hunt or Sir Samuel Meyrick, the enthusiasm of informed collectors like T.L. Parker, and the commercial products of designers and cabinet makers like Richard Bridgens and George Bullock was to provide a very interesting group of surviving interiors and furniture, expressing in all its variety and energy the spirit of the Regency. Perhaps the popular attitude can be demonstrated by a foreign tourist, Prince Pückler-Muskau, in 1826, 'I fancied myself transported back into by-gone ages as I entered the gigantic baronial hall, — a perfect picture of Walter Scott's; — the walls panelled with carved cedar; hung with every kind of knightly accoutrement; spacious enough to feast trains of vassals.'[54]

50. George Smith, *A Collection of Designs for Household Furniture and Interior Decoration,* 1808, p.9.
51. P.F. Robinson, *Designs for Ornamental Villas,* 1836, p.27.
52. See Robin Fedden, 'Neo-Norman', *The Architectural Review,* Vol. 116, No. 696, December 1954, pp.380-5, and the articles on Penrhyn by Douglas B. Hague and Christopher Hussey in *Country Life,* Vol. CXVIII, July 14th, 21st, 28th, 1955.
53. *The Architectural Magazine,* Vol. 1 1834, Art. IV. 'Design for a Villa in the Norman Style of Architecture', pp.333-48; Vol. II 1835, Art. VI. 'Design for a Villa in the Style of Architecture of the Thirteenth Century', pp.257-75.
54. Pückler-Muskau, Vol. III, p.216. (Warwick).

6. Exotics and Rustics

The development of later Regency design utilised motifs from a range of exotic sources including Chinese, Egyptian, Hindoo, Moorish and Etruscan, which have achieved far greater importance subsequently than the mainstream Greek and Roman styles. The Chinese taste, which was to be popularised through the preferences of the Prince Regent, had been very fashionable up to 1760 and lingered on through the later eighteenth century, but it was seen as essentially a Court Style and one emanating directly from the Royal Pavilion at Brighton, that pot-pourri of Chinese, Indian and Islamic taste. The only other contemporary example of such outlandish architecture was Sezincote in Gloucestershire which was built from 1805 in a quasi-Hindoo Moorish style by Samuel Pepys Cockerell, who was advised by the Indian topographical artists, Thomas and William Daniell, with the gardens designed by Humphrey Repton.

Although Henry Holland had designed a Chinese Drawing Room at Carlton House for the Prince of Wales in 1789 this was to be obliterated in subsequent alterations, as was Holland's original Marine Pavilion in Brighton whose inadequacies in the eyes of the Prince led to various extensions and redecoration schemes from 1795.[1] In 1801 the gift of some Chinese wallpaper fostered the Prince's interest and Holland introduced a 'Chinese Gallery' immediately to the north of the circular drawing room in the Pavilion and a 'Chinese Passage' Room with Chinoiserie stained glass panels.[2] Holland's Accounts for that year include 'making Designs for Chinese Decorations', using 'Works & Furniture by Messrs. Saunders, Hale & Robson, Marsh & Tatham, Morell, Crace'.[3] The firm of Crace were to be the Prince's main agent through the subsequent inevitable changes of mind and of architect, while Elward, Marsh and Tatham of Mount Street were to provide furniture in a suitably exotic style. A bill for expenses incurred for a total of £4,967.7s.6d. in 1802 included references to such characteristic items as 'India chairs', 'Indian Tables' with 'Fretts', sideboards 'on bamboo frames with frett rails', 'bamboo chairs japanned'.[4] Simple materials like beech simulating bamboo and lacquer were favoured rather than the ebony and ormolu that had been used at Carlton House, emphasising the gay informality of the new taste rather than the stylish and rich pieces made earlier. Authenticity was also provided by a proportion of the furniture and decorative accessories being imported directly from China.

Holland and William Porden, a pupil of Cockerell, both submitted designs for Chinese exteriors for the Pavilion in 1802 and although neither were executed, the Stables were built in Porden's interpretation of the Indian style in 1803, a new theme encouraged by the Daniells' publication, *Views of Oriental Scenery,* published 1795-1808, of which the Prince had a set. The Stables were approved of by Porden's rival, Repton, who described his reasons for choosing the Indian style for his new scheme in *Designs for the Pavilion at Brighton* in 1808, '. . . neither the Grecian nor

---

1. See John Dinkel, *The Royal Pavilion Brighton,* 1983.
2. John Morley, 'The Making of The Royal Pavilion, Designs and Drawings', 1984.
3. Royal·Archives 33528.
4. RA 25124-25125.

Mirror, gilded wood, c.1820. The convex shape was very popular in the Regency period and appeared in many forms, often with the addition of exotic animals, flora and other decoration.

the Gothic style could be made to assimilate with what had so much the character of an Eastern building. I considered all the different styles of different countries, from a conviction of the danger of attempting to invent anything entirely new. The Turkish was objectionable, as being a corruption of the Grecian; the Moorish, as a bad model of the Gothic; the Egyptian was too cumbrous for the character of a villa; the Chinese too light and trifling for the outside, however, it may be applied to the interior; and the specimens from Ava were still more trifling and extravagant. Thus, if any known style were to be adopted, no alternative remained but to combine from the Architecture of Hindustan such forms as might be rendered applicable to the purpose.'[5] Repton recommended the use of Indian motifs and designs because they had no resemblance to Grecian and Gothic forms, thus advocating a purity of style

5. Humphrey Repton, *Designs for the Pavilion at Brighton*, 1808, p. vi.

Chair, probably one of thirty-six dining room chairs made for the Pavilion in Brighton by Elward, Marsh and Tatham in 1802. Many designs in beech simulating bamboo were devised for the Pavilion from the 1790s until the 1820s.

One of a set of dining room chairs in beech simulating ebony with applied satinwood and brass inlay, supplied by Bailey and Saunders in 1817 for the Banqueting Room at the Pavilion, for £669. 12s.

Decorations in the Hindoo style from G. Cooper's *Designs For the Decoration of Rooms in the various styles of Modern Embellishment*, 1807.

The Saloon, c.1820, from Nash's *Views of the Royal Pavilion, Brighton, 1826,* showing the earlier chinoiserie scheme including some of the imitation bamboo chairs, lacquer cabinets and some of the fine collection of porcelain.

which was to be rejected by the Prince for a rococo fantasy, truly picturesque, as John Nash, the favoured architect, observed.[6]

In 1815 Nash began the remodelling of the Pavilion that was eventually, after a series of expensive adaptations due to his patron's changes of mind, to result in the present building. The interior underwent two distinct phases of decoration within six years which are recorded in Nash's *Views* of 1826, the first being more fantastical and Chinoiserie while the second was restrained and subtly rich. The contrast can be seen in two views of the Saloon, the core of Holland's building, the first showing it c.1820 with 'India' paper, fretwork cornices, and Chinoiserie chandeliers and pelmets, while after 1822 the paper had been replaced by crimson silk draperies and the pelmets and mirror frames had become distinctly more Indian in design.[7] Among the furniture designed for the room was a set of cabinets with a matching

6. In a draft for the unpublished preface to his *Views of the Royal Pavilion,* 1826, RA 34218-34219.

7. A full description of Nash's *Views* with a list of the plates and his unpublished preface were published by Henry D. Roberts, *A History of the Royal Pavilion Brighton,* London 1939, Chapter XVI.

Plate 24. The Saloon, Brighton Pavilion, from John Nash's *Views,* 1826, showing the room in its final transformation in 1823 by Robert Jones, a scheme of oriental sophistication with Oriental and Indian motifs, including a fine pair of painted and gilded open cabinets which are still in the room, and luxuriously upholstered ottomans.

chimney piece made by Bailey and Saunders, successors to Elward, Marsh and Tatham, between 1818 and 1825 to the designs of Robert Jones, the cabinets having central Indian arches with ormolu mounts and bell pendants.

The Music Room, the most spectacular of all the Chinese interiors at the Pavilion, was furnished with a set of four armchairs, twelve chairs and eighteen 'Runners' at a cost of £1,517 supplied by Bailey and Saunders in 1817.[8] The decoration included typically Chinese elements like the dragons carved on the crest rails, arm supports in the form of monsters' heads, dragons' wings under the side rails and scaling on the front rail. The Banqueting Room was furnished with a set of sideboards in pine and beechwood, veneered in rosewood and satinwood, decorated with fretwork panels in brass and dragons of carved and gilt wood, probably designed by Jones,

8. Details of the cost of the Decoration and Furnishing of the Music Room are given in Roberts, pp.134-5.

The North Drawing Room or Music Room Gallery, Brighton Pavilion, from Nash's *Views*, 1826. Among the rich furnishings are pieces from the Hervé set of seat furniture supplied for the Chinese Drawing Room, Carlton House, the two cabinets from the same room in the French style with two copies made by Bailey and Saunders, a pair of boulle tables made by Louis Le Gaigneur for the Prince Regent in the Louis Seize style, and more of the superb collection of Oriental and French porcelain, making this room one of the most elaborately furnished in the Pavilion.

and made by Bailey and Saunders in 1817 who also supplied a set of 36 chairs, with two matching elbow chairs with dolphin arm supports, in beech simulating ebony with applied satinwood and brass inlay. In the Corridor the original Chinese banners and mandarin figures were replaced by a set of Indian ivory and sandalwood chairs made c.1770 which were given by George III to Queen Charlotte, and bought by George IV after her death in 1819. The other rooms were furnished with an eclectic mixture of English, French and Far Eastern pieces, with the South Drawing Room containing Chinese export wares, Japanese lacquer commodes, and Holland furniture from Carlton House, the North Drawing Room the Hervé seat furniture and side tables from the Chinese Drawing Room at Carlton House, two boulle desks and more porcelain, both Chinese and Sèvres, and the King's private apartments English cabinets of Japanese lacquer, a boulle desk and a writing desk by Georges Jacob from Napoleon's study at the Tuileries.

Commode, beech simulating bamboo with japanned panels, early nineteenth century, of the type used to furnish some of the rooms in the Pavilion.

Chair in beech simulating bamboo and pine, another of the many variations in design produced in the Chinese style for the Pavilion and subsequently popularised.

The influence of the Pavilion on the taste of the period was not as persuasive as it might now appear and only one other interior seems to have been furnished in the same way. A room decorated at Ombersley Park, Worcestershire, for the Dowager Marchioness of Downshire between 1812 and 1814, was furnished with simulated bamboo furniture very similar to those pieces supplied by Elward, Marsh and Tatham for the Pavilion.[9] However, the Pavilion was the subject of much discussion, some favourable like Lady Bessborough, 'It is like Concetti in Poetry, in outré and false taste, but for the kind of thing as perfect as it can be...'[10] and other less enthusiastic, particularly about the amount of porcelain, 'All is Chinese, quite overloaded with china of all sorts, and of all possible forms, many beautiful in themselves, but so overloaded one upon another, that the effect is more like a china shop baroquement arranged, than the abode of a Prince. All is gaudy, without looking gay; and all is crowded with ornaments, without being magnificent.'[11] The influence of such a 'pattern card of royal folly and reckless expense'[12] was more to be observed in the fashion it set for the introduction of Chinese materials like bamboo, techniques like japanning and caning, and details like fretwork or trellis into furniture and interiors. The form of the furniture was usually of the conventional commode or bookcase with doors and sides of lacquer or japanned panels, the colour scheme being black and gold rather than in earlier styles of green and gold or red and gold, and some of the work being amateur rather than professional. A few of the pieces, like those supplied for the Pavilion, were obviously based on the form of Louis XVI commodes but with an imitation marble top and delicate fretwork in the frieze instead of the ormolu of the French originals. Even that arch populariser of the contemporary style, George Smith, included very few illustrations in the Chinese style in his *Household Furniture* and only one of these actually shows furniture (plate 81 Dejeune Tables), which is not one of his best designs.

Although the fashion for Chinoiserie continued into the 1820s, it was obviously part of the general desire for exotic fantasy, to be satisfied with the odd example as a foreign tourist found, 'Even from the very staircase everything is arranged as if in China itself; and when you enter, and see the ladies reclining, you may almost fancy yourself in Canton... Chinesiana, silk hangings, pictures, & ... The good creatures seem to me, in spite of their quality, to have brought a complete warehouse with them, for the moment a thing is sold it is replaced by another.'[13] Even George IV abandoned his maritime fantasy for the Gothic revival of Windsor Castle, and Britton pointed out in 1840 that the Pavilion did not become fashionable because 'it

9. Hugh Honour, *Chinoiserie The Vision of Cathay*, 1961, p.193, pl. 130.

10. Lady Bessborough to Lord Granville Leveson Gower, 9th October 1805, *Lord Granville Leveson Gower First Lord Granville*, Private Correspondence 1781 to 1821, ed. Castalia Countess Granville, vol. II, p.120.

11. *Extracts of the Journals and Correspondence of Miss Berry* from the year 1783 to 1852 Ed. Lady Theresa Lewis, 1865, Vol. II, 1811, p.490.

12. John Britton, *Graphic Illustrations, with Historical and Descriptive Accounts, of Toddington, Gloucestershire*, 1840, p.21 note.

13. Prince Pückler-Muskau, *Tour in Germany, Holland and England*, in the Years 1826, 1827, 1828, 1832, Vol. III, pp.362-3. Loudon's *Encyclopaedia of Cottage, Farm and Villa Architecture*, 1835, p.1073, also recommended 'articles of curiosity' like Chinese firescreens to be used occasionally in certain interiors.

Circular bookcase, japanned and gilded in the Chinese taste, c.1820.

failed to please even those who are generally too ready and eager to follow the worst examples of princes'.[14] However, the popularity of bamboo furniture particularly for bedrooms, and Chinese styles in garden design continued after the death of George IV.

The resurgence of interest in the Egyptian taste in the Regency period combined the archaeological study of antiquities with a popular craze for Egyptian motifs after Nelson's victory over Napoleon at the Battle of the Nile in 1798. There had been

14. John Britton, *Toddington*, p.21 note. Nathaniel Whittock, *The Decorative Painters' and Glaziers' Guide*, 1827, pp.114-5, commented that 'time has shewn but few imitators' of the Chinese style and only offered designs for decorating a summer room for entertaining.

The Green Closet, Frogmore House, from W.H. Pyne's *History of the Royal Residences*, 1819, showing cabinets and chairs of 'Indian cane' with wall decorations of 'original japan, of a beautiful fabric, on a pure green ground'. Princess Elizabeth, sister of The Prince Regent, decorated several rooms with japanned work.

Chair, painted and gilded, c.1810. An example of a conventional Regency form with decoration in the Chinese taste.

Table, kingwood with gilded pedestal carved with a lotus design, from the Drawing Room at Southill, c.1812-1815.

a tradition of interest in Egyptian or mock Egyptian culture in Europe since the Renaissance and motifs such as the anthemion, palmette, sphinx, pyramid and obelisk were all familiar details of the history of ornament and decoration.[15] Rome, because of the large number of Egyptian relics brought there after the fall of the Egyptian Empire, became the natural focus of attention for those interested in archaeological remains, and the publication of seven volumes on classical antiquities, *Recueil d'antiquités égyptiennes, étrusques, et Romaines,* 1752-7, by the Comte de Caylus, a source used by Hope, spread the knowledge of the contents of national collections through Europe. Perhaps the most noticeable influence on the Regency Egyptian taste were the fantastical designs of G.B. Piranesi, which decorated walls of the Caffè degli Inglesi in Rome and which were published in *Diverse Maniere d'adornare i Cammini* in 1769. Other printed sources of design included Bernard de Montfaucon's *L'Antiquité Expliquée. . . .* published in ten volumes 1719-24, on which Wedgwood and Bentley based their designs for the range of Egyptian wares that they produced from 1770. The drawings that C.H. Tatham sent to Henry Holland from Italy in 1796 included Egyptian ornament, one being for

15. Sir Nikolaus Pevsner and S. Lang 'The Egyptian Revival', *Architectural Review,* Vol. CXIX, 1956, pp.243-54; Patrick Conner (ed.), *The Inspiration of Egypt,* Catalogue of the exhibition, Brighton Museum, 1983; James Stevens Curl, *The Egyptian Revival,* 1982.

Cabinet, japanned and gilded in the Chinese taste, c.1820.

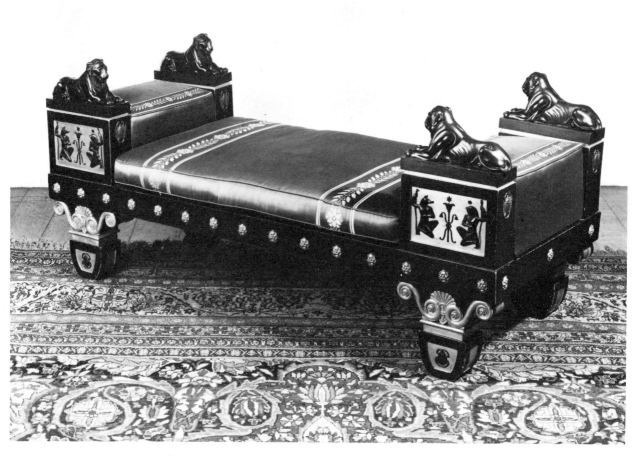

Couch, painted black and gold with bronzed and gilded ornaments, from the Egyptian Room, Duchess Street, London, and illustrated in *Household Furniture*, pl. 17.

a pair of candelabra with Egyptian figures made for Carlton House.[16] Holland's awareness of this trend can also be seen in the pair of side tables at Southill (p.206) which have gilt pedestals carved with the lotus design and stand either side of the drawing room fireplace carved with Egyptian terminal figures.

Thomas Hope created an Egyptian Room at Duchess Street, London, between 1799 and 1801, using his personal experience and sources like Piranesi's published designs to show how Egyptian antiquities could be combined successfully with appropriate decoration. The suite of seat furniture, of which one couch and two chairs are now at Buscot Park, were made of mahogany painted black and gold, and Hope described his sources for the decorative elements, . . .'the crouching priests supporting the elbows are copied from an Egyptian idol in the Vatican: the winged Isis placed in the rail is borrowed from an Egyptian mummy-case in the Institute at Bologna: the Canopuses are imitated from the one in the Capitol; and the other ornaments are taken from various monuments at Thebes, Tentyris, &c.'[17] The massive simplicity of outline of Hope's Egyptian furniture and the complicated iconography of its detail contrasts with the later indiscriminate use of Egyptian motifs on more conventional pieces. Hope also created an Egyptian room at his

16. H. Clifford Smith, *Buckingham Palace*, 1931, fig. 109.
17. Thomas Hope, *Household Furniture and Interior Decoration*, 1807, p.44.

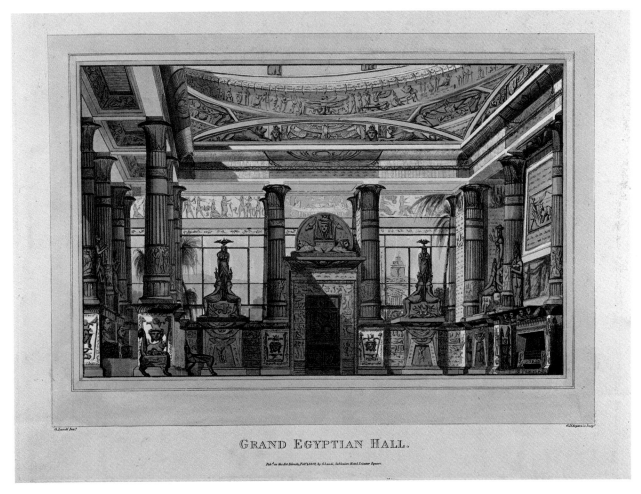

GRAND EGYPTIAN HALL.

Pub.ᵈ as the Act Directs, Feb.ʸ 1 1810, by G. Landi, Sablonier Hotel Leicester Square.

Plate 25. Grand Egyptian Hall from Gaetano Landi's *Architectural Decorations,* 1810, illustrating many of the Egyptian ornamental motifs popular for decorative detail on furniture. Edward Knoblock owned a pair of chairs very similar to the one on the left with animal armrests.

country house, The Deepdene, Surrey, where china and pictures were displayed and where Maria Edgeworth in 1819 saw a bed 'made exactly after the model of Denon's Egyptian bed'.[18]

The French vogue for Egyptiana evolved with Napoleon's campaigns from 1798, since he was accompanied by Baron Dominique Vivant Denon an archaeologist who recorded details of Egyptian topography and architecture and eventually became director of museums. Denon published *Voyage dans la Basse et la Haute Egypte* in 1802, and the English edition of the same year became an instant success, setting the fashion on which Southey commented 'Everything now must be Egyptian: the ladies wear crocodile ornaments, and you sit upon a sphinx in a room hung round with mummies, and with the long black lean-armed long-nosed hieroglyphical men, who are enough to make the children afraid to go to bed'.[19] Napoleon's defeat by Nelson resulted in a mass of commemorative motifs like crocodiles, sphinxes, ropes, anchors and other unsuitable decoration being applied to furniture, as in Sheraton's designs, and epitomised in the Dolphin suite of furniture on loan to Brighton Pavilion.

---

18. Maria Edgeworth, *Letters from England 1813-1844,* ed. Christina Colvin, 1971, p.197; David Watkin, *Thomas Hope . . .*, 1968, pp.179-80.
19. Robert Southey, *Letters from England,* 1807, vol. III, p.305.

Games table, mahogany with inlaid designs of lizards and other ornament, c.1820.

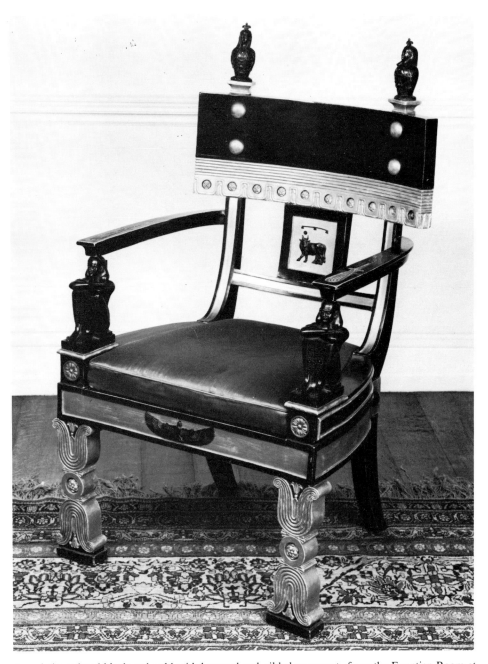

Armchair, painted black and gold with bronzed and gilded ornament, from the Egyptian Room at Duchess Street, illustrated in *Household Furniture*, pl.8.

The Egyptian style often amounted to no more than the addition of a crocodile, serpent, or sphinx head to pieces of otherwise conventional Greek Revival form, and the ambiguity of certain motifs like the lotus flower which could be used in a variety of ways ensured that Egyptian, Greek or other styles could be amalgamated successfully without adopting a purist approach as Hope advocated.[20] Sheraton's *Encyclopaedia* of 1804-8 was the first pattern book to use Egyptian motifs, although rather indiscriminately, with sphinx terminal figures for a Canopy Bed (p.74) and a bookcase decorated with similar figures combined with classical busts. A bookcase

20. *The Inspiration of Egypt,* 1983, pp.37-55.

DRAWING ROOM WINDOW CURTAIN & JARDINIERE.

Nº 39 of R.ACKERMANN's REPOSITORY of ARTS &c. Pubd. April 1.1810.

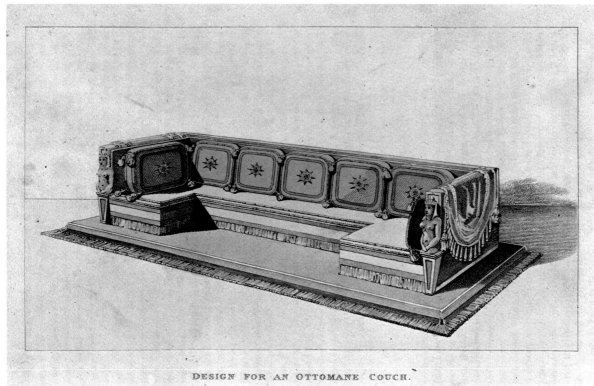

DESIGN FOR AN OTTOMANE COUCH.

212

Desk, mahogany with carved Egyptian and philosophers' heads, made by Thomas Chippendale the Younger for the library at Stourhead in 1805, costing £115.

Plate 26. Design for a Drawing Room Window Curtain and Jardinière from Ackermann's *Repository of the Arts,* Vol. VII, April 1819, pl. 15, a design influenced by the publications of Percier and Fontaine, the Empire architects and designers. The jardinière, which featured a bowl of gold and silver fish and a small aviary, is similar in concept to designs produced by the Danhauser factory in Vienna, one of the most famous of Biedermeier furniture manufacturers.

Plate 27. Design for an Ottomane Couch from Ackermann's *Repository of the Arts,* Vol. XII, July 1814, pl. 2. The use of Egyptian terminal figures refers to Egypt's then status as an Turkish Ottoman dominion while the terms "Ottoman" and "Turkey sofa" were used to describe any long, lowback, upholstered seat.

Pedestal cupboard, mahogany inlaid with ebonised stringing and Egyptian motifs.

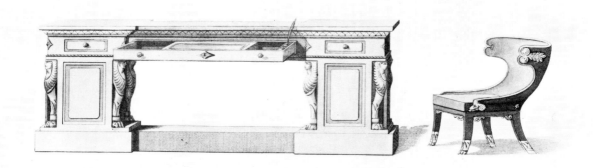

Library table and chair in the Egyptian style, Ackermann's *Repository of the Arts,* Vol. VII, May 1812, the decoration in ormolu and the top of the desk covered in green leather.

after this design survives with bronzed composition busts of Fox and Pitt at the top and plaster busts of Admirals Nelson and Duncan at the bottom (p.76).[21] Thomas Chippendale the Younger used the same motif in the furniture he supplied for Sir Richard Colt Hoare's library at Stourhead in 1804-5 where a pedestal desk, with both Egyptian and classical heads (p.213), writing table, eight armchairs (p.217) and two single chairs all incorporate sphinx heads in their design.[22] At Goodwood the dining room was furnished in the Egyptian style 1803-6, 'said to have been suggested by the works of Mons. Denon, particularly, his description of the Temple and Palace discovered at Tintyra'.[23] Although the furnishings included granite tables, porphyry vases and mirrors in marble frames, the dining chairs were more restrained, made of mahogany with ebony inlay and a bronze crocodile along the top rail. At Stowe there was an Egyptian Hall by 1805 and a bedroom which in August 1805 had been recently 'fitted up for the Duke of Clarence... in the Egyptian style'.[24]

George Smith was quick to take advantage of this fashionable taste and in his *Household Furniture* of 1808 included a range of designs in his personal interpretation with sphinx headed figures being much in evidence on library furniture, and the Egyptian heads and feet used as the terminations of pilasters on table legs and on bookcases and commodes. Some tables are pylon shaped with sides sloping towards the top, similar in shape to Egyptian porticoes, while sphinx heads are used to decorate the tops of mirrors and even small candlesticks are illustrated in the form of ancient lamps. Smith used a whole range of Egyptian motifs to decorate more conventional furniture including canopic vases, hieroglyphics, serpents, crocodiles and the winged disc of the sun. The ever popular lotus flower and bud appear as the feet of sofas, as a double motif dividing colonnettes, and as the capital and base of a column while cross framed stools often had the lotus motif used as a central decoration.

The divergence of scholarly and popular interest in Egyptian culture and decoration explains the critical attitude of architects and designers to what they saw as abuses of the style, as illustrated by C.A. Busby's remarks in 1808 'Of all the

21. Desmond Fitz-Gerald, 'A Sheraton-designed bookcase and the Giannellis', *Victoria and Albert Museum Bulletin,* Vol. IV No. 1, January 1968, pp.9-16.

22. John Kenworthy-Browne, 'Notes on the Furniture by Thomas Chippendale the Younger at Stourhead', *National Trust Year Book,* 1975-6, pp.93-102.

23. D. Jacques, *A Visit to Goodwood,* 1822, p.21. The decoration and furnishings were apparently removed in 1904, leaving only a few pieces of furniture including two side tables with lion monopodia legs made of lead.

24. *The Wynne Diaries,* ed. Anne Fremantle, Vol. 3, 1940, p.187.

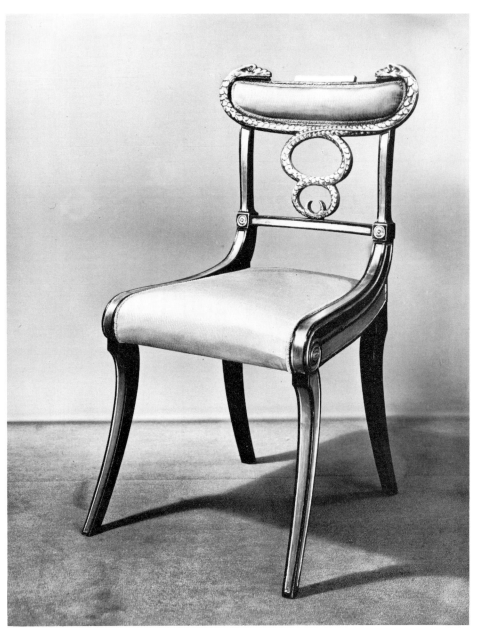

Chair, ebonised and gilded, c.1810, another example of a conventional shape with exotic decoration.

vanities which a sickly fashion has produced, the Egyptian style in modern Architecture appears the most absurd: a style which, for domestic buildings, borders on the monstrous. Its massy members and barbarous ornaments are a reproach to the taste of its admirers; and the travels of DENON have produced more evil than the elegance of the engravings and splendour of his publication, can be allowed to have compensated.'[25] Ackermann joined in the barrage of criticism, claiming in August 1809 that 'the barbarous Egyptian style, which a few years since prevailed,'[26] had been succeeded by classical elegance, but the *Repository* continued to respond to popular demand by publishing a library table with sphinx monopodia (p.215) in May

25. C.A. Busby, *A Series of Designs For Villas and Country Houses,* 1808, pp.11-12.
26. Ackermann's *Repository of the Arts,* Vol. II, p.132.

Chair, mahogany with carved Egyptian heads, made by Thomas Chippendale the Younger for the library at Stourhead as one of a set of eight in 1805, each costing £9.10s.

1812 and in July 1814 a couch with Egyptian terminal figures (p.212). Richard Brown also discriminated against the Egyptians who 'by the adoption of the pyramidal form, seem to have intended their works to outlast all record; but their productions are more to be admired for their sublimity than true elegance, and are more appropriate to monumental purposes than to furniture for apartments'.[27] However, he did include Egyptian among the list of styles recommended for the fitting up of a room with appropriate furniture and upholstery so as to present 'an accordance of ornament' unlike Sheraton whom he criticises for confusing Egyptian and Roman. In a typically restrained and elegant approach the Nicholsons suggested lotus leaves as decorative terminations for colonnettes on a basin stand and for

27. Richard Brown, *The Rudiments of Drawing Cabinet and Upholstery Furniture*, 1822, p.ix.

Cellaret, mahogany with ebonised and bronzed sphinxes and anthemion mouldings, c.1805. The sarcophagus form was recommended by George Smith for cellarets of mahogany with carved and bronzed ornaments. There is a similar example at Temple Newsam.

alternative schemes for the decoration of a cheval dressing glass, epitomising the way in which Egyptian motifs could be utilised effectively in Grecian Revival furniture. George Smith recommended the Egyptian style for a library in 1828, illustrating a bookcase (p.220) 'of the general form and character of the Egyptian temple' with appropriate Deities for decoration, although he was aware of the dangers of such barbarous taste and recommends the 'hand of an intelligent and clever Artist' for a 'light, yet imposing effect'.[28]

There were examples of a more exotic use of Egyptian motifs in interiors and in furniture at Craven Cottage, Fulham, created by Walsh Porter, 1805-6, with the help of Thomas Hopper. Walsh Porter was to become the Prince's adviser on the redecorations at Carlton House, presumably after Royal approval of his own fantastic interiors which included an Egyptian Hall (p.223), 'an exact copy from one of the plates in Denon's Travels in Egypt...'[29] with columns covered in hieroglyphics holding up the ceiling, palm trees in the corners, bronze figures, and furniture which included 'a lion's skin for a hearth-rug, for a sofa the back of a tiger, the supports of the tables in most instances were four twisted serpents or hydras...'[30] It was this

28. George Smith, *The Cabinet-Maker's & Upholsterer's Guide*, 1826, pp.168-9.

29. T. Faulkner, *An Historical and Topographical Account of Fulham*, 1813, p.432. Ackermann also described these 'grotesque and ridiculous' interiors, Vol. III June 1810, pp.392-3.

30. T.C. Croker, *A Walk From London to Fulham*, 1860, pp.190-1. Walsh Porter also created another set of unconventional interiors at Vine Cottage, Fulham, described by Croker pp.213-4.

Detail of library table, mahogany veneered with sabicu, with applied carvings also in sabicu, c.1810. The doors are carved with the wand of Aesculapius and the classical figures hold the emblems of architecture and music. Sabicu, a native of central America, was similar in appearance to certain kinds of mahogany and rosewood, being hard and heavy, and chestnut brown with darker stripes.

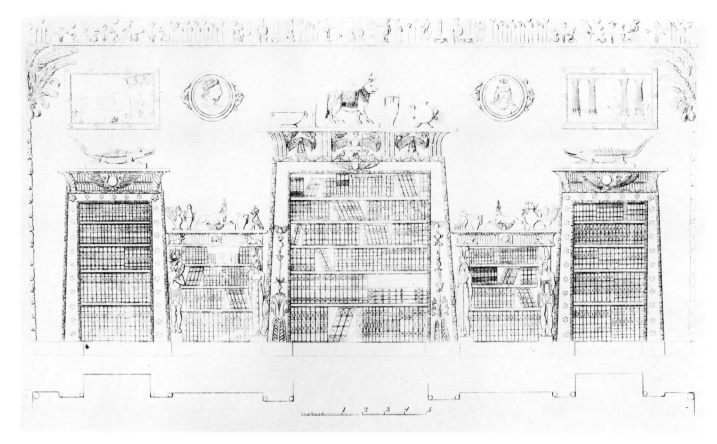

Design for a library in the Egyptian style, George Smith, *The Cabinet-Makers' and Upholsterers' Guide,* 1828, pl. CXLVII.

type of furniture which Richard Brown considered so 'disgusting and preposterous' because of the 'introduction of serpents and other obnoxious reptiles, to which we have a natural antipathy'[31] but contemporary opinion considered Walsh Porter's creation 'striking and characteristic'.[32] In 1810 Gaetano Landi published *Architectural Decorations:* A Periodical Work of Original designs Invented from the Egyptian, the Greek, the Roman, the Etruscan, the Attic, the Gothic, etc., for Exterior and Interior Decoration of Galleries, Halls, Apartments, etc., which included a plate of an Egyptian Hall (p.209), reminiscent of Piranesi's designs in its fantastical detail, although the 'lion' chairs shown in plate ii are more conventional and probably taken from Denon.

The interest in the exotic and in fantasy illustrated by the popularity of Chinese and Egyptian motifs could also be satisfied in a more familiar setting, that of the rustic retreat where the villa, cottage orné, temple, summer house or other romantic and picturesque creation, illustrated in a growing number of books of designs, could be furnished in appropriate style.[33] Various changes in fashion encouraged a more informal and less pretentious approach as was observed in 1817, 'The equality of expense, with the superiority of comfort, and independent privacy of the cottage

31. Brown, p.xii.
32. Faulkner, p.433.
33. Simon Jervis, 'Cottage, Farm and Villa Furniture', *The Burlington,* Vol. CXVII, No. 873, December 1975 Furniture Supplement, pp.848-59.

Side View.

Plan

1 Foot

Design for a cheval glass with alternative suggestions for lotus flower carvings, from Peter and Michael Angelo Nicholson's *The Practical Cabinet Maker*, 1826.

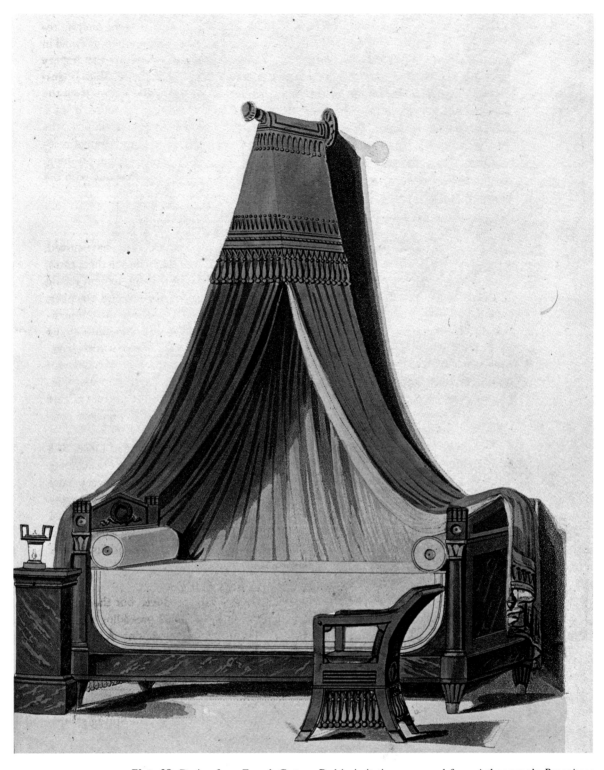

Plate 28. Design for a French Cottage Bed in imitation rosewood from Ackermann's *Repository of the Arts,* Vol. XIII, February 1815, pl. 7, an elegant example of the simpler styles suitable for fashionable villas and cottages.

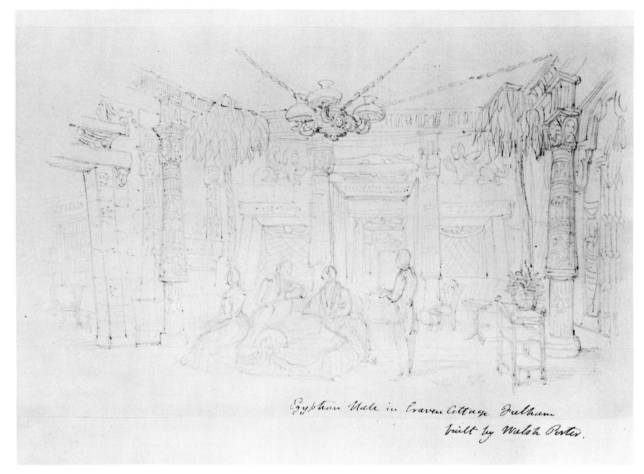

Egyptian Hall in Craven Cottage Fulham
built by Walsh Porter.

The Egyptian Hall, Craven Cottage, Fulham, created by Walsh Porter c.1805-6. Pencil drawing by Frederick Fairholt in an extra-illustrated copy of T.C. Croker's *A Walk from London to Fulham*, 1856.

style, is so congenial to an Englishman's modest retiring feelings, that it cannot fail of rendering it generally adopted'.[34] The growing interest in the Picturesque, in plants and gardens and the realisation of the important relationship between interiors and the landscape removed many of the barriers so that verandahs and conservatories became important additions to the living rooms of the house, a conservatory being 'frequently used as a breakfast or morning sitting-room'.[35] The furniture designed for these informal rustic settings reflected this flexibility with pieces constructed of more natural materials and sometimes used quite indiscriminately either inside or out.

The use of Chinese style in the landscape, a tradition of the eighteenth century in the designs of Edwards and Darly and of Sir William Chambers, continued in pattern books, in furniture supplied for retreats and in the illustrations of gardens. Charles Middleton illustrated some in 1799 (p.227) and the Thornery at Woburn, designed by Repton in 1808, was decorated with flowers and treillage and furnished with 'bamboo chairs japan'd as Botany bay wood' supplied by Tatham and Bailey, similar to the pieces they provided for the Royal Pavilion.[36] Repton's view of the Garden

34. *Annals of the Fine Arts*, Vol. I, 1817, No. II, p.26.
35. J.B. Papworth, *Rural Residences*, 1818, p.86.
36. Clive Aslet, Park and Garden Buildings at Woburn — I, *Country Life*, Vol. CLXXIII, No. 4467, March 31st 1983, p.775.

at Endsleigh, Devonshire, the cottage orné designed by Jeffry Wyatt for the Duke of Bedford, shows an armchair of the eighteenth century type with a Chinese trellis back[37] and J.B. Papworth recommended 'Small ornamental seats of China or porcelain'[38] for the furniture of the lawn while similar pieces, 'China barrel seats', were used along the verandah of the South Front and on the lawn at Whiteknights, these presumably being of bamboo in the Chinese style.[39] Papworth suggested more unusual designs, 'claiming a share of novelty, that perhaps may be allowed to them, both on account of the designs themselves, and the peculiarity of their construction'.[40] The first was based on an Indian temple and the second on a marquee, with some rather exotic decoration, and both were designed for easy assembly and removal.

The ideal furnishing of a rural retreat was also described by Papworth, combining plants, natural materials and Oriental decoration in the interior of a cottage orné: 'the little hall and staircase are decorated with trellising, composed of light lath and wicker basket-work, very neatly executed, and painted a dark-green: this is placed against the papering of the walls and ceilings, which are of a deep buff colour. Flower-stands and brackets are attached at various parts, from the bottom to the top of the staircase. The railing of the stairs being also of basket-work, the strings, &c. are painted buff or green, as the occasion required; for every part is so arranged, that the green may be relieved by buff, or the buff by the green . . . The parlour, the music-room and the lobby are very simply and neatly decorated by compartments coloured in tints resembling an autumnal leaf, the yellow-green of which, forms the pannels, and its mellower and pinky hues compose a very narrow border and stile that surround them. The draperies are of buff chintz in which sage-green leaves, and small pink and blue-and-white flowers prevail; the furniture is cane-coloured. Upright flower stands of basket-work are placed in each angle of the room, and the verandah is constantly dressed with plants of the choicest scents and colours. The drawing-room is fancifully ornamented with paper in imitation of bamboo and basket-work, in the colour of cane, upon a sky-blue ground, each side is divided into compartments by pilasters, which support a sort of roofing and transverse bamboo rods, to which seem to be suspended the most exquisite works of the Chinese pencil: these are the best that have appeared in this country, and consist of views of their apartments, representations of the costume of the people, and of the natural productions of China. A very able artist has further decorated this room, by painting a variety of Oriental plants, as supported by the pilasters, &c. about which they entwine, and arriving at the ceiling, they terminate, after spreading a short distance upon it. The furniture and draperies are the same as in the parlour. . . . In the whole of this cottage there is no portion of gilding; the glasses are let into the walls and

---

37. From the *Red Book* 1814, *Humphrey Repton Landscape Gardener 1752-1818,* Catalogue of the exhibition by George Carter, Patrick Goode and Kedrun Laurie at the Sainsbury Centre for Visual Arts, Norwich, 1982, Colour plate 4.
38. J.B. Papworth, *Hints on Ornamental Gardening,* 1823, p.95.
39. Mrs. Hofland, *A Descriptive Account of the Mansion and Gardens of White Knights,* 1819, p.29.
40. Papworth, *Rural Residences,* p.102.

Commode with book shelves, mahogany with gilt Egyptian ornament, c.1810.

covered by the paper decorations; and even the book-bindings are unornamented by gold, the lettering being merely stamped upon them.'[41]

There were other alternatives for furnishing cottages, including antiquarian schemes using the 'black furniture of ancient days, particularly chairs and tables, and even some of the same kind in modern use, when simple in their forms and of one hue (not picked out with a variety of gaudy colours) may be made to unite in no unpleasing manner to the general intention'.[42] Ackermann echoed this opinion in September 1813 by illustrating a cottage chair apparently composed 'after the designs which prevailed in the sixteenth century. . . . analogous to the purposes of a cottage ornee'[43] with similar strapwork decoration to that in Salvin's designs for the furniture at Mamhead. Jeffry Wyatt designed chairs in the Elizabethan style with bobbin turned spindle backs for the dining room at Endsleigh, a room appropriately

41. Papworth, op. cit., pp.50-1.
42. Edmund Bartell Jun., *Hints for Picturesque Improvements in Ornamented Cottages*, 1804, p.41, presumably some kind of ebonised furniture or pieces in oak.
43. Ackermann, Vol. X 1st Series September 1813, pp.175-6.

GARDEN SEATS.

Garden Seats designed by J.B. Papworth, *Rural Residences*, 1818, pl. XXV.

Designs for garden seats in Chinese and rustic styles from Charles Middleton's *The Architect and Builders' Miscellany*, 1799.

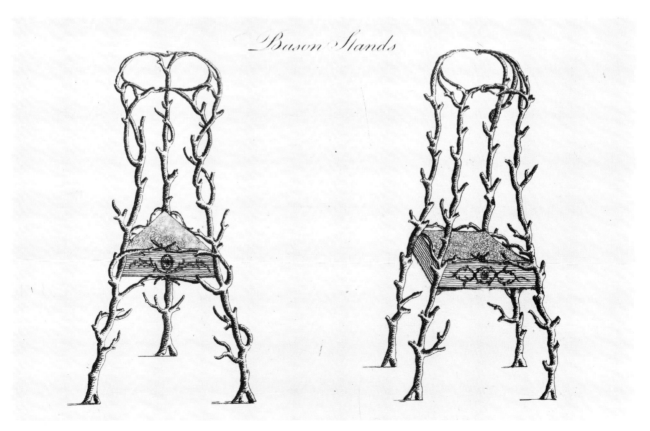

Design for Bason Stands from *Ideas for Rustic Furniture*, c.1790.

Design for mirror and side table from *Ideenmagazin für Liebhaber von Gärten* 1797, copied from the English publication *Ideas for Rustic Furniture*.

Design for Looking Glasses from *Ideas for Rustic Furniture* proper for Garden Seats, Summer Houses, Hermitages, Cottages, &c., c.1790.

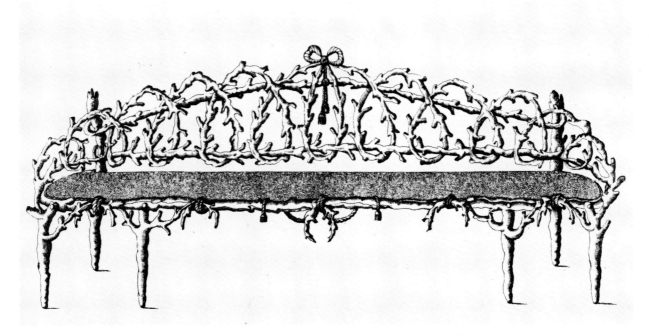

Design for seat, *Ideenmagazin für Liebhaber von Gärten* 1797, copied from the English publication.

Garden chair, wrought iron, in the Gothic style, late eighteenth century. Originally painted grass green and repainted over thirty times.

decorated with Gothic tracery en grisaille and grained woodwork.[44] Whatever furniture was chosen for the cottage orné it 'should correspond with the character of the building; chairs of yew-tree, elm, and tables of oak or wainscot, should take the place of mahogany'[45] which was considered too foreign for such natural settings that even the French had adopted the cottage orné and the English garden but the design of the French Cottage Bed (p.222) was obviously far too sophisticated since the French had 'preserved much of their own style'[46] for the kind of interior in which a simpler form of the Grecian style of furniture as produced by firms like Gillows and praised by Loudon would have been appropriate.

There was a wide variety of seats suitable for gardens, particularly those with covers, and as Loudon pointed out 'a great variety of names, such as root houses, heath houses, moss houses, huts, bowers, caverns, caves, grottos, temples, mosques, &c. besides plain covered seats either of wood or stone'.[47] Loudon recommended Grecian temples, Gothic porches, Chinese pagodas or other foreign or antique structures but rustic seats were considered rather childish by him who

44. Jervis, *Burlington,* pp.852, 855; Christopher Hussey, 'Endsleigh, Devon — II', *Country Life,* Vol. CXXX No. 3362, 10th August 1961, pp.296-9.

45. Bartell, 1804, p.47.

46. Ackermann, Vol. XIII 1st Series, February 1815, p.120, pl. 7.

47. John Loudon, *A Treatise on Forming, Improving and Managing Country Residences,* 1806, vol. I, p.328.

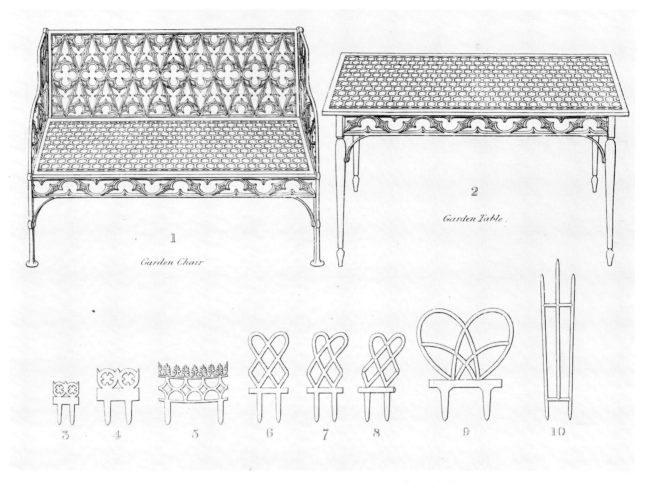

Designs for garden furniture from a pattern book of early nineteenth century metalwork designs.

illustrated examples of those designed by Papworth for Whiteknights, the Duke of Marlborough's house in Berkshire.[48] Rustic furniture, particularly that made of untrimmed branches and roots, appeared in the designs of Thomas Chippendale and Thomas Johnson and were featured in an anonymous work published by Josiah Taylor's Architectural Library, *Ideas for Rustic Furniture*, (pp.227, 229) Garden Seats, Summer Houses, Hermitages, Cottages, &c., about 1790-5.[49] This remained in print until at least 1820 and was reissued with no change in the plates by M. Taylor in 1835 while several of the plates were copied for use in J.G. Grohmann's *Ideenmagazin für Liebhaber von Gärten*, (pp. 228, 229) published in 1797. Picturesque settings for such furniture were composed of suitable materials as in the Duke of Buccleuch's bower where the 'inside was covered, walls, ceiling, chairs, and sofa, with moss, ingeniously woven into a solid velvetty matting; the tables and frames of seats were of rough sticks and roots...'[50] In spite of Loudon's contempt for such designs he did recommend adapting one of Thomas King's ideas for a circular ottoman with a central back support which could 'be made of straw, or, in

---

48. Loudon, *Encyclopaedia*, p.986-7; *The Architectural Magazine*, Vol. I, p.122.

49. Morrison Heckscher, 'Eighteenth Century Rustic Furniture Designs', *Furniture History*, Vol. XI, 1975, pp.59-65.

50. Louis Simond, *Journal of a Tour and Residence in Great Britain*, during the years 1810 and 1811. Vol. 1., p.344.

A typical garden seat of painted wrought iron after an early nineteenth century design. Examples with slightly diffferent patterns of wrought iron are in the Soane Museum and at Abbotsford.

some countries, of heath',[51] and appropriately placed in the centre of a large rustic summer-house. Tables and chairs made of untrimmed branches continued in popularity with designs illustrated by T.J. Ricauti in his *Rustic Architecture* of 1840 and in his *Sketches for Rustic Work,* while George Smith utilised the theme in the structure of his otherwise conventional four poster bed in 1805. However, the importance of the correct site for such furniture was pointed out by Edmund Bartell in 1804 as 'some attention is requisite, in allotting to them their proper situations . . . I have seen chairs made of the twisted branches of the oak or elm, truly grotesque, and well adapted to the cottage garden; for in that situation such fantastic seats may be admitted; but at a distance, where the pleasure is supposed to exist in the serenity or beauty of the scene, first impressions should not be broken; no frivolous ornament should impertinently intrude itself to interrupt the repose.'[52]

51. *The Architectural Magazine,* Vol. 11 1835, pp.512-3, review of *The Cabinet-Maker's Sketch Book of plain and useful Designs,* Vol. 1.
52. Bartell, 1804, p.77.

Gothic designs for garden furniture were produced by Repton for Brandsbury in 1789[53] and by Charles Middleton in 1799. Jeffry Wyatt designed a covered seat for the 6th Duke of Bedford at Woburn in 1811[54] and a very similar Gothic example was erected at Uppark, perhaps designed by Repton shortly after Wyatt's. Gothic garden furniture was particularly successful in wrought or cast iron which was also used from the early nineteenth century for more elegant designs with seats of strips of iron and delicate curves or trellis work for the backs and sides. The use of more naturalistic foliage for iron garden furniture was replacing this elegant design by 1840, but twisted wire was used for jardinières, hanging baskets and other pieces of lighter structure throughout the rest of the nineteenth century.

53. *Humphrey Repton* exhibition catalogue pl.56.
54. Aslet, *Country Life*, March 31st 1983, pl.3.

Design for a garden seat from John Porter's advertising leaflet, c.1840.

7. The Regency Revival

The Regency Revival is usually considered to have evolved in the two decades after the First World War but there are plenty of indications of a taste for late eighteenth century, Regency and Empire decorative arts from the middle of the nineteenth century, evidence of survival, rather than of revival. Clive Wainwright has shown how interest in the designs of Chippendale and his contemporaries developed in the 1830s, and by the 1860s designers, collectors and museums had moved on to Adam, Hepplewhite and Sheraton.[1] At the International Exhibition of 1862, the well-known firm of cabinet makers, Wright and Mansfield, showed furniture, the details of which were 'gleaned from the works of the Messrs. (Adelphi) Adam, and may be considered as indicating the style of English decorative furniture of the eighteenth century',[2] while in the Medieval Court at the same exhibition William Burges and William Morris were displaying painted furniture in the Gothic Revival style. Wright and Mansfield also exhibited at the Paris Exhibition of 1867 a very important cabinet (p.239) in the 'Adams' style (the contemporary term for designs influenced by the work of the Adam brothers), which was immediately purchased by the South Kensington Museum.

The development of the 'Queen Anne' Movement from the 1860s incorporated a move towards lighter and more delicate furniture than that designed by Burges or Seddon, an essentially English style rather than one influenced by Northern European Gothic. Mrs H.R. Haweis, author of several books on decoration and wife of a fashionable preacher, described this as 'the natural reaction among cultivated persons against the vulgarity of all the forms of furniture to which they have been for too long accustomed; these forms being in their turn a reaction against the excess of quietness, and artistic asceticism of seventy years ago'.[3] Whilst eclecticism was an important feature of Queen Anne interiors, the 'Adam' style was popular for drawing rooms and the contents of such rooms were equally varied, including Japanese screens, fans and prints, Persian carpets, and late eighteenth century furniture. There was a great deal of confusion about exactly what was meant by the term 'Queen Anne' exemplified in Mrs. Haweis's comment 'Only the other day I was shown a French mirror (Louis XIV.) by some really cultivated folks as Queen Anne ''Empire'', you know-genuine Chippendale!' She pointed out some of the problems since what 'people now call ''Queen Anne'' fashions with a charming indifference to the trammels of dates, are the fashions of the three Georges, Marie Antoinette... and especially everything which came in during the Empire (Napoleon I).'[4]

This range of styles available to the furniture designer was not as much employed as one might have thought, and period furniture was produced in either Adam, Sheraton or Hepplewhite styles until the 1880s. According to Herbert Cescinsky, 'Gillow of Lancaster, the Seddons, Edwards & Roberts, Wright & Mansfield, Jackson & Graham, Johnson & Jeans, and Copper & Holt, of Bunhill Row, all

1. Clive Wainwright, 'The Dark Ages of art revived, or Edwards and Roberts and the Regency revival', *The Connoisseur*, Vol. 198, No. 196, June 1978, pp.95-105.

2. *The Art Journal Illustrated Catalogue of the International Exhibition 1862*, p.104.

3. Mrs. H.R. Haweis, *The Art of Beauty*, 1878, p.244.

4. Mrs. Haweis, *The Art of Decoration*, 1881, p.42.

Chair, painted satinwood, c.1880, by Wright and Mansfield after a Sheraton design of the 1790s.

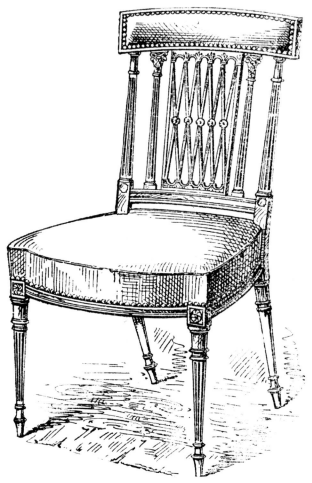

Chair after a Hepplewhite design, mahogany, c.1880.

Chair described as an 'admirable Sheraton specimen' by
Wright and Mansfield, *The Cabinet Maker & Art
Furnisher*, July 1st 1886.

Dressing table, painted satinwood, stamped Hindley & Wilkinson, c.1890. This is very similar to the example in the Victoria and Albert Museum which has been dated 1862-5.

specialised in ''Sheraton'' until about 1880'[5] but it was of Wright and Mansfield that the *Cabinet Maker* wrote in 1886, 'They must be accounted the leaders of that pleasing fashion which has happily brought back into our houses many of the charming shapes of the renowed eighteenth century cabinet makers.'[6] At the sale of furniture caused by the dissolution of the partnership in 1886 the South Kensington Museum purchased a pair of chairs (p.235), a card table and pembroke table, all said

5. Herbert Cescinsky, *The Gentle Art of Faking Furniture,* 1931, p.133.
6. *The Cabinet Maker & Art Furnisher,* Vol. VII, 1st July 1886, p.23.

Bergère chair, mahogany with cane back, sides and seat, with cushions covered in the 'Tulip' chintz, made by Morris & Co. c.1893 and probably designed by George Jack.

Plate 29. Detail of the marquetry, gilt mouldings and Wedgwood plaques on a satinwood cabinet designed by Mr. Crosse, made by Wright and Mansfield and shown at the Paris International Exhibition in 1867 as an example of the 'Adams' style.

to be in the style of Sheraton. By 1921 their furniture could be mistaken for the real thing since 'with the wear and tear of a household this furniture has acquired a tone or "patina" which renders its resemblance to its prototype very close'.[7]

Sources for reproductions included original pieces of which many survived, particularly the smaller pieces, and books of designs, including the various books of prices produced by the trade for costing their piece-work, which included Hepplewhite or Sheraton designs and were still being printed in the 1860s. According to J.H. Elder-Duncan, 'the reproduction of antique pieces, not, in the sinister sense, of forged or faked furniture, but of genuine and acknowledged copies of old pieces' was a special branch of the furniture trade, usually the antique dealers, since through their stock 'pass most of the genuine old pieces that are worth copying'.[8]

William Morris and his circle of friends had been interested in the late eighteenth century since the 1860s, when the firm of Morris and Co. moved to a Georgian house in Queen's Square and one of their most successful designs, the 'Sussex' chair manufactured in various forms from about 1865 onwards, was based on a typical

7. Frederick Litchfield, *Antiques Genuine and Spurious,* 1921, p.130.
8. J.H. Elder-Duncan, *The House Beautiful and Useful,* new edition 1911, p.123.

Dante Gabriel Rossetti in his Sitting Room at 16 Cheyne Walk. Watercolour by H. Treffry Dunn, 1882, showing an eclectic mixture of objects including a Sheraton style settee and two typical Regency convex mirrors.

Regency armchair with round cane seat, as shown in C.R. Leslie's painting of 1820, *Londoners' Gypsying*.[9] Although both Dante Gabriel Rossetti and Ford Madox Brown are believed to have been involved in the development of this design, E.W. Godwin also produced a very similar design for a 'Jacobean' armchair, and since the group all worked together so closely it is often difficult to identify one individual's work. The firm of Morris & Co. also featured in their catalogues from the 1890s, more familiar designs by Hepplewhite and Sheraton as well as a typical Regency bergère (p.238) with cane sides and back.

Both Dante Gabriel Rossetti and his brother William Michael were great enthusiasts of Regency art and literature, and Dante Gabriel moved to an eighteenth century house in Cheyne Walk in 1862 which he then proceeded to fill with a typically eclectic selection of objects, including blue and white porcelain, both Oriental and European, and English late eighteenth century furniture, both original and reproduction. His drawing room in 1863 was described by H. Treffry Dunn as 'one of the most curiously-furnished and old-fashioned sitting-rooms that it had ever

9. Simon Jervis, ' "Sussex" Chairs in 1820', *Furniture History,* Vol. X 1974, p.99.

Painted couch, probably designed by Rossetti and originally in his bedroom at 16 Cheyne Walk, c.1863.

been my lot to see'. Among the furniture was a 'cosy little sofa, with landscapes and figures of the Cipriani period painted on the panels', while the studio was furnished with 'Chippendale chairs and lounges' and his bedroom with 'an old-fashioned sofa, with three little panels let into the back, whereon Rossetti had painted the figures of Amor, Amans, and Amata.'[10] Whilst the sofa in the sitting room was probably an antique acquired by Rossetti after he moved in, the one in his bedroom, now in the Fitzwilliam Museum, is probably an early example of a Regency inspired design by him and slightly resembles the Morris and Co. 'Sussex' chair.

As a pioneer in the collecting of Sheraton and Regency furniture Rossetti was able to take advantage of the amount of cheap furniture available in antique shops. He 'delighted to take an evening's walk through Leicester Square, visiting the various curiosity shops in that neighbourhood, or through Hammersmith, a district where many a Chippendale chair or table could be met with and bought for next to nothing, such things not being then in the repute that they have become since the taste

---

10. H. Treffry Dunn, *Recollections of Dante Gabriel Rossetti and His Circle*, 1904, pp.18, 19, 36.

J.M. Whistler's studio in the Rue Nôtre Dame des Champs, Paris, from *The Westminster Budget*, 1894, showing two round tables of the type produced by Wright and Mansfield and part of a suite of Empire Revival furniture.

for Queen Anne houses and fittings sprang up.'[11] By the 1880s a great deal of publicity had been given to late eighteenth century furniture, and designs, either original or reproduction, were being regularly published in trade periodicals like *The Cabinet Maker* and in fashionable ones like *The Magazine of Art*. J. Elder-Duncan recommended 'The quaint little second-hand furniture shops in Wardour Street and elsewhere' in 1881 as useful sources but had to point out that 'ten or twenty years ago, before old furniture was as much sought after and as highly prized as it is now, it might have been possible to secure bargains, but your second-hand dealer of today knows to the last penny what the value of his stock is....'[12]

11. Ibid., p.29.
12. Elder-Duncan, p.221.

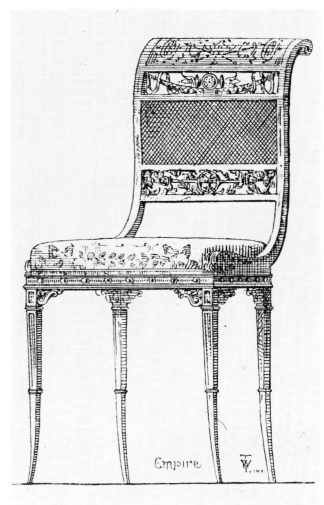

Jardinière, parcel-gilt bronze, c.1880, similar to designs by Hope.

Empire chair, *The Cabinet Maker & Art Furnisher,* August 1st 1884, described as either Empire or Grecian in style, and sanitary since the seat was removable for cleaning.

In 1867 E.W. Godwin was forced to design furniture for his house since he was unable to find what he wanted ready made, and for his dining room designed pieces in the Anglo-Japanese style, first in deal and then more successfully in mahogany. However, he realised that the effect was not 'calculated, to say the least, to make a room look cheerful or even comfortable' and decided, after considering various alternatives, 'to hunt up secondhand shops, for eighteenth century mahogany work inlaid with strips of satinwood. Whether it was that I had grown a trifle weary of modern designs in general, and my own in particular. . . the eighteenth century won the competition, and my dining room was refurnished with a bow-fronted sideboard, Chippendale chairs, flap tables, cabinets, bookcases, and a little escritoire, all of admirable colour, design, and workmanship.'[13] Godwin was to supervise the Costume Department of Liberty's, opened in 1884, and from 1887 the firm included a classic Greek gown called 'Athene' in their catalogue *Liberty Art Costumes.* The

13. *The Architect,* Vol. XVI, July 8th 1876, p.19.

Pedestal desk, mahogany with brass mounts in the Egyptian style, c.1890.

1892 catalogue announced a revival of Empire styles and included original sketches dated May 1813 of Empire dresses, commenting that they were able 'to offer to their clients the advantage of a prior and careful study of the Empire mode acquired by some years of experience in designing and fitting for Parisian Clients.' Grecian and Empire fashions continued to be included in the Liberty catalogues well into the 1920s.

Whilst Liberty's were supplying followers of the Aesthetic movement with suitable costumes, furnishing fabrics and objects, J.M. Whistler, friend of Godwin and one of the leaders of the movement, was collecting odd pieces of Sheraton and Empire furniture, either original or reproduction. In his Fulham Road studio in 1885-7 he had an old, painted Sheraton settee, while his Paris studio (p.242) in the 1890s was furnished with Empire and Sheraton furniture. Amongst a group of furniture bequeathed to the Hunterian Museum, Glasgow, by his sister-in-law, Miss R. Birnie Philip in 1953, are several pieces of Regency and Empire furniture,

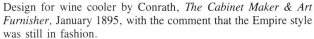

Design for wine cooler by Conrath, *The Cabinet Maker & Art Furnisher,* January 1895, with the comment that the Empire style was still in fashion.

Wine cooler, mahogany with brass mounts, very similar to Conrath's design, c.1895. Margaret Jourdain illustrated an almost identical cellaret, in *Regency Furniture,* fig.163.

probably reproductions of the late nineteenth century, including a Sheraton style settee which may once have been painted. Miss Birnie Philip also presented the Victoria and Albert Museum in 1933 with an Empire bed, with Napoleonic connections, which had belonged to Whistler.[14]

An interest in Empire as well as Regency styles was an essential part of the 'Queen Anne' Movement and, as Mrs. Haweis pointed out, 'the slang term "Queen Anne" means almost anything just now, but it is more often applied to the pseudo-classic fashions of the First Empire.'[15] By the 1880s interest in Empire styles was spreading among more conventional people and although Sheraton designs were still very popular, the availability of antique Empire furniture in private collections and

14. Other artists interested in Regency and Empire furniture include J.S. Sargent, whose painting of the Sitwell Family depicts an Empire table belonging to the artist, 'who was a collector of furniture, and showed great taste and knowledge' (Osbert Sitwell, *Left Hand Right Hand!* 1949, p.220).

15. Mrs. Haweis, *Beautiful Houses,* 1882, p.106 note.

Chair, mahogany with brass inlay and label of Edwards and Roberts, 1892-9, after a design by Thomas Hope.

Chair, mahogany with brass inlay, c.1895, after a design by Thomas Sheraton.

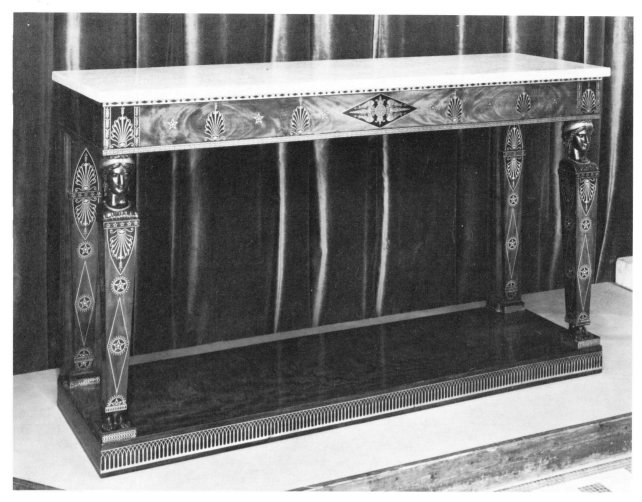

Side table, mahogany with inlay in brass and ebonised wood, and the label of Edwards and Roberts, 1892-6.

in the trade was noted by the *Cabinet Maker* in 1884 as many 'old pieces of Spanish mahogany brass mounted furniture, betraying an unmistakable "Empire" origin, still linger in English homesteads, or turn up in the sale rooms, and, for the most part, they are worthy of preservation, as respectable artistic relics.' Although the 'Adams' style of decoration and the designs of George Aitchison were both cited as evidence of a classical revival, it was obvious that the 'rage for reproducing late eighteenth century work is creeping on into this century... before long, we shall probably see, cropping up, some of the refined brass-mounted mahogany articles which were the outcome of Napoleon-the-Great's classic court...'[16] Designs for Empire furniture taken from the books of Thomas Hope and Percier and Fontaine, although only the latter were acknowledged, were included by Robert Brook in *Elements of Style in Furniture and Woodwork* in 1889 and he referred to the availability of Napoleonic relics for inspiration in Madame Tussaud's Exhibition in Baker Street. Alexander Henderson of Buscot Park, who purchased the 'Sleeping Beauty' series of paintings by Sir Edward Burne-Jones, asked Robert Christie of 102 George Street, Portman Square, to provide some furniture for his house, and

16. *The Cabinet-Maker & Art Furnisher,* Vol. IV, May 1st 1884, p.202; Vol. VI, March 1st 1886, p.225.

Commode, rosewood with brass inlay and mounts, stamped Edwards and Roberts, c.1894.

sketches of Empire pieces, including an octagonal table with female winged heads at the tops of the legs and lion paw feet, were illustrated in *The Cabinet Maker* in 1891.

By the 1890s the growing enthusiasm for Empire styles had become firmly established and 'wallpapers and tapestry hangings to dress goods, and even the patterns of women's clothes, all have shown a tendency to imitate the fashions of France in the days of the First Empire'.[17] As *The Cabinet Maker* pointed out in 1894 'Now that Louis Seize and Louis Quatorze have had a ''good run'' it seems to have become necessary for our leading upholders to ''make a change''. Failing the advent of some entirely new motif, there was nothing for it but to fall back on a respectable old one; and as the style of the first Napoleon came next in sequence to Louis Seize, it was quite natural to attempt once more to work that stately vein.' Several designs were illustrated which 'do not profess to be replicas, but they do possess a measure of that classicism which was the basis of the style'.[18] In 1895 the

17. *The Furnisher and Decorator,* Vol. VI, 1895, p.52. Relics of Nelson were also popular with his bedstead from the *Victory* being sold for 37 guineas and Lady Hamilton's fan for 68 guineas in 1896 (*Furniture and Decoration,* February 15th 1896, p.24.).

18. *The Cabinet-Maker,* Vol. XV, November 1894, p.117.

Pompeian Bedroom, The Waldorf Hotel, New York, *The Cabinet Maker & Art Furnisher*, February 1895, described as a 'praiseworthy attempt to adapt the Pompeian style to modern bedroom purposes.'

periodical devoted several pages to illustrations taken from Hope's *Household Furniture,* pointing out that these 'views, now ninety years old, are worth reading at the present time, for the Empire style comes to us in much the same way that it came at the beginning of the century.'[19]

The reproduction of Empire furniture created some problems for the cabinet makers interested in such styles and it was pointed out that 'the difficulties entailed by applying metal mounts and inlaying brass lines militate considerably against the extensive employment of this charming mode.'[20] Although brass founders provided exact facsimiles of Napoleonic ormolu mounts suitable for such pieces of furniture the chaste and restrained effect necessary prevented a 'lavish display of cheap ornament... any attempt to infuse cheap ornament into Empire work destroys its character.'[21] There was no overwhelming popularity for the style since despite its

19. *Cabinet Maker,* Vol. XV, January 1895, p.178.
20. *Furniture and Decoration,* February 15th 1896, p.22.
21. Op. cit., October 15th 1897, p.199.

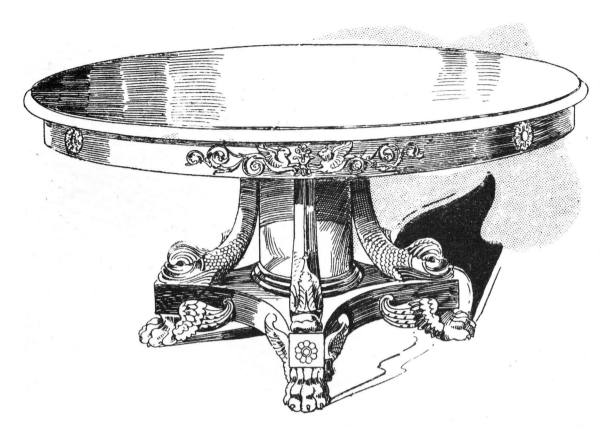

Design for table by the Brooks Household Art Company, The Cabinet Maker & Art Furnisher,
August 1895, similar to tables illustrated in the *Repository of Arts.*

Design for sideboard by the Brooks Household Art Company, *The Cabinet Maker & Art Furnisher,*
August 1895, typical of the debased Greek Revival styles of the later Regency.

Design for chair, 'unquestionably in Sheraton's style', *Furniture and Decoration,* September 15th, 1897.

beauty 'and the facility with which it may be employed by both chair and cabinet-makers, there is still a great paucity of examples to be seen in fashionable showrooms. It would almost seem that the style is too severe for English taste, and that it comes upon us as too great a contrast against the other extreme of the Louis Quinze.'[22]

In spite of this rather depressing attitude several firms did produce a number of Empire designs, including Edwards and Roberts who were founded in 1845, and by 1854 were trading as 'Edwards and Roberts 2 Wardour Street, Antique and Modern cabinet makers and importers of ancient furniture'. By 1892 they had expanded to

22. Op. cit., February 15th 1896, p.23.

The Ladies' Drawing Room, Hotel Cecil, London, 1896, as furnished by Maples.

a number of addresses in and around Wardour Street and a description of the firm in 1898 included the information that 'the "rage" during the last twelve years has been for furniture by "Chippendale", "Sheraton", "Hepplewhite", and "Adams" ', and that a 'fine and complete library of the works of these old designers is to be seen at Messrs. Edwards and Roberts'. 'The old French styles of the period of Louis XIV., XV., XVI., and of the "Empire" are much in request' and a representative of the firm also said that he 'believed that very little fraud was practised' as 'high class imitations of old furniture were very costly'.[23]

A number of pieces with the stamp of Edwards and Roberts have been studied

23. The Clergy of St. Anne's Soho, *Two Centuries of Soho*, 1898, pp.188-92.

The Empire Salon, Carlton Hotel, London, as decorated by Warings, *The Furnisher,* Vol. I, 1900.

Carlton House desk, mahogany, c.1900.

Dining chair, mahogany, c.1900, inspired by Regency styles.

Drawing room at Elmbank, York, with furniture designed by George Walton, *The British Home of To-day,* edited by W. Shaw Sparrow 1904. The chairs are very similar to ones Walton designed for Miss Cranston's tearooms in Glasgow in the 1890s.

PLATE XXVII. ADAMS DRAWING ROOM.   *Photographed at Warings.*

Adams Drawing Room, designed by Warings, *Our Homes and How to Beautify Them,* by H.J. Jennings, 1902.

recently (pp.246, 248, 249, 258), some after Hope designs and others typical of the brass-inlaid furniture of the 1820s while the firm also supplied more obvious reproductions of Sheraton and Regency furniture.[24] As they dealt in antiques, reproduction and modern furniture and stamped or labelled all these, it is often difficult to distinguish one of their reproduction pieces from a genuine one that passed through their hands. There seems to have been some contemporary confusion as well since in 1892 Frederick Litchfield wrote 'In order to supply the demand which has lately arisen chiefly in New York, but to some extent in England for the best "Empire" furniture the French dealers have brought up some of the old undecorated pieces and by ornamenting them with gilt bronze mounts cast from good old patterns have sold them as original examples.'[25]

24. Wainwright, *Connoisseur,* June 1978.

25. Frederick Litchfield, *Illustrated History of Furniture,* 1892, p.206.

Plate 30. Detail of the side table, mahogany with inlay in brass and ebonised wood, made between 1892 and 1896 by Edwards and Roberts as a sophisticated exercise in the neo-Regency style, inspired by designs by Percier and Fontaine.

Sheraton Bedroom, designed by Warings, *Our Homes and How to Beautify Them,* 1904.

Sofa, painted satinwood, made by Gillows, *The British Home of To-day,* 1904.

Sideboard, mahogany, in the Sheraton style by Robert Christie, *The British Home of To-day,* 1904.

Set of quartetto tables, mahogany, early twentieth century.

The drawing room of Charles Ricketts and Charles Shannon, Lansdowne House, London, c.1904, furnished with Hepplewhite and Sheraton furniture and Morris textiles.

Britain was not the only country to experience a revival of interest in late eighteenth century, Regency and Empire styles, and America 'greedily adopted the style of the ''Empire'' as soon as they saw modern public opinion was ripe for it...' and while England had been toying with the style, 'our more courageous relations have filled their showrooms with revivals'.[26] *The Cabinet Maker* described the various rooms and furnishings of the Waldorf Hotel in New York in 1895, including an Empire dining room and 'a praiseworthy attempt to adapt the Pompeian style to modern bedroom purposes' (p.250).[27] Also illustrated were a number of designs for furniture, said to be Empire although some were more typical of the debased classical styles of the later Regency, produced by the Brooks Household Art Company of Cleveland, Ohio. Mario Praz has described how unimportant the Empire Revival was considered to be in Italy, but that in France there were many allusions to it throughout the nineteenth century although not all were favourable.[28]

26. *Cabinet-Maker,* Vol. XV February 1895, p.208; Vol. XVI, August 1895, p.29.
27. *Cabinet Maker,* Vol. XV, February 1895, 205-212.
28. Mario Praz, *On Neoclassicism,* 1959, Chapter XV Resurrection of the Empire Style.

Hotels in England were also furnished in the Empire taste and the Hotel Cecil, London, was redecorated with several rooms in the style, including the drawing room (p.253) where the scheme had 'evidently received careful study' although it was pointed out that 'lavish uniformity of style is neither historically accurate nor artistically interesting. In style, a good deal of learning is often a dangerous thing'.[29] The furniture in the drawing room was of mahogany with ormolu mounts, upholstered in pale blue and silver cut velvet and the room furnished by Maples. Sheraton styles continued in popularity and the Carlton Hotel, London, decorated and furnished by Messrs. S.J. Waring from 1898 on, had both an Empire (p.254) and a Sheraton Salon. Both Sheraton's *Drawing Book* and Hepplewhite's *Upholsterers' Guide* had been reprinted by 1897 in order to meet the demand from 'our best furnishers for their showrooms, as original pieces have been so eagerly snapped up by connoisseurs that it is most difficult to obtain them'.[30] Even an Arts and Crafts designer like George Walton succumbed to contemporary fashion by producing designs for furniture for Miss Cranston's tearooms in Buchanan Street, Glasgow (p.256), based on a typical Regency design of an armchair with cane back and seat.

Empire and Regency furniture designs continued in popularity after 1900 with examples of reproduction and antique pieces being advertised by such firms as Gill and Reigate, Maples, Norman and Stacey, and Nicholls and Janes. Hermann Muthesius who worked in England (1896-1903) and later produced *Das Englishche Haus* 1904-5, a classic description of the architecture, interiors and furnishings popular at the time, described the popularity of Sheraton designs: 'Large factories, each employing hundreds of workers, devote all their efforts to the production of this furniture, furniture shops are full of new copies of Sheraton and Chippendale, for these are the pieces that the English public most desires. All the techniques of the late eighteenth century — inlay, satinwood veneer, painting on wood, have been recovered.'[31] Reproduction furniture was not considered any less attractive than antique pieces since it was believed that 'it is far better to possess modern copies of good old examples than either the antique but uninteresting work of a tasteless maker, or the spurious exhibits of Wardour Street'.[32]

One of the most interesting uses of neo-Regency styles in the early twentieth century was the interiors and furniture designed 1913-15 by Giles and Adrian Gilbert Scott for 129 Grosvenor Road, London, the home of the Hon. Sir Arthur Stanley, M.P. Giles Gilbert Scott, who designed most of the furniture after his brother left for military service, had already produced designs for neo-Regency interiors for his own house, 4 Campden Hill, Kensington, before the First World War, and for the house in Grosvenor Road, he was taken by his client to Italy where he sketched many details of furniture and decoration at Pompeii and elsewhere. The remarkable neo-Greek furniture that he designed included a marble topped table with legs copied from a bronze

29. *The Furnisher*, September 1900, pp.377-8.
30. *The Studio*, Vol. V, 1895, p.XLV.
31. Hermann Muthesius, *The English House*, English edition 1979, p.195.
32. H.J. Jennings, *Our Homes and How to Beautify Them*, 1902, p.23.

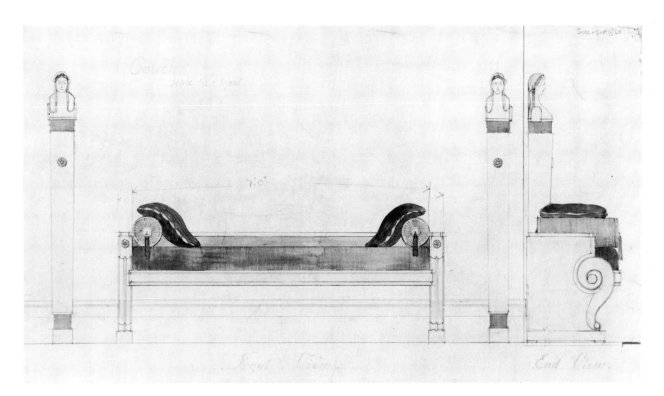

Design for couch by Giles Gilbert Scott for 129 Grosvenor Road, possibly for the River Room, c.1915. Similar scrolling forms were used for tub chairs and for side tables in the house by Scott.

Chair, mahogany, stamped Gill and Reigate, after a Hepplewhite design, 1920s.

The Painted Library, Beach House, Worthing, 1921, with The Deepdene bookcase in the background and imitation Empire drapery painted on the walls.

folding tripod sketched at Pompeii, tub chairs with scroll legs finished in dull silver, and an electric light based on a Roman oil lamp.[33] Contemporary comment on the house in Grosvenor Road stated that the 'decorative treatment and furnishings follow no orthodox style, though it draws its inspiration from Greek work, the architects having taken Greek forms and adapted them in a modern spirit'.[34] Scott produced similar designs for furniture for his own house, Chester House, Clarendon Place, Paddington, 1924-5, including a table decorated with anthemion scrolls around the top and lion paw feet.

Interest in Regency and Empire decorative arts in the first three decades of the twentieth century was associated with a group of collectors of whom perhaps the best known in England was the playwright, Edward Knoblock. He decorated and furnished

33. Jill Lever, *Architects' Designs for Furniture,* RIBA Drawings Series 1982, p.121, pl. 102. (I should like to thank Jill Lever for her help with Giles Gilbert Scott's neo-Regency schemes.)

34. *Architectural Review,* Vol. XXXVIII 1915, pp.80-1.

Drawing Room, Edward Knoblock's house ,11 Montague Place, London, 1931. On the left a chair after George Smith's design, in the centre a sofa after Hope, and on the right one of a pair of amazing Egyptian inspired chairs.

several homes in the Regency style and formed a fine collection of suitable furniture and furnishings, including some of the furniture designed by Thomas Hope and sold in the sale of the contents of The Deepdene in 1917, his country house that still belonged to his descendants.[35] Knoblock may have obtained his Hope pieces cheaply since they were not identified as such in the catalogue, and one of these, the bookcase with sphinx heads and winged beasts, now in the Bowes Museum (p.97), was apparently acquired 'for a ridiculously low sum during a period when people were afraid of bombings and had no wish whatever to buy furniture, so the same piece, after Knoblock's death during the Second World War, was sold to its present owner on conditions highly advantageous to him, and for the same reasons'.[36] After the First War Knoblock bought Beach House, Worthing, which he redecorated and furnished in such a way so as to 'produce

35. Knoblock's autobiography, *Round the Room*, 1939, is a fascinating account of his collection, attitude to interior decoration and various homes.
36. Mario Praz, *The House of Life*, 1964, p.40.

Back drawing room, 11 Montague Place, 1931, showing the pole and shield fire screens and round table from The Deepdene, and the side cupboards flanking the fireplace which belonged to William IV.

something which would form a permanent example of the Regency days'[37] but the financial and practical problems forced him to sell the house seven years later, and he subsequently lived in smaller homes in Brighton, and in London in Titchfield Street and Ashley Place. Some of his pieces of Hope furniture are now in the Victoria and Albert Museum.

Another familiar name in this group of connoisseurs was the Italian art historian, Mario Praz who began his collecting of Empire objects in England in the 1920s and visited Knoblock in his last home in Ashley Place in 1937, having discovered his collection of Hope furniture through Margaret Jourdain's publications. He described in his autobiography, *The House of Life*, the contents of his flat and their associations, and also commented on the problems of finding suitable pieces since 'the antique-dealers were far from well stocked with Empire furniture; the vogue for this style was only just beginning, and while secretaires could always be found, fine sofas were strangely difficult to come by'.[38] Two other collectors in this group were Lord Gerald Wellesley, later 7th Duke of Wellington, and Sir Albert Richardson, both architects and both owners of Hope pieces sold at The Deepdene.

Lord Gerald owned a variant of the Hope round table, several versions of which apparently existed, Hope black and gold wall lights and chimney garnitures, all acquired at The Deepdene sale, and first met Knoblock in Rome in 1917. As an architect he worked many times in the Regency style, notably at Hinton Ampner, Hampshire, where his client Ralph Dutton also had a fine collection of Regency furniture, but Lord Gerald's most important schemes were carried out at Stratfield Saye after he succeeded to the title in 1943. The distinctive quality of the interiors at this house with their many original light fittings, furnishings and furniture is a memorial to his taste, knowledge and experience.[39] Sir Albert Richardson also owned wall lights designed by Hope which are now in Brighton Pavilion, but he had been collecting late eighteenth century and early nineteenth century furniture, pictures and objects for some years before that, with which he furnished two Georgian houses, Cavendish House, St. Albans, and Avenue House, Ampthill.[40] His collection included several fine pieces like the furniture designed by Henry Holland for Oakley House, but his particular delight was in objects with the same historical association which he then arranged in a particular design. Mario Praz described how he hung 'a portrait of Nelson, in an oblong frame in the form of a piece of rope with loops at the upper and lower extremities, close to two models of the Victory, and near by, portraits of Napoleon and Josephine, a bronze sphinx and a chess board, together with its chess men to symbolise the struggle between the Emperor of the French and the great English Admiral.'[41] Trafalgar Day was celebrated by Sir Albert with special dinners from 1909 onwards, where the dining table was laid with porcelain and silver

37. See 'Beach House, Worthing, Sussex', *Country Life*, Vol. XLIX, No. 1256, January 29 1921, pp.126-133.
38. Praz, *House of Life*, p.271.
39. James Lees-Milne, 'Stratfield Saye House', *Apollo*, Vol. CII, No. 161, July 1975, pp.8-18.
40. Simon Houfe, *Sir Albert Richardson — The Professor*, 1980.
41. Praz, *House of Life*, pp.314-5.

Front drawing room of Lord Gerald Wellesley's house at 11 Titchfield Terrace, London, 1931, showing part of a set of French satinwood seat furniture, a typical Regency dwarf bookcase and black and gold sconces from The Deepdene illustrated by Hope.

of the period of 1805, busts of Nelson and Napoleon, and bone or straw models made by French prisoners of war.

By the 1920s Regency furniture had become topical enough for *House and Garden* to devote several articles to it, including one on Professor Richardson's home, Avenue House, Ampthill, in 1923. The coverage was justified by the fact that 'Neo-Georgians are now discovering in these once neglected pieces quality and character that goes far to condone the faults... it is interesting to note how well some of the pieces with their gilding, rosewood, redundancy, and brass, all mellowed and glazed over by the hand of time, blend well into modern interiors.'[42] Certain types, like chairs, were very plentiful, although care had to be taken to avoid later imitations, while library tables were difficult to find because of their adaptability for modern interiors. Items recommended as being both safer to collect and more interesting were those no longer in daily use like work or games tables, X-frame window seats for dressing table use with pembroke or sofa tables, marble topped pier tables, canterburies and dwarf bookcase or secretaire combinations. The availability of

---

42. *House and Garden,* July 1923, pp.11, 23. By the 1920s several ship interiors had also been decorated in revival styles including the 'Kinfauns Castle', launched in 1899 with a Georgian first-class saloon, the 'Olympic', sister ship to the 'Titanic' and launched in 1910, with an Empire suite containing beds of satin brass and Lurex silver, and the 'Viceroy of India', launched 1929 with neoclassical decoration in the First Class reading and writing room.

Sofa, ebonised and gilded beech, c.1820, from the collection of
Lord Gerald Wellesley.

Chair, ebonised and gilded frame, c.1820, as shown in the back
drawing room, 11 Montague Place.

The Library, Henry Channon's house, 5 Belgrave Square, London, 1938. The bookcases were designed by Lord Gerald Wellesley and Trenwith Wills and the curtain drapery copied from originals at Clandon.

Chair, one of a set, mahogany with inlaid decoration, 1936. Designed by Eric Ravilious and made by H. Harris for Dunbar Hay Ltd.

many types of Regency furniture, particularly the smaller, lighter pieces made for ordinary domestic interiors also helped to increase their popularity since prices were still low although not as low as before the First War.

Interest in the period was still tempered with caution by some members of the antiques trade and when Lenygon and Morant decided to feature Regency decorative arts in an exhibition in the late 1920s, calling it 'the last of the great English periods', they arranged a separate entrance to their gallery so that their collection of earlier furniture would not be contaminated through association with the Regency display. Having spent a year in preparing the display, the firm discovered that the subject was very popular and the exhibition a great success, being patronised by Royalty and remaining open for six months.[43]

Some interesting Regency designs were used by Sir Edwin Lutyens when working on the furniture for the Viceroy's House, New Delhi, 1925-30. Committees had been set up to advise on the furnishings for these interiors and to choose examples of antique styles suitable for reproduction by Indian craftsmen. Among other historical designs Lutyens produced a cane seated armchair for a guest bedroom similar to

43. Queen Mary was very interested in the Regency period and made many gifts to Brighton Pavilion, including some original furnishings.

The Dining Room, The Holme, Regent's Park, 1940 (the home of Edward James's sister, Mrs. Peter Pleydell-Bouverie), showing the Empire scheme devised by M. Jansen of the Paris firm of Boudin with white and gold painted furniture including a side table supported on Egyptian figures.

those designed by Walton in the 1890s for Miss Cranston's tearooms, and occasional chairs for the ballroom based on a typical chair of about 1805 with a twisted top rail and back partly filled with an amalgam of classical ornament.[44]

One of the first interior decorators to use Regency furniture in her schemes was Mrs. Dolly Mann who established her business in 1923 and was a friend and professional colleague of Edward Knoblock.[45] Since Regency furniture was so plentiful and cheap she always included examples in her stock, particularly painted pieces, and worked for several clients interested in Regency or Empire styles. Edward James, who had first shown an interest in Empire design at Oxford by papering one of his rooms with a Napoleonic paper, employed Mrs. Mann at his home, Monkton, on the West Dean estate where he introduced drain pipes shaped like bamboo lengths, and a bed copied from Napoleon's hearse with green curtains and silver fringe and palm trees holding up the tester. James's London home in

44. Lever, *Architects' Designs*, pls. 94, 95.

45. He described her as 'one of the rare women decorators who knows her job from A to Z.' (*Round the Room*, p.175).

Wimpole Street also contained some fine pieces of original Empire furniture.[46]

By the 1930s Regency and Empire styles had become fashionable enough for a number of modern interiors in a style of compromise incorporating various Regency or Empire features to be illustrated in chic periodicals. The Regency style was the last of the classic styles before the confusions of the mid-nineteenth century and was therefore popular with modern designers since it went so well with many of their schemes. It also offered the opportunity of greater profits, since although the furniture could be acquired reasonably and installed cheaply it demanded harmonising wallpapers, elaborate window drapery, carefully hung pictures and careful arrangements of ornaments, all of which required time and money to be spent on them. The scale of Regency furniture also made it eminently suitable for 'the restricted spaces in which we now live compared with those of the 18th century. And Regency furniture is snapped up at the sales where many of the bigger and finer things go begging.'[47]

The 1920s and 1930s have traditionally been seen as the period of revival of interest in Regency and Empire decorative arts but since the 1860s these styles have been in vogue with collectors, museums and makers of furniture with many antique examples being acquired and reproductions, either faithfull or in the same spirit, produced. Although Sheraton designs seem to have been more popular in the 1860s and 1870s, styles of the later Regency and Empire periods were certainly fashionable in the 1880s and 1890s. Even today both antique examples and reproduction pieces are still popular since the furniture is stylish, space-saving and flexible enough to be absorbed easily with interiors and furniture of quite different design.

---

46. Edward James, *Swans Reflecting Elephants,* ed. George Melly, 1982; Philip Purser, *Where is He now? The Extraordinary Worlds of Edward James,* 1978. Some of his Regency and Regency Revival furniture is now in Brighton Pavilion.
47. *Vogue House and Garden Book,* Spring 1937, p.9.

8. Upholstery

During the Regency period the interest in and use of upholstery developed enormously, almost equalling the role of furniture in the interior, and affecting not only seat furniture and beds, but also cabinet furniture and tables, screens, doors and windows. Fashionable interest was epitomised by the Prince Regent, later George IV, of whom it was written, 'The King has the greatest contempt for the Ministers, but thinks nothing but upholstery & his Buildings...'[1]. He was responsible for encouraging one of the forerunners of the modern interior decorator, Walsh Porter, who replaced Henry Holland's delicate designs at Carlton House with florid and elaborate effects achieved with the help of complex upholstery, having impressed his royal patron with the exotic effects of his home, Craven Cottage, in Fulham.[2] The importance of the role of the upholsterer and of upholstery can also be seen in the expansion of their profession in trade directories and in the growing number of pattern books either wholly or partially devoted to the subject, including George Smith's *Household Furniture* of 1808, the number of designs which appeared in Ackermann's *Repository of the Arts,* 1809-28, John Taylor's *The Upholsterer's and Cabinet Maker's Pocket Assistant,* c.1825, and in the various publications of Thomas King in the 1830s.[3] By 1834 the upholsterer was no longer subordinate to the cabinet maker, nor part of the same business but an independent craftsman acknowledged as such by the *Architectural Magazine* 'The furnishing of large houses is generally committed to the UPHOLSTERER, who employs the CABINET-MAKER',[4] a reversal of their roles fifty years earlier.

Materials used for upholstery between 1790 and 1840 included woven, printed and painted and some embroidered fabrics, but by far the most numerous were chintzes, block or roller printed cottons with colourful, sometimes large, designs which were then glazed, and there are many contemporary references and surviving examples to illustrate their popularity and superiority of design and technique.[5] Although not considered suitable for the state rooms of the grandest houses, chintzes were fashionable enough to appeal to the Prince of Wales who commissioned a 'rich furniture chintz', the contemporary description, from Abraham Allen, a prominent merchant in Pall Mall, for his bedroom at Carlton House in 1811. Chintzes were obviously suitable for furnishing villas and cottages, where more elaborate or heavier materials would have been obtrusive, and the Duchess of Bedford chose a rose pattern chintz for her rural retreat, Endsleigh, in Devonshire, while Chiswick House, the Duke of Devonshire's villa, was furnished with a great deal of chintz,

1. *The Journal of Mrs. Arbuthnot 1820-1832.* Edited by Francis Bamford and the Duke of Wellington, 1950, vol. ii, entry for December 2nd 1827.

2. T.C. Croker, *A Walk from London to Fulham,* revised and edited by T.F. Dillon Crofton, 1860, pp.190-1. Walsh Porter's other exotic creation, Vine Cottage, is also described in this book, pp.213-4.

3. *Modern Designs for Household Furniture, Fashionable Bedsteads with Hangings, The Upholsterer's Sketch Book of Original Designs, The Modern Style of Cabinet Work exemplified,* generally published without dates.

4. *The Architectural Magazine,* Vol. I, 1834, pp.8-9.

5. See *English Printed Textiles 1720-1836,* Victoria and Albert Museum/H.M.S.O. 1960, and F.M. Montgomery, *Printed Textiles* English and American Cottons and Linens 1700-1850, 1970.

Plate 31. Octangular Tent Room from George Smith's *Cabinet-Maker's and Upholsterer's Guide*, 1826. The idea of a tent room originated in France and was particularly suitable for rooms like boudoirs or bedrooms. There is a surviving design for a tent room at Brighton Pavilion among the Crace drawings.

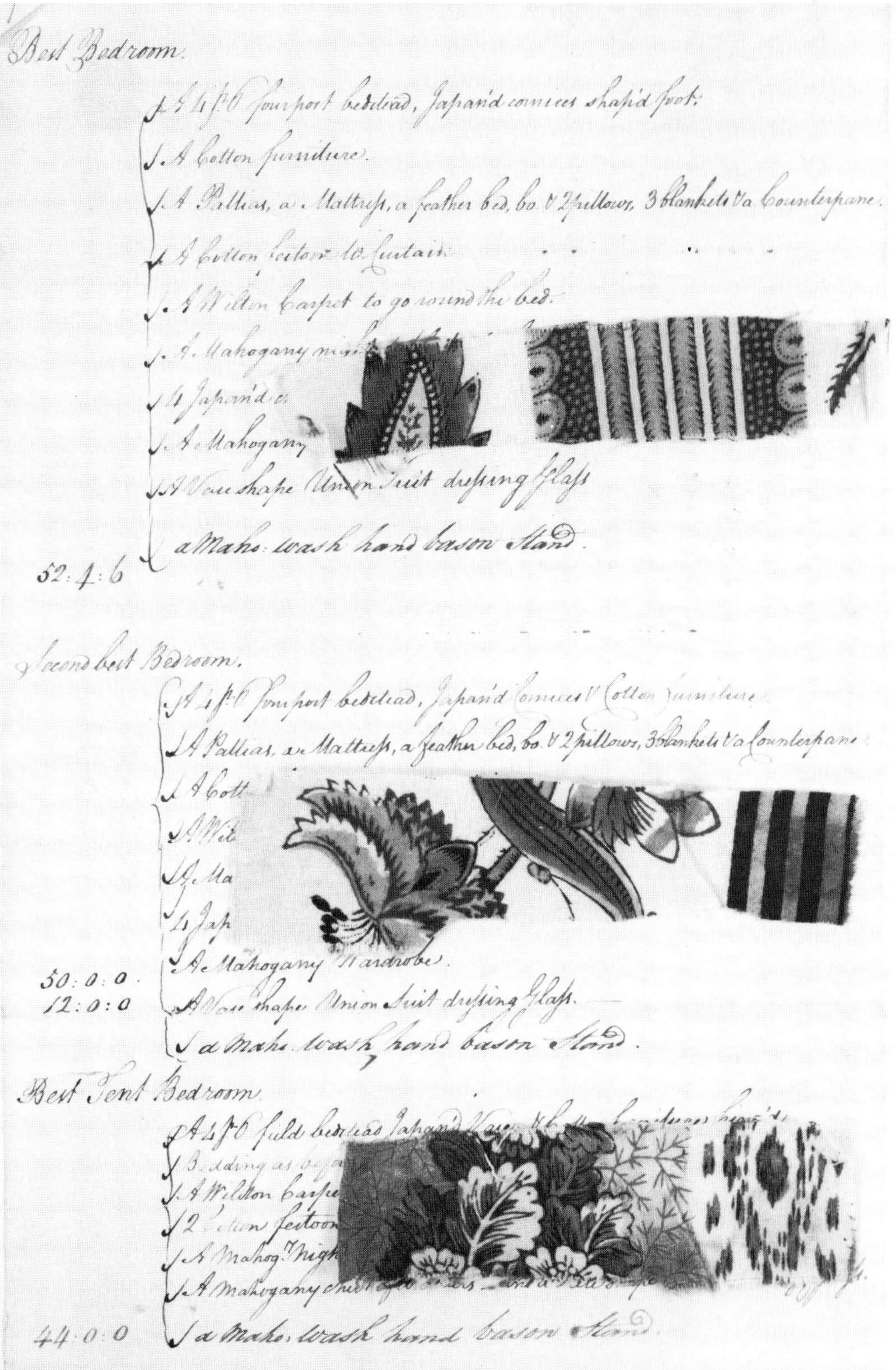

Best Bedroom.

£4.4..0 four post bedstead, Japan'd cornices shap'd foot:

A Cotton furniture.

A Pallias, a Mattress, a feather bed, bo. & 2 pillows, 3 blankets & a Counterpane.

A Cotton festoon do Curtain

A Wilton Carpet to go round the bed.

A Mahogany night

A Japan'd e

A Mahogany

A Vase shape Union Suit dressing Glass

a Maho. wash hand bason Stand.

52:4:6

Second best Bedroom.

A 2 f..0 four post bedstead, Japan'd Cornices & Cotton furniture.

A Pallias, a Mattress, a feather bed, bo. & 2 pillows, 3 blankets & a Counterpane.

A Cott

A Wil

A Ma

A Jap

A Mahogany Wardrobe.

A Vase shape Union Suit dressing Glass. —

a Maho. wash hand bason Stand.

50:0:0.
12:0:0

Best Tent Bedroom.

A 4 f..0 field bedstead Japan'd

Bedding as

A Wilton Carpe

2 Cotton festoon

A Mahog.y Night

A Mahogany chest

a Maho. wash hand bason Stand

44.0.0

Upholsterer's estimate for Winchmore Hill, 1790, with samples of printed cottons for bed hangings attached.

Plate 32. Borders of printed cotton, with designs in Classical and Gothic styles, from the Duddings pattern book, 1800-14. These borders, which were supplied in a range of widths, were intended to decorate curtains and seat upholstery and give some impression of the strong colours popular in the early nineteenth century.

Plate 33. Border of printed cotton, with a Chinoiserie design, similar to designs by Robert Jones or the Crace firm for Brighton Pavilion, from the Duddings pattern book, 1800-14.

Cotton, block-printed with pillar and floral design, c.1805.

both for beds and for seat furniture, in 1811.[6] Although used extensively for beds, window hangings and seat upholstery, chintzes were also found covering footstools, and cushions on cane seated chairs, and as loose covers.

Between 1790 and 1810 designs painted in watercolour on silk were also very popular, since the light effect achieved complemented the more delicate styles of furniture then fashionable. Some of these fabrics were imported from China while others were produced in London by firms like that of Francis and George Eckhardt in the King's Road who took out a variety of patents from 1780 onwards for painted and printed silks, linens and papers. Hepplewhite and Sheraton both recommended the use of small panels of painted or printed silk for the decoration of chairs and similar oval, rectangular or shield-shaped panels were used for fire screens and other pieces with floral, figurative or decorative designs in suitable neoclassical taste. Embroidery in coloured silks on pale coloured silk or satin grounds was used to produce the same effect both in small panels and for bed hangings, and later after 1810 there was a revival of tent stitch embroidery on canvas, echoing the introduction of less delicate styles in furniture, for seat upholstery and for smaller pieces like pole screens. In the period after 1810 the backs of sofas or couches and loose cushions, often covered with velvet or plain silk, would be embroidered with

6. Ackermann's *Repository of the Arts*, Vol. X, October 1813, p.244. MS. Inventory of the contents of Chiswick House 1811, now at Chatsworth.

designs of classical devices in coloured silks or gold and silver thread, probably imitating the woven Empire patterns produced by the Lyons silk weavers. After 1825 embroidery in coloured silks in architectural or heraldic designs was used for upholstered furniture in the Gothic taste.

There was no equivalent range of designs in patterned woven fabrics to those produced by the cotton printers and plain fabrics like satins, velvets, worsteds and other woollen materials, and cheaper linen and cotton mixtures like dimity were used extensively for all forms of upholstery. There were some patterned fabrics but their designs were subdued and included some modified eighteenth century floral damasks, small polychrome flowers on pale grounds for silks and small diaper patterns stamped by machine on 'Manchester Velvets' made of cotton rather than of silk. Plain worsteds and some silks were decorated with patterns made by pressing the material under engraved rollers to give the watered effect popular in the eighteenth century and plain velvets were occasionally painted with naturalistic and other decorative designs. The upholsterer achieved the desired decorative and

Borders, in two sizes, block-printed with Egyptian design, from a pattern book 1800-14.

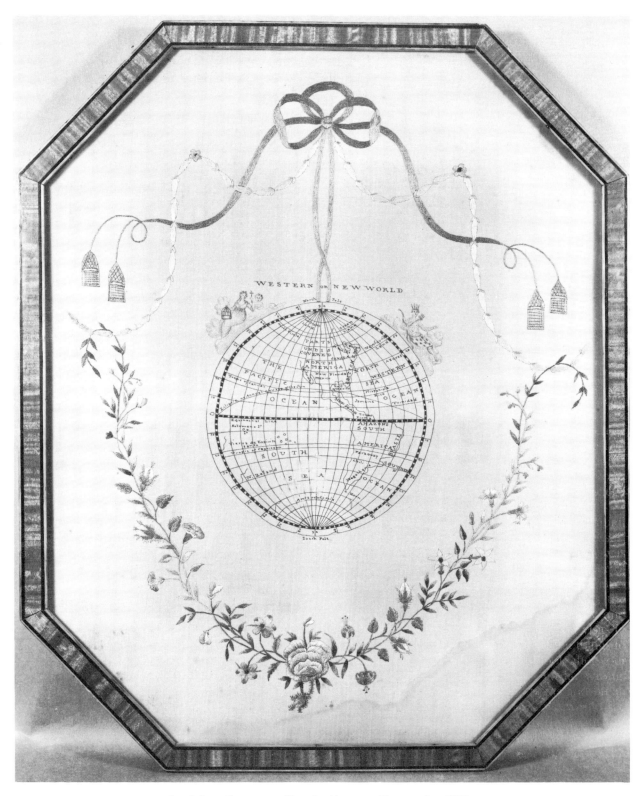

Panel from firescreen, silk embroidery on silk ground, c.1800.

Illustration from *A Series of twenty-nine designs of Modern Costume*, 1823, by Henry Moses, showing a Greek Revival couch with classical embroidery on the back and cushions, and a typical Regency fringe along the front.

elaborate effects by the use of complicated drapery, involving great yardages, and ornamental fringes, gimps, tassels, cords and braids, made of coloured silks, wools, and some gold or silver thread. 'Parisian' or 'Turkish' tassels, 'Parisian' or 'Egyptian' fringe and 'silvered bell fringe' were all obviously more expensive trimmings while galloons and gimps seem to have been cheaper, depending of course on the yarn. The Gillow records include both samples of narrow gimps in different colours, usually corresponding to one of the colours in the chintz covers, and samples of narrow silk tapes, described as 'bindings' for use with chintz covers.[7] One of the most distinctive trimmings used is the network of silk or wool with tassels along the bottom attached to a braid heading and this appears on seat furniture, bed hangings and window curtains in different widths.

Every upholsterer was expected to be aware of the appropriate material for each room in a house if he was to appeal to the fashionable patron, and George Smith lists the fabrics considered suitable 'for Eating Rooms and Libraries, a material of more substance is requisite than for Rooms of a lighter cast; and for such purposes superfine cloth, or cassimere, will ever be the best; the colours as fancy or taste may direct; yet scarlet and crimson will ever hold the preference: undress morine may be substituted for cloth, although it does not suit for every description of drapery: calico when used should be of one colour, in shades of moreen or scarlet.

In elegant Drawing Rooms, plain coloured satin or figured damask assumes the first rank, as well for use as for richness: lustring and tabarays the next; the latter, however, makes but indifferent drapery. Calico, the next in choice and of so great

7. Gillow Decorators and Upholstery Estimate Book 1817-24 from the Gillow Archive at the Westminster City Library Archives Department, No. 344/142. Sheraton describes different bindings in his *Cabinet Dictionary*, 1803, p.51.

Gothic chair, carved and gilded mahogany, with original upholstery of velvet with wool and silk embroidery, c.1830.

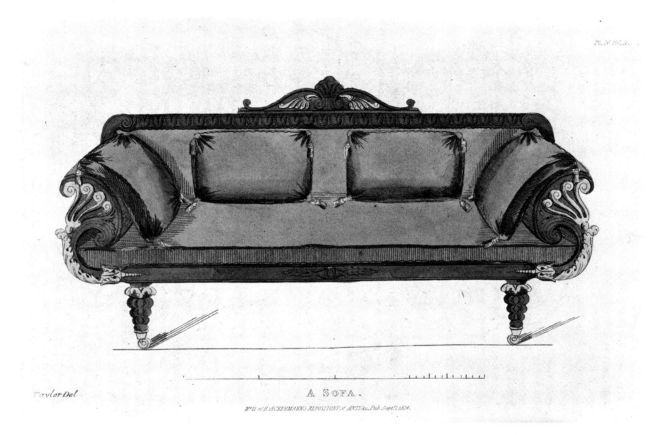

A SOFA.

Plate 34. Design for a Sofa from Ackermann's *Repository,* Vol. IV, 3rd Series, September 1824, pl. 16, which was intended to be made of gilded rosewood with silk or merino damask upholstery trimmed with silk cords and tassels. The design is by John Taylor, upholsterer, Bedford Court, Covent Garden, who previously worked for George Oakley of Bond Street and who provided several designs for the *Repository* 1821-4.

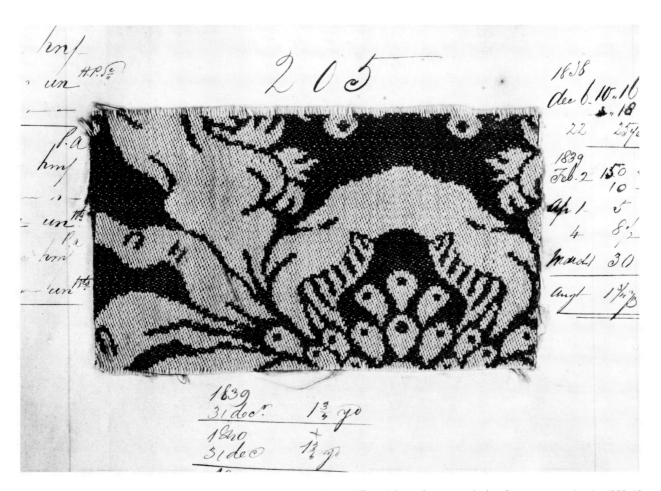

Sample of woollen damask with modified eighteenth century design from a pattern book, 1830-43.

variety of patterns, should, where good drapery is required, be glazed mellow: the small chintz patterns hold a preference in point of effect, especially for draperies.'[8] Seat upholstery and window curtains usually were of the same colour or a similar range of colours while the materials were either the same or complementary and, as Loudon pointed out, if there was little or no seat upholstery then 'if the furniture be chiefly mahogany, the material of the curtains should be moreen or cloth; and the colour should be of the same tone, and strong or dark . . . the furniture be chiefly of oak or of different coloured foreign woods . . . light coloured cloth, or moreen, or some description of chintzes or cottons, will be more suitable'.[9]

Sheraton recommended figured satins or silks for drawing room chairs and also 'French printed silk or satin, sewed on to the stuffing, with borders round them'.[10] At Chatsworth in 1783 the Music Room was furnished with flowered tabouret for the curtains and upholstery and in the Drawing Room the seat furniture was covered

8. George Smith, *Collection of Designs for Household Furniture and Interior Decoration*, 1808, pp.xii- xiii. Superfine cloth and cassimere were both smooth faced woollen fabrics, morine or moreen a worsted or long stapled woollen fabric with a pronounced rib, calico a printed cotton usually with a small all-over pattern, lustring a bright, glossy silk, tabaray or tabouret a silk or silk and linen mixture with alternate satin and watered silk stripes with occasionally a floral spring pattern.

9. J.C. Loudon, *The Encyclopaedia of Cottage, Farm and Villa Architecture*, 1835, Curtains for Villas, pp.1074-5.

10. Thomas Sheraton, *The Cabinet Makers' and Upholsterers' Drawing Book*, 1791-4, p.317, pls. XXXII, XXXIV.

in green damask while the Prince of Wales's Chinese Drawing Room at Carlton House was furnished in 1792 with chairs covered with brocaded satin covers and borders, all in the appropriate taste.[11] Hepplewhite also mentions woven materials, tabouret or moreen, for japanned furniture for a drawing room. Tabouret was also used for cushions for mahogany chairs and japanned chairs with cane seats for two rooms at Trinity College, in Cambridge in 1807.[12] Ackermann suggested velvet for a chaise longue and window seat in 1809, and green velvet with blue or black appliqué or a rich figured silk for drawing room chairs, while light blue silk, Persian fringe and broad lace was shown for a gilded boudoir chair in 1823.[13] The Rococo Revival encouraged more patterned materials with the pair of sofas supplied by Robert Hughes for Syon House in 1829 whose silk upholstery matched the original wall hangings of the 1760s in the room for which they were intended.[14] Coloured floral patterns printed on velvet were supplied for chair covers in the French taste[15] and woollen materials like moreens, either plain or patterned were also suggested.

Less sophisticated materials were also considered suitable for Gothic furniture and the sale of the late Mr. Bullock's stock in 1819 included 'A Gothic pattern chair of oak, the back with twisted columns, mounted with ormolu, stuffed, the back seat covered with scarlet cloth, laced and fringed' a very similar chair to the one Ackermann illustrated in 1817 (p.185) and to the chair from Battle Abbey.[16] Crimson serge with black velvet borders was used for oak armchairs in the Great Hall of Speke Hall, an interior scheme apparently designed by Bullock,[17] and black velvet for ottomans at Newstead Abbey.[18] Loudon suggested chintz for a cushion for an oak parlour chair and damask for both Gothic dining room and drawing room chairs.[19] Plain materials like cloth and moreen were much used for all but the grandest chairs in libraries, parlours and bedrooms and Ackermann observed in 1809 that for Dining Parlours 'morone continues still in use, and the more so, where economy is requisite; which article also has experienced an improvement by being

11. Ivan Hall, 'A neo-classical episode at Chatsworth', *The Burlington Magazine,* Vol. CXXII, No. 927, June 1980, pp.400, 403-14. Geoffrey de Bellaigue, 'The Furnishings of the Chinese Drawing Room, Carlton House', *The Burlington Magazine,* Vol. CIX, No. 774, September 1967, pp.518-28.

12. Robert Williams, 'A Cambridge Family of Furniture Makers and The Furnishing of the Master's Lodge Trinity College, Cambridge, 1795-1820', *Furniture History,* Vol. XII, 1976, pp.64-85.

13. Ackermann's *Repository,* Vol. 1 January 1809, pp.54-5, pl. 3; Vol. 11 3rd Series July 1823, p.59, pl. 3.

14. Victoria and Albert Museum No. W21 1975, the design being derived from an Adam suite of neo-classical furniture supplied for the same room in the 1760s. The original Adam settees were also re-upholstered in 1829.

15. *The Architectural Magazine,* Vol. I p.244, coloured flowers printed on velvet for chair covers 'at Mr. Nixon's Show Rooms, John Street, Oxford Street, imported from France — newly invented and practised by the French'.

16. Christie's Sale Catalogue of 'The stock of the late Mr. Bullock at 4, Tenterden Street, Hanover Square', May 3-5 1819. Ackermann, Vol. IV New Series September 1817, p.18, pl. 14.

17. Catalogue of furniture of the 'ancient Speke Hall, and of that admired large antique Feudal-Hall, the Furniture of which is quite new, and but just finished in great taste, and never has been used' 1-3 September 1812. According to an advertisement in the *Liverpool Mercury* August 14 1812 the furniture of the Hall was designed and made by George Bullock.

18. 'Catalogue of the contents of Newstead listed for sale October 1815 by Mr. Farebrother on the premises'. The sale did not in fact take place.

19. Loudon, *Encyclopaedia,* p.2156, figs. 2007, 2008; p.2162, fig. 2015.

Plate 35. Border of printed cotton, with a design of drapery with tassels, a very popular pattern in Regency chintzes, from the Duddings pattern book, 1800-14. The pattern book bears the label of George Oakley who had purchased the printing blocks and patterns of Mr. Dudding and had a fashionable shop in Bond Street.

A FRENCH WINDOW CURTAIN

& GRECIAN SETTEE.

French window curtain and Grecian settee, *Repositiory of Arts,* Vol. 2, October 1809, pl. 26, showing 'Parisian' fringe on both the curtain and the settee with the latter covered in leather with a printed border.

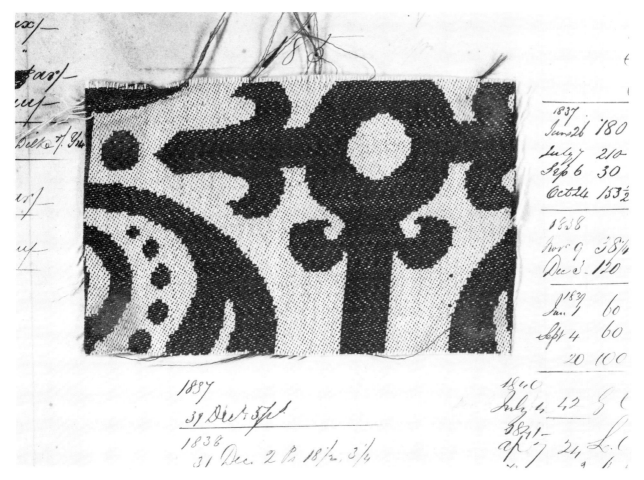

Sample of woollen damask, very similar to patterns designed by Thomas Willement for wallpapers and furniture covers, from a book of samples, 1830-43.

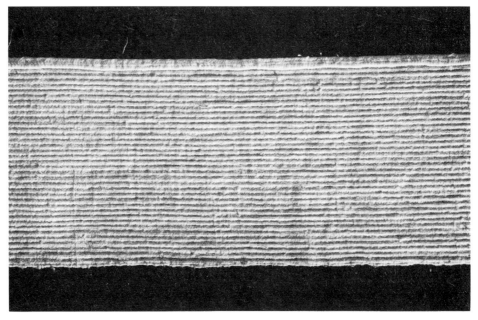

Sample of dimity, linen and cotton mixture, late eighteenth century. This was one of the most common upholstery materials of the Regency period.

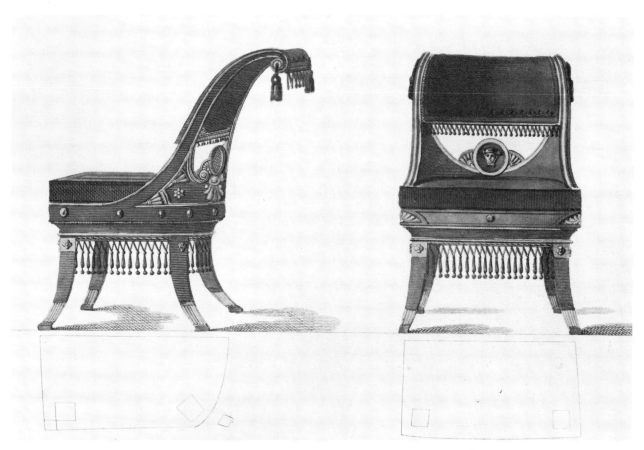

Drawing room chairs, *Repository of Arts,* Vol. 2, December 1809, pl. 39, described as made of mahogany, carved and gilt, covered with morocco leather, velvet or damask, and trimmed with 'Persian' fringe.

embossed in a variety of patterns.'[20] Cheaper and washable materials like dimity, a linen and cotton mixture with a pronounced rib, were obviously suitable for covers for easy chairs in bedrooms, as at Lee Priory in 1834.[21]

Also used principally for library and dining chairs were leather and horsehair, both in a range of different colours and both fastened with double or single rows of decorative brass nails around the seat. Hepplewhite observed that 'Mahogany chairs should have the seats of horse hair, plain, striped, chequered, &c, at pleasure'[22] and 'sattin' horsehair, in a satin weave was also popular. Horsehair was also recommended by Hepplewhite for an easy chair and continued in use right through the Regency period. Leather was equally popular with red or blue morocco tied down by silk or wool tassels noted by Hepplewhite, green leather for mahogany dining chairs at Chiswick in 1811 and yellow and buff for mahogany and oak dining chairs in Mr. Bullock's stock in 1819. Morocco was also used for loose cushions on cane seated chairs, and for parlour chairs in the Grecian style Ackermann recommended red morocco leather with appropriate printed black designs.

20. Ackermann, Vol. 1 March 1809, p.188. Moreen was often stamped with a pattern made by an engraved roller.

21. Catalogue of all the 'superb Antique and Modern Household Furniture...which will be sold by Auction by Mr. W. Sharp, on the premises, Lee Priory', 11-21 August 1834.

22. A. Hepplewhite and Co., *The Cabinet Maker and Upholsterer's Guide,* 3rd edition 1794, p.2.

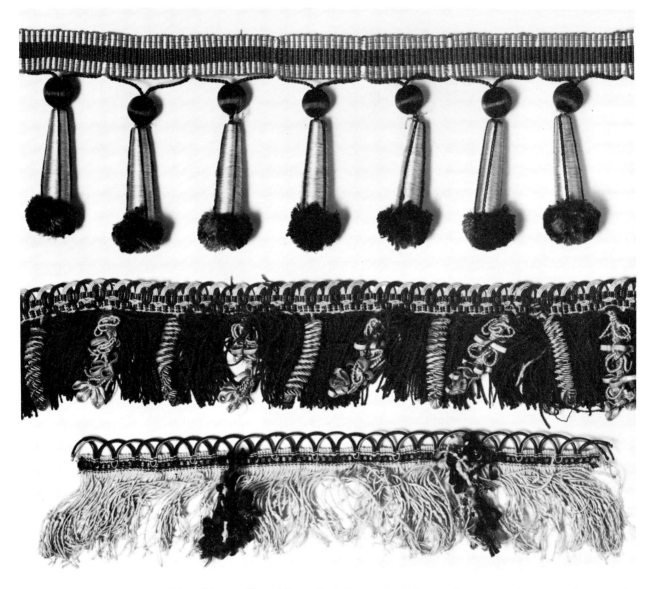

Three fringes, silk and linen, the bottom and middle ones late eighteenth century, the top early nineteenth century and similar to the Persian fringe illustrated by Ackermann.

Chintz 'which may now be had of various patterns on purpose for chair seats, together with borders to suit them'[23] was recommended by Sheraton for drawing room chairs and mahogany chairs with cane bottoms and cushions, 'the cases of which should be covered with the same as the curtains', were mentioned by Hepplewhite[24] as were japanned chairs with cane bottoms and linen or cotton cases for the thin cushions. At Chiswick in 1811 there were several chintz, calico or cotton cases mentioned including chintz for cushions for a set of white and gold elbow chairs with cane backs in the Saloon, and a 'Scarlet Ground chintz cotton case' for a mahogany easy chair in the Duchess's bedroom, while at Newstead in 1815 the Chintz Room contained a set of japanned chairs with rush seats and cushions covered

23. Sheraton, *Drawing Book,* p.374, pl. VI Drawing Room Chairs.
24. Hepplewhite, p.2.

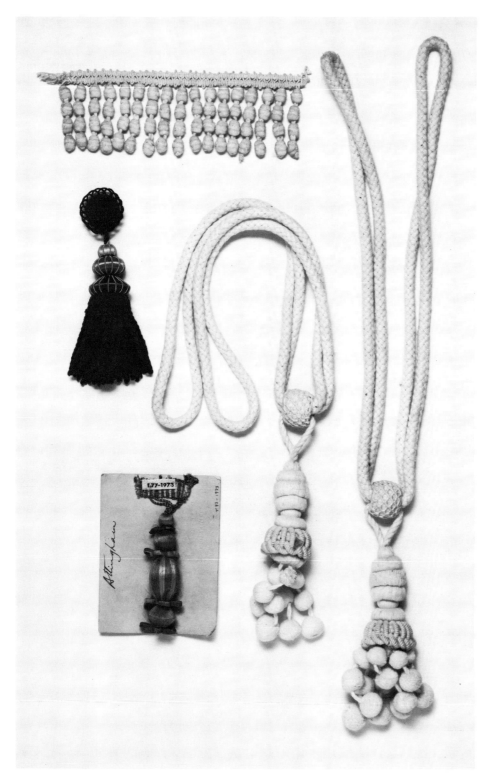

White cotton tassels and fringe from a bed, c.1820, silk and wool tassel with cloth rosette from a cushion, early nineteenth century, and silk tassel from Attingham, Shropshire, late eighteenth century, which could have been used for a bed or for seat furniture.

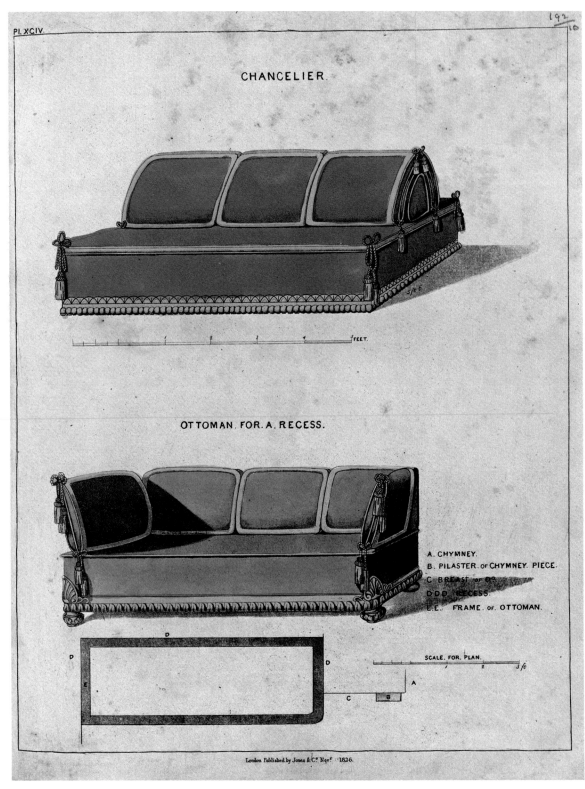

CHANCELIER.

FEET.

OTTOMAN. FOR. A. RECESS.

A. CHYMNEY.

B. PILASTER. of CHYMNEY. PIECE.

C. BREAST. or DO.

D.D.D. RECESS.

E.E. FRAME. of. OTTOMAN.

SCALE. FOR. PLAN.

3 ft

London Published by Jones & Co. Nov.r 1826.

Plate 36. Designs for a Chancelier and Ottoman for a Recess from George Smith's *Cabinet-Maker's and Upholsterer's Guide*, 1826, pl. XCIV. The chancelier was based on the Lord Chancellor's seat in the House of Lords and the upholstery on both pieces was intended to match that on other seat furniture in the room.

Samples of printed cottons for borders, classical and chinoiserie, c.1805.

LADY'S WORK TABLE.

Nº2. of R. ACKERMANN's REPOSITORY of ARTS &c. Pub. Feby 1823.

Plate 37. Design for a Lady's Work Table from Ackermann's *Repository*, Vol. I, 3rd Series, February 1823, pl. 9, which could be positioned in a sitting room, boudoir or drawing room. The piece was to be made of rosewood with ormolu mounts and could be used for drawing, reading and writing as well as for needlework which could be stored in the blue silk bag with its silk fringe.

Part of a curtain, showing the field and border, printed cotton, c.1805.

en suite with the chintz bed hangings, and the Drawing Room contained a couch with scroll ends covered with cotton furniture, matching the rest of the seat upholstery and the window curtains.[25] At Attingham in 1827 there was a similar sofa 'with thick hair squab, three square back cushions and two round bolsters, in canvas, and handsome crimson and morone flower-pattern chints cotton cases, with Grecian border'[26] and the continuing popularity of borders was acknowledged by Loudon in 1833 'A very cheap and yet tasteful loose sofa cover may be made of glazed self-coloured calico, with a narrow piece of different coloured calico, or shawl bordering, laid on about a couple of inches from the edge. This kind of cover lasts clean much longer than one of common printed cotton; and when the bordering is carried round the corners of the cushions, bolsters, &c., it has a pretty and even

25. Chiswick Inventory 1811, Newstead Sale Catalogue 1815.

26. 'A Catalogue of the Superb Furniture...which will be sold by auction, by Mr. Robins,...Attingham Hall', July August 1827, Lot 105.

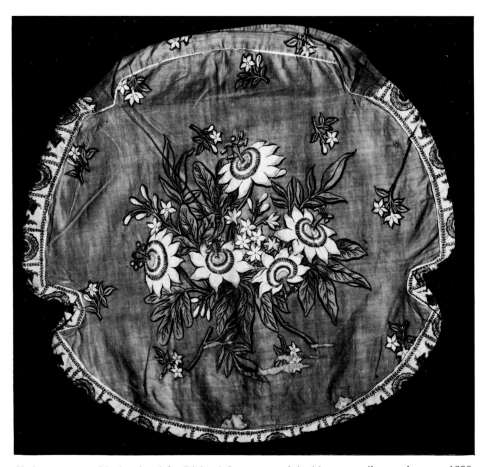

Chair seat cover, block printed for Richard Ovey, one of the biggest textile merchants, c.1800.

elegant effect.'[27] Designs for chintzes were normally designed and printed so that the material could be used either for bed and window curtains or for seat upholstery. The patterns included three parts: the 'furniture-print' for the curtains, the 'filling', a small overall print used indiscriminately for the background, and the chair seat with the flowers of the curtain design rearranged either as a bouquet or as a wreath. Borders were printed with matching or dissimilar patterns in vertical strips to be cut apart and applied.[28]

Most pieces of good furniture, and every piece in grand houses like the Royal Palaces, Chatsworth or Attingham, were supplied with loose protective covers known as 'throwovers' or 'cases' removed only for special occasions in some places. Chintzes were also used for these as were plain and 'Manchester' striped cottons and simple materials like holland, used for covers for curtains and chairs at Attingham in 1827, and linen, mentioned for ottomans by Loudon. Woollen materials were used like green baize for sideboards at Chatsworth and for covering carpets, white serge for chairs in the Drawing Room at Chatsworth and green cloth for library tables and music tables. Sheraton referred to 'Covers for pier tables, made of stamped leather and glazed, lined with flannel to save the varnish of such table tops. Lately they have

27. Loudon, *Encyclopaedia*, Furniture for Cottage Dwellings, p.325, No. 650.
28. Montgomery, *Printed Textiles*, fig.359.

introduced a new kind of painted canvas, varnished, and very elastic in its nature, and will probably answer better than leather.'[29] Damask leather covers lined in green baize were used for pier tables at Chatsworth while 'wash leather and Manchester strip' covers were listed for candelabras at Lee Priory.[30]

One of the most familiar pieces of Regency seat furniture, the Grecian couch with scroll ends, was illustrated by Sheraton in the *Cabinet Dictionary* but later elaborated into a variety of forms by George Smith including some with one end like a chaise longue. He also included sofas with solid backs and ends and both forms continued to develop through the Regency with their assemblage of squabs, the flat mattress, square or oblong back cushions, and bolsters, sometimes with a flat cushion laid over them. Loudon included designs for both couches and sofas, both with bolsters and thin pillows, observing that 'Couches in small rooms are generally preferred to sofas' and that the 'coverings and finishings of couches and sofas should harmonise, in colour and material, with the window curtains.'[31] Chairs of the period before the publication of Smith's *Household Furniture* in 1808 generally only had upholstered seats or loose cushions secured with tapes underneath on cane seats, while the backs, if upholstered at all, only had a small padded area, but Smith included designs for the bergère or curricle type where the padded back curves round to form the arm rests. Although wing chairs appeared earlier, arm chairs with padded backs and sides developed in the 1820s and 1830s, sometimes with cane seats and loose cushions, sometimes tufted or buttoned on the back and seat, on the back only or on the seat only. Chairs without arms, and the back upholstered with a gap between it and the seat became very popular and there were many variations, some with tufting or buttoning in the back and seat, some in the seat only, and some with no tufts but with the outline of the seat edged with cord and tassels attached at the corners.

An interesting development in seat furniture of the late eighteenth and early nineteenth century is that of the ottoman, described by Francis Hervé as 'Angle Confidants' when he supplied them for the Drawing Room at Chatsworth in 1782.[32] Sheraton mentions their exotic connotations 'These are genteel seats introduced in the most fashionable houses, and are an imitation of the Turkish mode of seating...'[33] and suggests a beech frame, webbed and strained with canvas to support the cushions. Other terms used for the same piece of furniture included 'Turkey sofa' or 'Turkey couch', some of which were fitted into alcoves or corners like those of Sheraton's, those at Chatsworth or those at Chiswick, where in the Blue Room there was 'A Turkish couch fitted to the Angle of the Room with Squab, 4 back cushions and Blue callico cases trimmed with fringe'.[34] Ottomans could also be free-standing and as Smith pointed out, 'Ottomans are particularly useful in Picture Galleries, their projection from the wall preventing the pictures being

29. Sheraton, *The Cabinet Dictonary*, 1803, p.336.
30. Presumably leather with a protective striped cotton lining.
31. Loudon, *Encyclopaedia*, Grecian and Modern Villa Furniture, p.1059.
32. Hall, *Burlington* 1980, p.413.
33. Sheraton, *Drawing Book*, Turkey Sofa pl. LII, p.412.
34. Inventory 1811.

Dress sofa designed by John Taylor, *Repository of Arts,* 2nd Series, Vol. XI, February 1821, pl. 9, showing one of the many variations for cushions. Materials suggested for covers included satin, damask or velvet with gold lace and tassels for a gilded frame and simpler materials, presumably a wool mixture, for less elaborate frames.

Couch, mahogany with modern upholstery copying original designs, c.1840.

Designs for chairs by John Taylor, *Repository of Arts,* Series 3 Vol. IV, November 1824, pl. 28.
The left hand example is described as a library chair, in oak, covered with crimson wool cloth with
tufts of the same material. The one on the right, described as a drawing room chair, either painted
and gilded or of zebrawood, is intended to have covers of silk or damask with an appropriate gimp.

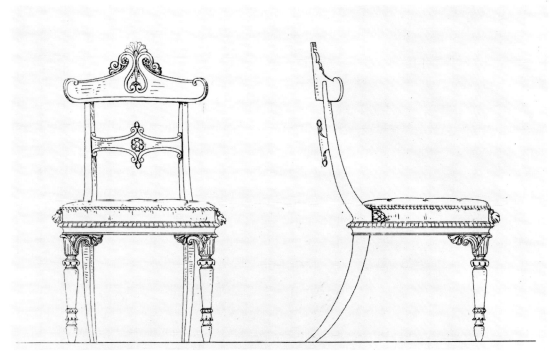

Design for a chair from Henry Whitaker's *Designs of Cabinet and Upholstery Furniture,* 1825,
showing an edging of cord with tassels at the corners of the seat and tufting.

Design for a chair from P. and M.A. Nicholson's *Practical Cabinet-Maker,* 1826, with the edge of the upholstery bordered with a lace or gimp and fringe with a bullion twist placed along the side of the seat rail.

fingered, which is too often practised' and he recommended covers 'of superfine cloth, or chintz pattern calico; the fringe worked in fine worsteds'.[35] Ackermann, responding to the taste for the exotic, illustrated a design for 'an Ottomane Couch' in 1814 (p.212) and circular and fitted ottomans are shown in Nash's *Views of the Royal Pavilion 1826,* included in both schemes for the Saloon but with different upholstery.[36] At Attingham there was a Turkish ottoman in a recess in the Small Drawing Room and one in the Picture Gallery with a large middle cushion and two pillows, upholstered in chintz. Loudon included several designs for fitted and free-

35. Smith, *Household Furniture,* p.12, pls. 67, 68.
36. Ackermann, Vol. XII July 1814, p.56, pl. 2.

Design for a chair from John Taylor's *The Upholsterer's and Cabinet Maker's Pocket Assistant*, c.1825, showing a typical armchair of the later Regency with tufting in the seat. The cover could have been of wool, leather or horsehair.

standing ottomans which are similar to those shown in the watercolour of the Striped Drawing Room at Apsley House by Thomas Shotter Boys, c.1852.[37] While Loudon recommended a fine wool cloth as suitable for covering ottomans their Eastern origins attracted more luxurious decoration and Ackermann illustrated a Dress Sofa in 1821 intended to have a white velvet cover with a painted design, an apparently popular technique mentioned by Nathaniel Whittock since 'the downy surface of the velvet and the brilliancy of the liquid colours used to produce fruit and flowers, give it a decided superiority over any other kind of flower painting, for ornamenting bell

---

37. This watercolour, now at Apsley House, was the model for pl. 3 of the volume of lithographs entitled *Apsley House and Walmer Castle* published in 1853.

ropes, ottomans, &c.'[38]

Stuffing materials for chairs, sofas, couches and ottomans included curled horsehair, sheep's wool, or cheaper materials like 'chaff, chopped hay, or straw, or bran'[39] or even sea wrack grass, laid on a piece of hessian tacked down to strips of webbing stretched tightly across the seat frame. The curled hair was stitched down to the webbing with string to prevent movement and covered with linen, hessian or canvas with sometimes a separate roll of hessian or canvas enclosed hair attached to the front rail to prevent collapse of the stuffing due to the sitter's weight. Various patents were taken out for springs in the late eighteenth and early nineteenth centuries, but Samuel Pratt's suggestion for an Elastic and Swinging Seat in 1826 was far closer to the kind of upholstered springing necessary for seat furniture than his predecessors', including that of Sheraton for a Chamber Horse with springs of very limited extension.[40] By 1833 sprung upholstery had become accepted since Loudon observed that 'seats of this description are now, however, made by upholsterers generally'. Loudon also referred to the other development of seat upholstery, the replacement of the eighteenth century silk or wool tufts arranged in decorative patterns on the backs and seats of chairs and sofas for buttoning, when he illustrated mahogany dining chairs with morocco seats which 'are quilted, but, instead of tufts, small rings are used, covered with the same leather as the chair; these rings being found to look as well as, and wear better than, tufts, of silk; at the same time that they do not harbour dust'.[41]

Sheraton included many designs for cabinet furniture which included drapery, 'a curtain of green silk, fixed on a brass wire at top and bottom' for a pot cupboard, and green silk fluting and drapery behind the doors of the Cylinder Desk and Bookcase, repeated for other pieces like bookcases and dressing tables.[42] As he pointed out 'Wire Doors are much introduced at present in cabinet work...they have generally green, white, or pink silk fluted behind', the drapery and fluted silk being attached together before being fixed to a rabbet left inside the door for that purpose.[43] Fluted silk in various colours was also used for pianos and for chiffoniers where the fluted silk 'should correspond or harmonise in colour with the curtains of the room'.[44] Bookcases were furnished with protective covers for the books, described by Ackermann in 1813 as 'a drapery of silk, suspended within side and at the top of the case by a spring roller, in the manner of a blind, and is made to draw to the bottom of the case, where spring locks are placed to receive the means

38. Ackermann Vol. XI 2nd Series January 1821 pl. 9 Dress Sofa, with a reference to a painted velvet state cover for an Oriental couch for the Sovereign of Russia. For the technique see Nathaniel Whittock, *The Art of Drawing and Colouring Flowers, Fruit and Shrubs...Painting on Velvet*, 1829.

39. Loudon, *Encyclopaedia*, Furniture for Cottage Dwellings, p.325.

40. Siegfried Giedion, *Mechanisation Takes Command*, 1948, pp.379-83.

41. Loudon, p.1049.

42. Sheraton, *Drawing Book*, pls. XLIII, XLVII, XLVIII, XLIX.

43. Sheraton, *Cabinet Dictionary*, p. 332. The drapery for Sheraton's Chaise Longue in the *Drawing Book* was attached in the same way.

44. Loudon, *The Surburban Gardener, and Villa Companion*, 1838, p. 102.

FRENCH SOFA BED.
N.º.3. of R·ACKERMANN'S REPOSITORY of ARTS &c.Pub.March.1816.

Plate 38. Design for a French Sofa Bed from Ackermann's *Repository,* Vol. I, 2nd Series, March 1816, pl. 14, illustrating the way beds could be arranged standing parallel to the wall with drapery falling over a rod projecting at right angles from the wall.

for confining it; they are connected at the side by grooves, and thus become as protecting as doors would be, without their weight or inconvenience.'[45] Ackermann also recommended 'Curtains of cloth or silk, or of other coloured materials', as being 'more ornamental, and more readily made to harmonise with the woodwork' than glass doors, for a Study Bookcase and Medal Cabinet in 1824.[46]

Silk was suggested for work tables by Sheraton, 'The drapery which hides the work-bag is tacked to a rabbet at the under edge of the frame all round...connected with the lower one by small upright pieces tenoned in, after which the bag is formed of silk, and tacked to each frame, and ornamented on the outside with drapery.'[47] Loudon also mentioned fluted silk for covering the bag frame with fringe at the bottom. Fire screens were covered in fluted silk, satin, tammy, moreen or other materials 'of the same colour as that of the other furniture in the room'[48] and also with embroidered or painted panels, maps or prints. Bedsteps were generally covered with carpet, matching that of the bedroom while at Attingham in 1827 there

45. Ackermann, Vol. X July 1813, p.42.
46. Ackermann, Vol. III 3rd Series January 1824, pl. 3.
47. Sheraton, *Drawing Book,* Pl. XXVI p.403 Ladies Work Tables.
48. Loudon, *Encyclopaedia,* p.2128 fig. 1973.

was 'A set of three tier mahogany Library Steps, lined crimson carpet'.[49]

The many designs for beds in pattern books of the Regency period illustrate the contemporary fascination with complicated drapery and trimmings which could be shown to advantage particularly on the heavily curtained four posters which were fashionable from 1790 right through to 1840. Generally the upholstery consisted of a tester or roof, a curtain for the back of the bed, four curtains to draw around, two at the head and two at the foot, which ran between inner and outer valances, a valance around the bottom and, sometimes, extra drapery along the tester and on the back curtain. The second type of bed, the light 'tent' or 'field' bed was more suitable for small rooms, for the fashionable cottages and villas, and for those involved in travelling, particularly the military, since it was relatively easy to collapse and re-erect. Usually the posts, lower than those on a four poster, were united by curved rods which were then covered by drapery to form a tent or canopy with draped curtains around the posts. Variations on this type included tent beds with shaped rods for the canopy. The third type, the 'French Bed' was in fact a couch, generally placed sideways against the wall with the drapery suspended from a pole at right angles to the wall about 10 feet above, or from a small canopy attached to the ceiling. There were alternatives to these three, including the half tester bed where the tester only extended half way over the base and there were no posts at the foot, couch beds with loose testers and pillars which could be removed and stored underneath the couch during the day, sofa and chair beds where the base unfolded like a modern sofa bed, press beds which concealed the mattress and frame inside a piece of furniture like a wardrobe or cabinet, and stump beds with very short posts at the foot and slightly longer ones at the head supporting a board. The press and stump beds were used particularly in simpler bedrooms and by servants.

Although few beds survive with their original drapery from the Regency period it is possible to gain some impression of their complicated nature from contemporary comments and illustrations. Sheraton referred to drapery 'of the French kind; it is fringed all round, and laps on to each other like unto waves'[50] while the ingenious Mr. Oakley 'invented a new arrangement of beds, which merits notice. Instead of the clumsy and cumbrous four-post bedstead, he disposes the hangings, in the form of drapery, against the side of the room, whence they are made to extend themselves at pleasure, by sliding tubes, or unfolding frame work. The bed itself, when not used as such, serves the purpose of an ordinary couch or sofa. Nothing can be more convenient or elegant, and the price is less than that of a four post-bed of equal decoration.'[51] There were obviously many variations on the way in which material could be draped over the tester and around the posts, the shape of the valances and the decoration of the back curtain or headcloth, tester and foot board. Loudon suggested one alternative, 'The headcloth and tester are fluted in a particular

49. Attingham Sale Catalogue 1827, lot 112.
50. Sheraton *Drawing Book*, p.379.
51. Ackermann, Vol. XIII May 1815, p.278. Mr Oakley was George Oakley who had a 'Manufactory and Magazin' for fashionable furniture at 8 Old Bond Street.

Design for a chair from Richard Bridgens' *Furniture with Candelabra,* 1838, showing the arrangement of buttons, now replacing tufts, and the use of a long fringe with small rosettes, presumably metal or material, and a gimp.

Pl. LX.

FRENCH DOME BED.

A. The Plan of Canopy and Dome.
B. Plan of Teaster.
C. Plan of Bedstead.

Scale for Plan.

Feet.

London, Published by Jones & Co. Aug. 19. 1826.

Plate 39. Design for a French Dome Bed from Smith's *Upholsterer's Guide*, 1826, pl. LX, showing the alternative position for the sofa bed, with a tester above fixed to the wall.

Interior at Repton Cottage, Hare Street, Essex, by Humphrey Repton, c.1815, showing ottomans
fitted neatly in the corners beside the fireplace and a pair of charming little hanging fitments.

manner; that is, with one wide flute and a narrow one on each side of it, leaving a space between it and the next flute. The footboard which is made to slide out and in, is fluted to correspond with the headcloth and tester.'[52] Full or half sunburst fluted patterns were also popular but the most important thing was that 'all best beds and drapery for sitting rooms should be put up by regular upholsterers, as it requires much correctness of eye, added to taste and knowledge of the prevailing fashion'.[53]

The range of materials used for bed drapery and curtains, known as furniture, and usually matching the window curtain and seat upholstery fabric, was as wide as that used for seat upholstery, as Hepplewhite observed, 'They may be executed of almost every stuff which the loom produces. White dimity, plain or corded, is peculiarly applicable for the furniture, which, with a fringe with a gymp head, produces an effect of elegance and neatness truly agreeable. The Manchester stuffs have been wrought into Bed-furniture with good success. Printed cottons and linens are also very suitable; the elegance and variety of patterns of which, afford as much scope for taste, elegance, and simplicity, as the most lively fancy can wish. In general, the lining to these kinds of furniture is a plain white cotton. To furniture of a dark pattern, a green silk lining may be used with a good effect... In state rooms, where a high degree of elegance and grandeur are wanted, beds are frequently made of silk or satin, figured or plain, also of velvet, with gold fringe, &c.'[54] As Sheraton noted, it was possible to obtain printed borders and motifs for appliqué on to the valances, curtains and counterpanes, and these were produced with contrasting designs on a smaller scale intended for the ground material. The popularity of washable materials like linens and cottons was noted by Robert Southey in 1807 'My bed, though neither covered with silk nor satin, has as much ornament as is suitable; silk or satin would not give that clean appearance which the English always require, and which I have already learnt to delight in. Hence, the damask curtains which were used in the last generation have given place to linens. These are full enough to hang in folds; by day they are gathered round the bed posts, which are light pillars of mahogany supporting a frame work, covered with the same furniture as the curtains; and valances are fastened round this frame, both withinside the curtains and without, and again round the sides of the bedstead.'[55] While chintzes and dimity were favoured for four posters, tent and French beds in most bedrooms, lesser rooms and those of servants were furnished with more old fashioned fabrics like cheney, a relatively humble worsted material, or checked cottons.

By 1833 dimity, muslin, printed cottons, Manchester stripes and chintzes were all acceptable for bed furnitures while moreen which 'used to be employed for the hangings of best beds and bed-room windows...is now considered as apt to harbour moths and other vermin; and therefore, in these economical times, it is much less used than formerly. It has, however, the advantage of not taking fire so readily as

52. Loudon, *Encyclopaedia,* Grecian and Modern Furniture for Villas, 2132 fig. 1981.
53. *The Workwoman's Guide* By a Lady, 1840, p.193.
54. Hepplewhite, pp.17-18.
55. Robert Southey, *Letters from England:* By Don Manuel Espriella, 1807, vol. 1, pp.160-1.

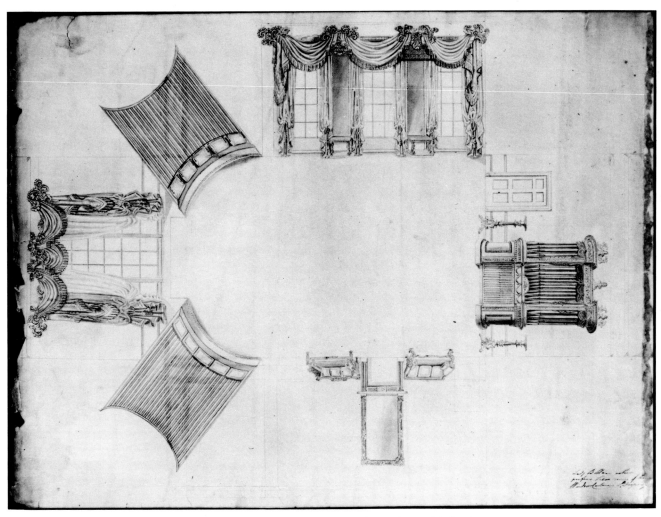

Design by Gillows for a music room, c.1825, showing ottomans built into alcoves hung with fluted silk, each ottoman fitted with cushions.

chintz or dimity. . .'[56] Bed curtains of chintz or dimity were generally lined with a different coloured plain or spotted cotton harmonising with the colour of the bed curtains while the thicker materials like damask, linen or moreen did not require lining. White dimity was 'sometimes lined with coloured calico with turned up hems, sometimes merely coloured hems, at others finished with white fringe, or frills with white cords and tassels'.[57] Other decoration for bed hangings included fringes, tassels, gimp and festoons of cords, often matching the colour of the lining.

Bed frames were made of mahogany, rosewood or oak for best bedsteads, sometimes with japanned or gilded posts or cornices, while beech, stained or painted was used for simpler styles like field or stump beds and iron for hospitals and prisons. Brass bedsteads appear to have been used for travelling since at Newstead there were two mentioned in 1815, each with 'military chest to hold the same' and

56. Loudon, *Encyclopaedia*, p.1080 fig. 1982.
57. *Workwoman's Guide*, p.193.

The Gallery leading to the drawing room, Fairlawn, Kent, watercolour dated 1842, showing typical freestanding ottomans trimmed with tassels and probably covered with some sort of woollen material.

The Workwoman's Guide in 1840 commented that they were 'used abroad, especially by travellers, and are ornamental and durable, but very expensive'.[58] The bedding was supported on sacking laced tightly to the sides of the base frame or on laths laid across the frame and fitting into grooves on either side. Bedding usually consisted of a hair, straw or flock mattress, feather bed, three blankets, linen or calico sheets, feather bolster and two down pillows or variations on these depending on the status of the bed and of its occupant. Blankets, the most famous coming from Witney, were 'of the natural colour of the wool, quite plain; the sheets plain also. I have never seen

---

58. Newstead Sale Catalogue 1815, lots 43, 57. *Workwoman's Guide*, p.191.

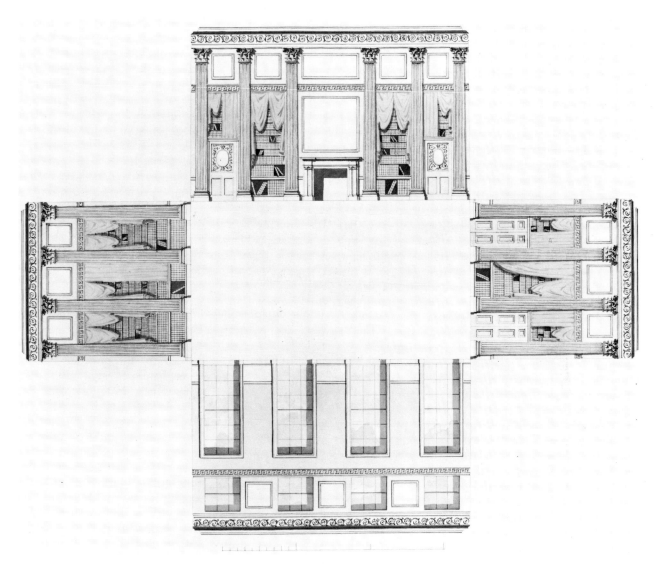

Design for the Outer Library, Attingham Park, by George Stewart, c.1780, showing the way in which curtains hung over bookshelves could be looped back, presumably with some sort of cord system. They were probably made of silk.

them flounced nor laced, nor ever seen a striped or coloured blanket.' However Southey was not so impressed with his counterpane which was 'of all English manufactures the least tasteful; it is of white cotton, ornamented with cotton knots, in shapes as graceless as the cut box in a garden'.[59] This was presumably a Marseilles quilt, a woven copy of hand quilting, which was much the most popular type of counterpane, listed everywhere including best bedrooms at Attingham and Chiswick, while other covers included silk or sarcenet for state beds, brown holland and superfine for four posters and white cotton or rugs for servants.

59. Southey, vol. 1, pp. 160-1.

PLATE 22

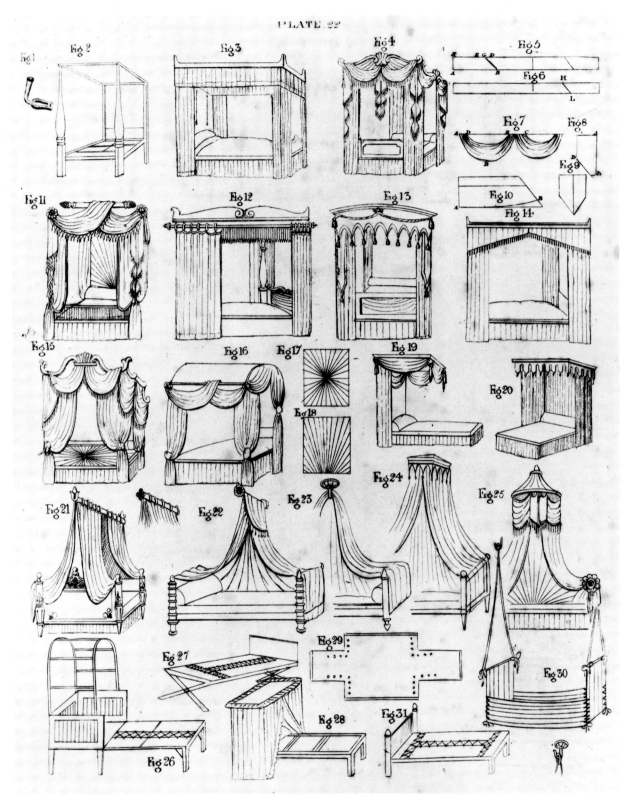

Designs for beds from *The Workwoman's Guide*, 1840, including four-posters, tent and camp (Nos. 15, 16), half-tester (19), French pole and arrow (21, 22), turn-up bed (26) and stump bed (31).

Design for four-poster from George Smith's *Cabinet Maker's Guide*, 1826, apparently with chintz bed hangings lined in blue, with the curtains arranged behind the bed posts, a sunburst pattern at the back and fluted material in the footboard.

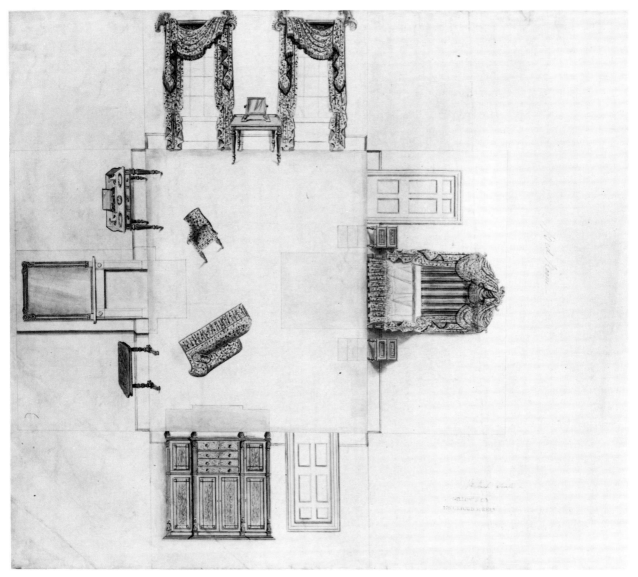

Design for a bedroom by Gillow & Co., 1830s, showing matching chintz for all upholstery materials and a complete bedroom suite of typical later Regency furniture.

9. Techniques and Materials

One of the most interesting technical innovations of Regency cabinet making was the introduction of wood working machinery in the 1790s, due almost entirely to the inventions of Sir Samuel Bentham, brother of the philosopher Jeremy Bentham. In 1791 he patented a mechanical planing machine, and in 1793 issued a comprehensive patent (No. 1951) covering planing, moulding, rebating, grooving, mortising, and sawing machinery, originally intended for use in prisons. In 1802 Joseph Bramah patented inventions for planing and thicknessing, and in 1803 James Bevans added machinery to cut mouldings, and other decoration in relief. In spite of these inventions there is little evidence that woodworking machinery was in general use for furniture making in the Regency period, and Thomas Martin, who includes cabinet making in *The Circle of the Mechanical Arts* 1813, only mentions Bentham's invention applied to pulley block making and to the use of steam engines or water mills for driving large lathes, suggesting that manual power was more commonly used.

There was no organised system for the industrial production of machine tools and most furniture making was still carried out with hand tools. In larger workshops there was an increased separation of processes and each craftsman was responsible for an even more selected number of commoner operations than formerly. The economic situation created by the Napoleonic Wars and other factors resulted in the cost of living doubling between 1795 and 1820 and this undoubtedly affected demand for complicated carving and inlaying, further exaggerated by the changes in fashion. T. Martin in *The Circle of the Mechanical Arts* referred to the paucity of master carvers and of journeymen, describing them as very old and retired with no professional workshops. Carved and inlaid decoration were replaced by cast ornaments, lines and beads of brass and although the animal monopodium legs popularised by Tatham and Hope required more skilled carving, the square section or scroll-shaped type could be easily cut with a bow saw by semi-skilled labour. The revival of repetitive carved ornament as part of the revival in eighteenth century French styles was facilitated by the invention of Jordan's patent wood carving machine in the 1820s. There was a corresponding increase in the number of carvers and gilders listed in the trade directories although some of these may have carved frames for pictures, mirrors and screens.

Veneering. Almost all Regency furniture that was not painted or lacquered was veneered rather than made of solid wood with the exception of chairs and some dining tables. Sheets of wood of particular richness of colour and figure of grain were cut very thinly with special saws and then glued to a base of a more common wood. This technique was used not only for large flat surfaces, like the tops of tables or fronts of cabinets, but also for shaped members like those which supported tables, or brackets for shelves. Veneering was used not only for economic reasons, because of the smaller amount of expensive wood necessary but also as a method of obtaining the best effects with woods of a fine colour and grain, which became scarce and expensive during the Napoleonic Wars when the difficulties of sea trade made supplies uncertain. Special methods of cutting also enabled complex figures of grain to be obtained which could not economically be obtained from solid timber.

Tea caddy, mahogany veneered with rosewood, satinwood, amboyna, kingwood and tulipwood, c.1804.

The invention of machinery for cutting woods for veneers by Mr. Marc Isambard Brunel resulted in a great saving of cost since cutting them by hand was laborious, expensive and often resulted in uneven veneers. Mr. Brunel, who established his factory in Battersea in 1819, designed a machine using circular saws driven by steam power. Apparently, skilled cabinet makers could get 8 or 9 thicknesses out of an inch of timber but those less professionally inclined and therefore indifferent to the quality of the timber and the durability of the finished veneers could cut 15 or 16 thicknesses out of an inch. Woods used for veneering included mahogany, rosewood, and satinwood as well as some of the more exotic types like zebrawood or calamander while the basic timbers were usually made of oak, beech or pine.

Woods. There was a constant demand throughout the Regency period for new patterns in woods, particularly those with fine colouring and graining which could be used to advantage in the fashionable designs set off by lines or beads of brass.[1] Although mahogany and satinwood were more fashionable, oak, beech and pine were used for carcases as well, with elm for cheaper and more provincial pieces. Oak was particularly suitable for Gothic designs because its close grain made it suitable for carving, and beech for painted, grained and japanned furniture, a type produced

---

1. For information about the various woods see *The Library of Entertaining Knowledge A Description and History of Vegetable Substances,* Used in the Arts, and in Domestic Economy, 2nd edition 1832, pp.167-181 Fancy Woods.

Table, calamander base and top of calamander,
rosewood, satinwood and other exotic woods,
c.1820.

Tea caddy, satinwood inlaid with various woods,
c.1800.

Table, zebrawood with gilding and ormolu mounts, c.1825.

by certain specialised makers and known as Fancy Furniture. George Bullock popularised the use of English native woods like larch and oak, combined with brass marquetry and metal mounts.

Mahogany. Imported from Honduras and used from the mid-eighteenth century and was dark, reddish brown in colour and very hard. After 1790 Honduran mahogany was replaced by supplies from the West Indies and Cuba, known as Spanish mahogany, and with a lighter, more brownish colour fading to a dusky yellow. Mahogany was comparatively cheap because of the extreme thinness into which veneers could be cut, and the coarser types could be used for the bottoms of drawers and other less important details of interior construction. The wood was particularly used for furniture for dining rooms, including tables and sideboards, and as Robert Southey pointed out, 'the tables were made of the solid plank; but English ingenuity has now contrived to give the same appearance at a far less cost of materials, by facing common deal with a layer of the fine wood not half a barley corn in thickness'.[2] Mahogany remained popular with cabinet makers right through the Regency period.

Satinwood. Imported from Brazil, Guiana and the West Indies from the 1760s, and pale to deep yellow in colour with a fine grain and sometimes richly figured. Also imported from Ceylon from the 1780s, pale to golden yellow in colour and used for

---

2. Robert Southey, *Letters from England*, 1807, vol. 1, p.154.

Plate 40. Table, mahogany with brass mounts and penwork top signed by Henzell Gouch and dated 1815.

Ornaments for Painting on Wood & Fancy Work, *Repository of Arts,* 3rd Series Vol. III, January 1817, pl. VI.

Ornaments for Painting on Wood & Fancy Work, *Repository of Arts,* 2nd Series Vol. III, February 1817, pl. 12.

Plate XXVII

GREEK AND ROMAN ORNAMENTS.

Gilding on Rose Wood &c.

Designs for Greek and Roman Ornaments for painting and gilding, *The Decorative Painters' and Glaziers' Guide*, 1827.

Designs for Chair Painting, *The Decorative Painters' and Glaziers' Guide,* by Nathaniel Whittock
1st edition 1827, pl. XXIII.

veneers, inlays and in solid timbers for small articles. Satinwood was used for some of the finest pieces of furniture from the 1790s until about 1810 and was recommended by Sheraton in the *Cabinet Dictionary* for its 'cool, light, and pleasing effect in furniture, on which account it has been in much requisition among people of fashion for above 20 years past'.[3]

Rosewood from Brazil. Reddish brown with dark brown or black streaks. Used from the late eighteenth century, first for bands of inlay in imitation of Louis Seize patterns and later for veneers, and as solid timbers for smaller pieces like caskets or legs of chairs and details like knobs and buttons. Because of its very attractive appearance it was intended for ornamental pieces, and gilt bronze and brass ornaments were thought to look particularly good on it. It was considered more fashionable than mahogany and remained popular until the 1840s.

3. Thomas Sheraton, *The Cabinet Dictionary,* 1803, p.314.

Settee, cane back and seat with painted design in black and gold, c.1815.

Zebrawood from Guiana and Brazil. Heavy wood of light brown colour, close grained with darker brown, straightish streaks. Chiefly used for veneers over mahogany carcases and presumably in short supply around 1820 when Miss Edgworth referred to tables made of it by George Bullock at Aston Hall.[4] Seddon and Shackleton, the partnership in existence 1793-1800, were particularly known for their use of zebrawood.

Calamander or Coromandel from Ceylon. Similar to zebrawood but the ground colour of a yellowish buff with a greater variety of mottling and streaking in the grain. Very rare, hard and heavy. Used for veneers and also for chairs, tables and sometimes doors.

Amboyna from the Moluccas. Hard wood with close grain, light red brown with

4. *The Life and Letters of Maria Edgeworth,* ed. A.J. Hare, 1894, vol. 1, pp.275-6 description of Bullock's tables at Aston Hall.

Pier glass, giltwood with under-glass painted panel, c.1810.

small bird's eye figure. Fashionable from about 1810 until the 1830s. Used for veneers and for beading. Similar to thuya wood in colour and markings, thuya being imported in the eighteenth century from North Africa.

Kingwood from Brazil, light yellowish brown with darker streaks. Very hard and similar to rosewood. Used for veneers and for crossbanding.

Other woods that were less commonly used include sandalwood, snakewood, harewood, maple and Botany Bay oak and for stringing lines, bands and decorative motifs, ebony and white holly. Ebony, imported from Madagascar, was also used for furniture in the Rococo Revival style. Pearwood, stained black with a mixture of gall and ink, was used as a substitute.

Commode, pine decorated with penwork, c.1810.

Painted and Stained Furniture

Furniture with painted designs and cheaper woods grained or stained to look like more expensive ones were both popular in the Regency period, particularly for interiors of villas or cottages, and for bedrooms, and many examples still survive. Instructions for implements, colours, stains and designs were given in a number of technical manuals including Sheraton's *Cabinet Dictionary,* Nathaniel Whittock's *The Decorative Painters' and Glaziers' Guide,* 1827, and *The Complete Cabinet Maker* by J. Stokes, c.1829. Designs and also suitable objects for painting could be obtained at specialist shops like 'The Temple of Fancy' run by S.J. Fuller at 34 Rathbone Place, London, where the stock included 'an extensive collection of handsome screens, both Plain and Ornamental, Screen-Poles, elegant Stands for

Table-Tops and Chess-Boards, Card-Racks, Flower Ornaments, and White-Wood Boxes, in a variety of shapes, for painting the inlaid Ebony and Ivory, with every requisite useful for Painting and Ornamenting the same'.[5] Sheraton recommended a pencil or brush of camel's hair while the hair of the marten, or of children, and even swansdown were also suggested for the more delicate painting, while brushes of hog's bristle or more unusually badger's or goat's hair, were used for larger areas.

There were plenty of illustrations of painted furniture in Ackermann's *Repository* including, in its first number in January 1809, a reference to the popularity of bronzing since it still prevailed 'as a ground-work for chairs, sofas, cabinets, &c. and will always be classic when delicately and sparingly assisted with gold ornaments'. Furniture painted black with simple gilt and red palmette motifs and stringing lines was also popular, particularly for bedrooms, and Ackermann illustrated in 1814 'three designs for light chairs intended for best bed-chambers, for secondary drawing-rooms, and occasionally to serve for routs. These chairs may be stained black, or, the present tase is, veined with vitriol, stained with logwood, and polished to imitate rosewood.'[6] Other pieces of bedroom furniture made of cheap woods like beech, pine, or deal and then painted, include beds, chests of drawers, dressing tables and wardrobes.

Whittock suggested several different ways of imitating woods particularly rosewood and 'excellent imitation of rosewood chairs, which are now so commonly sold at every broker's shop:- the chairs are made of beech...the stain is almost as permanent as the real rosewood'. Imitation rosewood satin was made by boiling logwood with water and salt tartar and then adding the streaks with deep black stain. Whittock also suggested that chairs 'may be painted in imitation of any fancy wood' and for 'light grounds, the lines must of course be dark, in general black, and this colour is so thin that it will run with greater freedom than any other. For dark grounds, such as pollard oak, rose or coral wood, white lines on common furniture have a good effect.'[7] Marbling effects could be achieved for the tops of tables, cabinets and washstands by mixing indigo and Roman ochre and adding light and dark green spots for verd-antique, raw terra de sienna and burnt umber with veins of burnt umber for Sienna marble, and indigo, Venetian red, and lake with dark green veins for Mona marble. Even a recipe for a green paint for garden furniture and Venetian blinds was included, the ingredients being mineral green and white lead ground in turpentine mixed with turpentine varnish and a little Prussian blue for a brighter colour.[8]

Verre-Églomisé. This term applies to the kind of decoration carried out in gold leaf applied to the underside of the glass and then engraved with a design. The backgrounds of the designs were usually black but could also be in blue, white or maroon. Designs could also be painted on the underside of the glass with a brush,

---

5. Quoted by Clifford Musgrave, *Regency Furniture*, 1961, p.136.

6. Ackermann, vol. 1, January 1809, p.55; vol. XII, August 1814, pp.98-9.

7. Nathaniel Whittock, *The Decorative Painters' and Glaziers' Guide*, 1827, pp.72, 80.

8. J. Stokes, *The Complete Cabinet Maker, and Upholsterer's Guide*, 1829, pp. 30, 127.

Detail of music stand, wood and brass with penwork decoration on gold and black ground. Made by Erard & Co., c.1810.

and sometimes this technique in various colours was combined with verre- églomisé in black and gold. Under-glass painting usually depicted figures and landscapes and floral motifs while verre-églomisé was nearly always used for designs with formal or abstract motifs.

Japanning. One of the most popular techniques was japanning, the European imitation of Oriental lacquer, first popularised in the seventeenth century, which was revived in the 1790s and mentioned several times by Sheraton in his *Drawing Book*. The basic technique involved preparing the ground surface with plaster of Paris or whiting and size which is then polished, and then covering this with several coats of lamp black, turpentine and lac or copal varnish. Designs could then be traced on to the surface and if raised japanning was required the details built up with a mixture of whiting or egg yolk and size, each outline being worked separately, and after the surface was dry it was polished with a soft camel hair pencil (or brush) and water. The technique became so popular for decoration of pseudo Oriental furniture that by 1800 there were over 60 japanners listed in London street directories but the vogue for this type of furniture declined by the 1820s and in 1827 there were only 27 japanners listed.

One of the uses of japanning was for ornamental decoration known as penwork, found on the tops of tables, panels of cabinet furniture, and smaller pieces like boxes and trays, and used to make cheaper wood carcases like pine, beech or faulty mahogany much more attractive. Thomas Sheraton referred to this kind of ornamental japanning and suggested some of the more fashionable patterns in Instructions for Drawing Ornaments in the *Drawing Book*. Other designs were produced by professional pattern drawers and copied by artists skilled in penwork and also published in such fashionable periodicals as Ackermann's *Repository,* (p.320) presumably for amateur use of which some examples survive. The surface was first varnished, japanned black, varnished again, and the designs painted all over with white japan and the lines added in Indian ink drawn with a quill pen and fine brushes. In some examples the ground was entirely of white japan with the design carried out in fine black lines, but in both black and white japanned surfaces the white japan and varnish have aged to a dirty yellow. Designs popularised by Sheraton included formal arrangements of flowers and foliage while later patterns used motifs from Greek, Roman or Egyptian styles as well as the pseudo-Oriental decoration associated with the Pavilion at Brighton.

Metal inlay and Buhl-work. Lines and stringings of rosewood or ebony, fashionable in the early Regency period were replaced by about 1812 by brass inlay and stringing and after 1815 brass marquetry or buhl work became very popular. Although not exactly the same technique as that practised by A.C. Boulle, since the Regency equivalent used wood veneer of rosewood or mahogany instead of the original tortoiseshell, the technique was used in similar continuous decoration covering whole panels of cabinets or table tops as well as for more simple details and motifs. By 1829 Mr. Stokes described buhl work as 'the art of inlaying in brass, silver, ivory, tortoiseshell, &c.... introduced into this country some years since, and is now brought to a state of perfection which equals anything of foreign manufacture'. He then gave detailed instructions for the technique, including inlaying with shaded wood which remained popular, various glues, polishes and cheaper imitations of precious metals.[9]

Ormolu. Many of the metal workers in England during the Regency period were French refugees, and one of the more well known designers for ormolu was John James Boileau of Sloane Square, a French decorator employed by the Prince of Wales at Carlton House. The expensive and dangerous technique favoured by the French which involved casting the mount in brass or bronze which was then gilded with mercury and gold under heat, was abandoned by the English craftsmen for a cheaper type of ormolu achieved by covering brass in lacquer gilding, sometimes without any gold, and firms in London and Birmingham like Boulton and Fothergill were known for their production of this type of ormolu. Often the same piece of furniture contains a mixture of mounts, some in bronze and lacquer gilded and others brass. There were of course plenty of examples of early eighteenth century French ormolu mounts which could be copied for furniture mounts in this style.

Composition and Papier Mâché Ornaments. Composition, a mixture of whiting, resin and size, could be moulded for ornaments to be applied to furniture as well as for architectural details and from about 1790 these were used particularly for details in the Egyptian taste such as mummy heads. Although prefabricated composition mounts could be obtained from specialist suppliers such as John Jaques of 13 High

9. Ibid., p.43.

Holborn, a cabinet maker could make his own from existing bronzes.[10] From about 1820 papier mâché moulded in the whole began to be used for ornaments on furniture, although Henry Clay's patent of 1772 for heat resistant panels of layers of specially prepared paper, known as 'paper ware' and later named papier mâché by the firm of Jennens and Bettridge, had introduced japanned and painted tea trays and other small objects of papier mâché.

French Polish. Although a variety of recipes is given for polishes and varnishes in the various technical manuals, perhaps the most well known was French polish, supposed to have been introduced into this country after the peace of 1814. Several variations were given, notably by Richard Brown where the ingredients included spirits of wine, mastic, sandarac, seed lac, shell lac, gum lac, gum arabic, and virgin wax, and by Stokes where spirits of wine, gum copal, gum arabic and shellac were suggested.[11] Whatever the ingredients the method of application remained the same, using the polish on a ball of cloth which was then wrapped in a piece of calico, moistened with linseed oil, and rubbed hard on to the surface of the wood with a circular motion, decreasing the amount of polish and increasing the amount of spirit until a perfect thin gloss was achieved.

---

10. Thomas King in Designs for *Carving and Gilding* c.1830 commented on the fashion for designs 'in the old French style, owing to the prevalence of which, composition ornaments, of the greatest beauty, may now be obtained, adapted for the small and intricate work'.

11. Richard Brown, *The Rudiments of Drawing Cabinet and Upholstery Furniture*, 1822, p.56; Stokes, p.102.

Appendix: Prominent Regency Craftsmen and Designers

BECKWITH, Samuel, and FRANCE, William, 101 St. Martin's Lane, London.
The firm was founded in 1764 and during the period 1784-1810 were one of the important suppliers of furniture to King George III. Among their other commissions was a suite of giltwood seat furniture for the King James I Drawing Room at Hatfield in 1781. They are listed as subscribers to Sheraton's *Drawing Book* 1791-4.

BAILEY, Edward, and SAUNDERS, Richard, 13 Mount street, London.
Partners 1817-27 in the firm that succeeded Marsh and Tatham (q.v.) at the same address and continued Marsh and Tatham's important role as cabinet-makers to the Prince Regent, later George IV. They are known particularly for the furniture, drapery, carpets and all other aspects of the cabinet-maker's and carver's work supplied for the final phase of furnishing at Brighton Pavilion under the direction of the Crace family of designers and Robert Jones, particularly in the Saloon, Music Room and Banqueting Room. They also supplied George IV with furniture for Windsor Castle and made repairs and alterations to the ebony and ivory suite of library furniture supplied for Carlton House by Marsh and Tatham in 1806. Edward Bailey continued to supply furniture and furnishings for the Royal Collection at least until 1840, including the chair of state for Queen Victoria's wedding in 1840.

BOGAERT, Frederick
Carver, from the Low Countries, employed by Thomas Hope for furniture at Duchess Street, London, and his country house, The Deepdene, and by Samuel Rogers, 1803-4. He may be the same person as Frederick Boeges, one of the Prince of Wales's debtors in 1795, and possibly connected with Peter Bogaerts, carver and gilder, recorded from 1804 at 23 Air Street, Piccadilly, in association with Paul Storr. George Smith in his *Cabinet-Maker's Guide*, 1826, mentioned his involvement in designing furniture and other areas of interior decoration.

BOILEAU, John James, Sloane Street, London.
Came over from France c.1787 to London and was employed as a painter and decorator under Henry Holland (q.v.) at Carlton House. Well known as designer of furniture including Turkish tripods for Fonthill, and ormolu, and praised by George Smith in *Cabinet-Maker's Guide*, 1826, for his 'airy and classic style of design'.

BRIDGENS, Richard
Designer, in contact with George Bullock (q.v.) in Liverpool from 1810 and used Bullock's address when exhibiting at the Royal Academy in 1813. Designed furniture for Battle Abbey, including a chair in the Elizabethan style made by Bullock and illustrated by Ackermann in 1813 (two examples of this survive, one in the Victoria and Albert Museum and one in Birmingham Museum), for Abbotsford in collaboration with Bullock, and for Aston Hall more Elizabethan furniture and

decoration 1819-24. Author of *Furniture with Candelabra*, first edition 1833, later edition 1838, the most influential pattern book of the Elizabethan revival.

BROWN, Richard
Had a small London practice as an architect, published several works on architecture and ran an 'architectural academy' at 4 Wells Street, London. Author of *The Rudiments of Drawing Cabinet and Upholstery Furniture* (1822, reprinted 1835) with many designs in a heavy Grecian style. This pattern book refers to the originality of George Bullock's (q.v.) designs (whose partner, Joseph Gandy was a friend of Brown) and illustrates some pieces of furniture with distinct similarities to Bullock's style.

BULLOCK, George, died 1818
Appeared in the Liverpool Trade Directories in 1804 as Modeller and Sculptor, Lord Street, and was joined by Joseph Gandy 1809-10 as partner when the firm is listed as architects, modellers, sculptors, marble masons, cabinet makers and upholsterers, Church Street, Liverpool. Appeared in the London Directories in 1813 as upholsterer, Grecian Rooms, Egyptian Hall, Piccadilly, and moved to 4 Tenterden Street, Hanover Square, with a subsidiary address, Mona Marble and Furniture Works, Oxford Street, in 1815 where he remained until his death. Particularly noted for his use of native British woods and marbles (he was proprietor of the Mona Marble Works, Anglesey) and for the prominence of boulle and inlaid woods and metal in his furniture. Much of his brass work used British flora like hops and oak leaves instead of the more conventional classical motifs. Associated with the designer, Richard Bridgens (q.v.), particularly for the furniture supplied to Abbotsford and Battle Abbey, and with Richard Brown (q.v.) who made favourable mention of Bullock's furniture. Bullock supplied designs of furniture and chimney pieces for Ackermann's *Repository* 1816-17 and the sale catalogue of his stock, May 1819, included a cabinet sofa very similar to Brown's plate XIII and Ackermann's plate 26, May 1816. Pieces of furniture made by Bullock survive at Blair Castle, Abbotsford and the Victoria and Albert Museum

BUTLER, Thomas, 13 and 14 Catherine Street, Strand, London.
Upholsterer and cabinet-maker who established a business as supplier of patent furniture at No. 14 in 1787. Employed both Thomas Morgan and Joseph Sanders (q.v.) prior to their establishing their own, very similar, business in 1801. After briefly closing in 1801, he reopened 1802-10, closed 1810-13 and finally reopened 1813-14. Three of his leading employees began business as Pryer, Steaines & Mackenzie, 30 Brydges Street, in 1812 offering a similar range of other furnishings. The number of firms offering patent furniture and the uncertain nature of their survival is very typical and many of the firms pirated each other's designs.

CAMPBELL, Robert, c.1777 King's Arms, Queen Street, Seven Dials, c.1790 Marylebone Street, Golden Square, and c.1800 33 Marylebone Street.

Took out patent for library steps enclosed in tables, chairs and stools in 1774 and examples were supplied to John Parker of Saltram in 1777 and apparently for George III. Supplied furniture for the Prince of Wales, including the upholstery of the seat furniture for the Chinese Drawing Room, Carlton House, and for the Duke of York.

CHIPPENDALE, Thomas, the younger, 60 St. Martin's Lane, 57 Haymarket and c.1821 42 Jermyn Street.

Continued his father's business in St. Martin's Lane after 1779 until bankruptcy in 1804 when he began a new business which continued until at least 1821. Known to have visited Paris and influence of French design seen in pieces supplied for Stourhead 1795-1820. Designed chair c.1820 made from elm used as Wellington's command post at Waterloo. Praised after his death by George Smith in 1826 for 'his great degree of taste'.

DURHAM, John, 16 Catherine Street.

Member of the Carpenters' Company who became foreman to Joseph Morgan of Morgan and Sanders (q.v.), patent furniture makers, and continued their business from 1820. Supplied two designs for Ackermann's *Repository*, September 1822 and February 1824 and several pieces of furniture survive with his label, including a field bed in Brighton Museum. His business closed in the late 1820s.

ELLIOTT, Charles

The firm of Elliott and Davis, later Charles Elliott, and finally Elliott and Francis, was in business at 97 New Bond Street 1775-1807, and No. 104, 1808-26. They were were one of the principal Royal cabinet makers and appear in the Royal Accounts from 1784 and are also known to have supplied furniture for Lord Berwick at his London house and at Attingham and for William Tuffnell's house, Langleys, Essex, 1797-8.

GILLOW, the firm of

Founded by Robert Gillow in Lancaster in 1729 who opened London premises in 1769 at 176 Oxford Road after his sons Richard and Robert had joined the firm. In 1772 the firm was known as Gillow and Taylor, in 1776 as Gillow, in 1790 as Robert Gillow and Company and in 1811 as G. & R. Gillow and Company. After Robert Gillow's death in 1772, his son Richard ran the Lancaster branch and Robert the London end of the business. Richard Gillow is credited with the invention of the telescopic dining table and took out a patent for the Imperial Dining Table in 1800. The firm is credited with many other pieces of innovative furniture, including the what-not c.1790 and the davenport c.1816, which are illustrated in the Estimate Sketch Books, records of the firm's designs which survive among the Gillow Collection in the Westminster Public Library. The last member of the family associated with the

firm, Richard Thomas Gillow, retired in 1830 but the firm survived and flourished, finally amalgamating with Warings c.1900. Many pieces of furniture made by the firm survive and can be identified by their stamp which they began using in the 1780s or from the Estimate Sketch Books.

HERVÉ, François or Francis, John Street, Tottenham Court Road.

Listed as 'cabriole chairmaker' or 'French chairmaker' from 1790. Known to have worked at Carlton House (Chinese Drawing Room and elsewhere), Althorp and Chatsworth c.1782 where he supplied not only seat furniture but also side tables, light fittings and the State Bed. Some of his seat furniture survives at Chatsworth and there is a set of library steps with his label in the Victoria and Albert Museum. Another set with the label 'Meschain & Herve No. 32 in Johns Street, Tottenham Court Road' was sold at Sotheby's 7th July 1985, lot 167.

HOLLAND, Henry (1745-1806)

Important and distinguished architect who had great influence over the design of the contents of his houses. He had profoundly French sympathies and was partly responsible for the spread of Anglo-French taste, particularly among his clients with Whig leanings. His most important work was for the Prince of Wales at Carlton House, and Brighton Pavilion, the Duke of Bedford at Woburn, Lord Spencer at Althorp and Samuel Whitbread at Southill, where much of the decoration and furniture remain as Holland designed them.

HUGHES, Robert

Partner of Nicholas Morel (q.v.) at 13 Great Marlborough Street, 1805-26, and later supplied furniture for the Duke of Northumberland for Syon House, 1826 and 1829.

INCE, William, and MAYHEW, John

Partnership formed 1759 and continued after Ince's death in 1804, at Broad Street, Soho, and later Marshall Street, Carnaby Market. Considerable reputation throughout the later eighteenth century, partly through publication of their *Universal System of Household Furniture* 1759-63 but few pieces from their workshops have been identified although they are known to have supplied aristocratic clients including Lord Palmerston. Ince was concerned with the design of pieces while Mayhew provided capital and managerial experience.

LE GAIGNEUR, Louis Constantin, Buhl Manufactory, 19 Queen Street, Edgware Road.

Is known to have specialised in the production of boulle furniture and supplied a number of pieces for the Prince of Wales at Carlton Housee 1815-16, including two kneehole writing tables in contre-partie boulle which bear his signature. A similar table is in the Wallace Collection, also with his signature, and a small ebonised table with brass decoration and a label of the Conyngham family, very similar to one shown in Nash's view of the North Drawing Room, Brighton Pavilion, 1826, has recently appeared (H. Blairman & Son).

LICHFIELD, William, and Graham
Listed in Trade Directories from 1786 at 1 St. Martin's Lane,
1 Long Acre and from 1788 at 72 St. Martin's Lane. Last
listing is in 1808 at 22 St. Martin's Lane and 1 Long Acre. The
firm supplied furniture and furnishings for Croome Court from
1779-85 and worked under Henry Holland's direction in the
early redecoration schemes at Brighton Pavilion and at Southill
from 1796.

McLEAN, John, Upper Terrace, Tottenham Court Road and
34 Marylebone Street, Piccadilly.
Listed in the Westminster Poll Book in 1774 and included in
Sheraton's list of cabinet-makers in the *Cabinet Dictionary*,
1803. Trade Directories 1809-14 give John McLean & Son,
upholders, 58 Upper Marylebone Street and from 1814-25
William McLean at the same address who may be a relative.
McLean is known particularly for his fine cabinets and desks
in the French taste with brass mounts and inlay and advertised
that he specialised in 'Elegant Parisian Furniture'.

MARSH, William, and TATHAM, Thomas, 13 and 14
Mount Street.
The firm began c.1785 with the partnership of George Elward
and Marsh, joined 1793 by Edward Bailey and 1798 by
Thomas Tatham. Before 1803 the name Elward, Marsh and
Tatham was used and from 1803-11 the firm was known as
Marsh and Tatham, Richard Saunders joining in 1811. The
firm's title was Tatham and Bailey or Tatham, Bailey and
Saunders until Tatham's death in 1818 when it became Bailey
and Saunders (q.v.). The firm was one of the most important
and influential suppliers of furniture and furnishings to the
Prince of Wales and to other fashionable clients and supplied
a great many pieces for Carlton House and Brighton Pavilion
from 1783. Tatham's brother, the designer C.H. Tatham
(q.v.), probably supplied the firm with ideas for much of their
furniture, including notably a set of ebony inlaid yewtree
bookcases for Carlton House in 1806 (one is in the Victoria
and Albert Museum, one sold by Christie's November 1985,
others are still in the Royal Collection).

MERLIN, John Joseph (1735-1803)
Native of the Low Countries who came to England in 1760 and
worked for the goldsmith and inventor, James Cox, before
establishing himself as a mathematical instrument maker at 42
and later 66 Queen Anne Street East. In 1783 he moved to 11
Princes Street, Hanover Square, and opened Merlin's
Mechanical Museum in the late 1780s. He specialised in the
production of automata and other mechanical toys and in
ingeniously designed furniture which often combined two or
more functions. His name is particularly associated with the
'gouty' chair, an early form of wheelchair, but early designs
of the same type of chair are known to have existed on the
Continent. Ackermann illustrated Merlin's Mechanical Chair
in his *Repository* in 1811 using a design supplied by Morgan
and Sanders (q.v.).

MOREL, Nicholas, and HUGHES, Robert, 13 Great
Marlborough Street.
Morel was among the debtors of the Price of Wales in 1795,
listed as an upholsterer and cabinet-maker of Tenterden Street,
Hanover Square, having probably worked at Carlton House and
Brighton Pavilion and among the group of fashionable
cabinet-makers who supplied furniture for Southill from the
1790s. From 1802 his address was in Great Marlborough
Street where he is listed with Robert Hughes (q.v.) and they
continued to provide the Prince with a great deal of furniture
and furnishings for his houses until 1826 when the partnership
ended. Other major commissions were for the Earl of Bradford
at Weston Park, 1802-3 and 1805-6, and for Northumberland
House, London, in 1823. From 1827-33 Morel formed a
partnership with George Seddon to provide a whole range of
services for the new schemes of interior decoration at Windsor
Castle, the Seddon firm (q.v.) providing workshops and
craftsmen while Morel used the experience of his journeys to
France to introduce new designs in the rich, florid taste of the
1820s.

MORGAN, Thomas, and SANDERS, Joseph, 16 and 17
Catherine Street, Strand.
Established c.1801 as upholsterers and by 1809 had become
'Patent Sofa-Bed & Chair-Bed manufacturers, Upholsters &
Cabinet-Makers' which they are listed as until 1821.
Ackermann illustrated a view of their showrooms in his
Repository in August, 1809 and there are many subsequent
references in the magazine to the firm who were one of the
most famous promoters of multipurpose and 'patent
metamorphic' furniture. Several pieces of furniture have
survived with their nameplate.

NELSON, Sefferin, Marshall Street, Golden Square and 4
Carnaby Market.
Carver and gilder who gilded the chair frames for the Chinese
Drawing Room, Carlton House, 1791, and was also employed
at Chatsworth in the 1780s, Audley End in 1787 and Althorp
in 1791.

OAKLEY, George, 22 South Side of St. Paul's Churchyard
and 8 Old Bond Street.
Established business as upholder, 1782, 2 Clements Lane and
had moved to St. Paul's Churchyard by 1786 and Old Bond
Street by 1798. First partner was Henry Kettle in 1796 and by
1800 the firm was known as Oakley, Shackleton & Evans,
Thomas Shackleton being a son-in-law of George Sedddon.
Between 1802-5 Oakley, Dudding & Co., Furniture Printers,

67 Old Bond Street, are listed in the Trade Directories since Oakley had acquired the printed textiles business of Dudding & Co. By 1819 Oakley & Evans are still in partnership at 22 St. Paul's Churchyard and 8 Old Bond Street. They are known to have supplied furniture for the Prince of Wales and for other important clients like Charles Madryll Cheere of Papworth Hall and were recommended for fashionable furniture by P.A. Memnich when writing of his English travels in 1807. Smith in his *Cabinet-Maker's Guide*, 1826, refers to furniture supplied by Oakley and Evans for Alexander Copeland's house, Great George Street, Westminster.

PAPWORTH, John B. (1775-1847)
Trained with the architect, Sir William Chambers, and began a prolific architectural career in the late 1790s. Many designs contributed to Ackermann's *Repository*, later reprinted as *Select Views in London* 1816, *Rural Residences* 1818, *Hints on Ornamental Gardening* 1823. Also designed Ackermann's new premises 1826 and furniture for the cabinet-makers Edward and William Snell and George and Thomas Seddon in the 1830s. His son Wyatt Papworth later stated that many of the designs in John Loudon's influential *Encyclopaedia of Cottage, Farm and Villa Furniture*, first edition 1833, were taken from his father's work.

PARKER, Thomas, 19 Air Street, Piccadilly, 1808-17, 22 and 32 Warwick Street, Golden Square, until 1829.
Known to have specialised in the production of boulle furniture and several pieces survive with his stamp, including a pair of marriage coffers on stands and a small table, later converted into a display case, in the Royal Collection.

PUGIN, Augustus Charles (1769-1832)
Established himself as an architectect and topographical artist and was responsible for the original watercolours of the interiors of Brighton Pavilion, later engraved for Nash's *Views* 1826. Contributed designs of furniture in the Gothic style to Ackermann's *Repository* 1825-7, later reprinted as *Gothic Furniture*. Father of A.W.N. Pugin (q.v.).

PUGIN, Augustus Welby Northmore (1815-52)
Commissioned as a very young man in 1827 to design Gothic furniture for Windsor Castle which was made by Morel and Seddon. Established his own cabinet-making firm in Hart Street, Covent Garden, 1829-31, and produced furniture in the Gothic, Elizabethan and Jacobean styles (a table with his stamp is in the Victoria and Albert Museum). Later designed furniture for various patrons including Lord Shrewsbury and Charles Scarisbrick and published his first book, *Gothic Furniture in the Style of the Fifteenth Century*, in 1835. His most important and extensive later work was responsibility for the design of all the internal decorative furniture and furnishings for the New Palace of Westminster.

ROBINS, John
First appears in the Directories in 1778 at 28 Chancery Lane, later moving in 1793 to Beak Street, Golden Square, 1796 Chancery Lane and Warwick Street, Golden Square, 1817 2 Beak Street and Warwick Street, 1825-8 170 Regent Street. Business associate of Sir John Soane who designed Robins' own house in Park Lane and a large block of business premises for him in Regent Street. Robins supplied furniture, presumably to Soane's design, for the Bank of England and for Soane's houses at Pitshanger 1801-2 and for Lincoln's Inn Fields.

SEDDON, the firm of
Very large and important firm founded by George Seddon in Aldersgate at 151 and 158, c.1750. The firm changed its name several times, being known as George Seddon & Sons in 1789, George Seddon, Sons & Shackleton 1793-1800 (Thomas Shackleton later joined George Oakley (q.v.)) and Thomas and George Seddon 1820-36. The firm expanded to 16 Lower Grosvenor Street in 1826 and branches of the family had businesses at 10 Charterhouse Street and 24 Dover Street from 1791. From 1827-33 the firm was in partnership with Nicholas Morel (q.v.) to provide furniture for Windsor Castle, the total cost being just under £180,000. In 1833 Thomas and George Seddon opened premises in Gray's Inn Road and in 1837 vacated the workshops in Aldersgate. The firm produced fashionable and innovative furniture including the croft, a small cabinet with lockable drawers and writing surfaces. Several pieces survive from the furniture supplied for D. Tupper of Hauteville House, Jersey, in 1790.

SHERATON, Thomas (1751-1806)
Said to have worked for many years as a journeyman cabinet-maker but made his reputation as a drawing-master specialising in furniture design. His first book, *The Cabinet-Maker and Upholsterer's Drawing Book*, published in parts 1791-4, included designs strongly influenced by the Anglo-French style of Henry Holland. The only surviving views of the Chinese Drawing Room, Carlton House, in its original state, are illustrated in the *Drawing Book* which also included a list of master cabinet-makers. His second book, *The Cabinet Dictionary*, 1803, illustrated designs incorporating animal motifs first published by C.H. Tatham (q.v.) and his final work, *The Cabinet-Maker, Upholsterer and General Artist's Encyclopaedia*, 1804-7, was uncompleted on his death in 1806. Although the text was rather eccentric, the plates included some of the first pieces of furniture using Egyptian motifs. Sheraton's influence on the furniture trade can be seen in the number of his designs copied by Gillows (q.v.) and in the popularisation of furniture in the styles he illustrated.

SMITH, George, Brewer Street, Golden Square.
From 1806 he produced plates for his *Designs for Household Furniture and Interior Decoration* 1808. The illustrations

included designs in the Greek, Gothic, Egyptian and Chinese styles. From 1809 Smith contributed designs and text concerning fashionable upholstery to Ackermann's *Repository* and published *A Collection of Ornamental Designs* in 1812 with illustrations in the Grecian style. His last book, *the Cabinet-Maker's and Upholsterer's Guide*, 1826, described him as 'Upholsterer and Drawing Master to His Majesty' and included plates in the Egyptian, Greek, Etruscan, Roman, Gothic and Louis XIV styles. No firm evidence of his cabinet-making business has yet been found.

TATHAM, Charles Heathcote (1772-1842)

Trained with his relative, John Linnell, and joined Henry Holland's (q.v.) office in 1789. Holland sent him to Rome in 1794 to collect architectural fragments and provide Holland with source material for his designs which Tatham supplied in a series of illustrated letters (Victoria and Albert Museum Print Room). His first book, based on his experiences in Rome, *Etchings of Ancient Ornamental Architecture...* published in 1799 and reprinted several times up to 1843, was very influential and several pieces of furniture survive after his designs. His later book, *Etchings Representing Fragments of Grecian and Roman architectural ornaments*, was published in 1806. Linnell's collection of drawings was left to Charles Heathcote Tatham's brother, Thomas, partner in the firm of Marsh and Tatham (q.v.) for whom Charles probably designed many pieces, including the council chairs from the Throne Room, Carlton House. C.H. Tatham also designed furniture for Castle Howard as well as the whole decoration of the gallery which he published in 1811. In the same year he published interiors · of Brocklesby Park for which he had designed furniture and interiors.

TAYLOR, John, 16 Bedford Court, Covent Garden.

Worked for George Oakley (q.v.) before establishing his own business, 1824-9. Contributed several designs to Ackermann's *Repository* 1821-4, and published *The Upholsterer's and Cabinet-Maker's Pocket Assistant* c.1825. His second book, *Designs for Decorative Household Furniture*, also included some of his designs for Ackermann.

Bibliography

Acloque, Guy, and Cornforth, John, 'The Eternal Gothic of Eton', *Country Life* Vol. CXLIX, Part I No.3844, February 11, Part II No.3845, February 11, 1971.

Agius, Pauline, and Jones, Stephen, *Ackermann's Regency Furniture and Interiors*, 1984.

Austen, Brian, 'Morgan & Sanders and the Patent Furniture Makers of Catherine Street', *The Connoisseur*, Vol. 187, No.753, November 1974.

Cescinsky, Herbert, *The Gentle Art of Faking Furniture*, London 1931.

Curl, James Stevens, *The Egyptian Revival*, London 1982.

de Bellaigue, Geoffrey, 'The Furnishings of the Chinese Drawing Room, Carlton House', *The Burlington Magazine*, Vol. CIX, No.774, September 1967; 'George IV and French Furniture', *The Connoisseur*, Vol. 195, No.784, June 1977.

de Bellaigue, Geoffrey, Harris, John, and Millar, Oliver, *Buckingham Palace*, 1968.

de Bellaigue, Geoffrey, and Kirkham, Pat, 'George IV and the Furnishing of Windsor Castle', *Furniture History*, Vol. VIII 1972.

Devonshire, The Duchess of, *The House A Portrait of Chatsworth*, London 1982.

Devonshire, The Sixth Duke of, *Handbook of Chatsworth*, 1844.

Dinkel, John, *The Royal Pavilion Brighton*, London 1983.

Edwards, Ralph, 'Review of *Sheraton Furniture*', *The Burlington Magazine*, Vol. CV, No.718, January 1963.

Elder-Duncan, J.H., *The House Beautiful and Useful*, new edition, London 1911.

English Printed Textiles 1720-1836, Victoria and Albert Museum/H.M.S.O., 1960.

Fastnedge, Ralph, *Shearer Furniture Designs*, London 1962; *Sheraton Furniture*, London 1963.

Fedden, Robin, 'Neo-Norman', *The Architectural Review*, Vol. 116, No.696, December 1954.

Fitz-Gerald, Desmond, 'A Sheraton-designed bookcase and the Giannellis', *Victoria and Albert Museum Bulletin*, Vol. IV No.1, January 1968.

Gilbert, Christopher, 'London and Provincial Books of Prices: Comment and Bibliography', *Furniture History*, Vol. XV, 1979.

Glenn, Virginia, 'George Bullock, Richard Bridgens and James Watt's Regency Furnishing Schemes', *Furniture History*, Vol. XV, 1979.

Hall, Ivan, 'Patterns of Elegance: The Gillows' Furniture Designs—I', *Country Life*, Vol. CLXIII, No.4222, June 8 1978; 'Models with a choice of leg. The Gillows' Furniture Designs—II', *Country Life*, Vol. CLXIII, No.4223, June 15 1978; 'A neo-classical episode at Chatsworth', *The Burlington Magazine*, Vol. CXXII, No.927, June 1980.

Hardy, John, and Wainwright, Clive, 'Elizabethan-Revival Charlecote Revived', *The National Trust Year Book*, 1976-77.

Harris, John, *Regency Furniture Designs 1803-1826*, London 1961.

Haweis, Mrs. H.R., *The Art of Beauty*, London 1878; *The Art of Decoration*, London 1881; *Beautiful Houses*, London 1882.

Heckscher, Morrison, 'Eighteenth-Century Rustic Furniture Designs', *Furniture History*, Vol. XI 1975.

Honour, Hugh, *Chinoiserie The Vision of Cathay*, London 1961.

Houfe, Simon, *Sir Albert Richardson—The Professor*, Luton 1980.

James, Edward, *Swans Reflecting Elephants*, (ed.) George Melly, London 1982.

Jennings, H.J., *Our Homes and How to Beautify Them*, London 1902.

Jervis, Simon, ' "Sussex" Chairs in 1820', *Furniture History*, Vol. X 1974; 'The Pryor'sbank Fulham', *Furniture History*, Vol. X 1974; 'Cottage, Farm and Villa Furniture', *The Burlington*, Vol. CXVII, No.873, December 1975, Furniture Supplement.

Jourdain, Margaret, *Regency Furniture 1795-1820*, 1934.

Joy, Edward T., 'Georgian Patent Furniture', *The Connoisseur Year Book*, 1962; 'A Versatile Victorian Designer J.B. Papworth', *Country Life*, Vol. CXLVII, No.3802, January 15 1980; *English Furniture 1800-1851*, London 1977.

Kenworthy-Browne, John, 'Notes on the Furniture by Thomas Chippendale the Younger at Stourhead', *National Trust Year Book*, 1975-6.

Knoblock, Edward, *Round the Room*, London 1939.

Lever, Jill, *Architects' Designs for Furniture*, R.I.B.A. Drawings Series, London 1982.

Litchfield, Frederick, *Illustrated History of Furniture*, 1892; *Antiques Genuine and Spurious*, 1921.

McClelland, Nancy, *Duncan Phyfe and the English Regency 1795-1830*, 1939.

Mavor, Elizabeth, *The Ladies of Llangollen*, London 1971.

Montgomery, F.M., *Printed Textiles* English and American Cottons and Linens 1700-1850, London 1970.

Morley, John, 'Early Chinese Interiors at Brighton Pavilion', *Apollo*, Vol. CXVI, No.247, September 1982; *The Making of the Royal Pavilion Brighton*, London 1984.

Musgrave, Clifford, *Regency Furniture*, London 1961; *Adam and Hepplewhite and other Neo-Classical Furniture*, London 1966.

Muthesius, Hermann, *The English House*, English edition, London 1979.

Pevsner, Sir Nikolaus, and Lang, S., 'The Egyptian Revival', *Architectural Review*, Vol. CXIX, 1956.

Praz, Mario, *On Neoclassicism*, London 1959; *The House of Life*, London 1964.

Proudfoot, Christopher, and Watkin, David, 'The Furniture of C.H. Tatham', *Country Life*, Vol. CLI, No.3912, June 8 1972.

Purser, Philip, *Where is He Now? The Extraordinary Worlds of Edward James*, London 1978.

Reade, Brian, *Regency Antiques*, London 1953.

Redburn, Simon, 'John McLean and Son', *Furniture History*, Vol. XIV, 1978.

Richardson, A.E., *et al*, *Southill A Regency House*, London 1951.

Roberts, Henry D., *A History of the Royal Pavilion Brighton*, London 1939.

Robinson, John Martin, *The Wyatts: An Architectural Dynasty*, Oxford 1979.

Sitwell, Osbert, *Left Hand Right Hand!*, London 1949.

Smith, H. Clifford, *Buckingham Palace*, 1931.

Stroud, Dorothy, *Henry Holland: His Life and Architecture*, 1966.

Udy, David, 'The Neo Classicism of Charles Heathcote Tatham', *The Connoisseur*, Vol. 177, No.714, August 1971.

Wainwright, Clive, 'Specimens of Ancient Furniture', *The Connoisseur*, Vol. 184, No.740, October 1973; 'A.W.N. Pugin's Early Furniture', *The Connoisseur*, Vol. CXXI, No.767, January 1976; 'Walter Scott and the Furnishing of Abbotsford', *The Connoisseur*, Vol. 194, No. 779, January 1977; 'The Furnishing of the Royal Library, Windsor', *The Connoisseur*, Vol. 195, No.784,

June 1977; 'The Dark Ages of art revived, or Edwards and Roberts and the Regency revival', *The Connoisseur*, Vol. 198, No.196, June 1978; 'Myth and Reality', *Country Life*, Vol. CLXXII, No.4439, September 16 1982; 'Object of Natural Curiosity', *Country Life*, Vol. CLXXII, No.4440, September 23 1982; 'Charlecote Park, Warwickshire', I and II, *Country Life*, Vol. CLXXVII, No.4566, February 21, No.4567, February 28, 1985.

Ward-Jackson, Peter, *Victoria and Albert Museum English Furniture Designs of the Eighteenth Century*, London 1958.

Watkin, David, *Thomas Hope 1769-1831 and the Neo-Classical Idea*, London 1968.

Watson, F.J.B., 'George IV as an Art Collector. Some Reflections on the Current Exhibition at the Queen's Gallery', *Apollo*, Vol.

LXXXIII, No.52, June 1966; 'Holland and Daguerre: French Undercurrents in English Neo-Classic Furniture Design', *Apollo*, Vol. XCVI, No.128, October 1972; 'The Great Duke's Taste for French Furniture', *Apollo*, Vol. CII, No.161, July 1975.

Welleseley, Lord Gerald, 'Regency Furniture', *The Burlington Magazine*, Vol. LXX, No.410, May 1937.

Williams, Robert, 'A Cambridge Family of Furniture Makers and The Furnishing of the Master's Lodge Trinity College, Cambridge, 1795-1820', *Furniture History*, Vol. XII, 1976.

Wills, Geoffrey, 'The Carlton House Writing-Table', *Apollo*, Vol. LXXXIII, No.50, April 1966.

CONTEMPORARY SOURCES OF DESIGNS FOR FURNITURE AND INTERIORS

Ackermann, R., *Gothic Furniture*, 1827; *The Repository of Arts*, published in volume form from 1809 to 1828; *Selection of Ornaments*, 1817-1819.

Bartell jun., Edmund, *Hints For Picturesque Improvements in Ornamented Cottages*, London 1804.

Bridgens, Richard, *Furniture with Candelabra*, 1838.

Britton, John, *The Union of Architecture, Sculpture and Painting*, 1827; *Graphic Illustrations, with Historical and Descriptive Accounts, of Toddington, Gloucestershire*, 1840.

Brown, Richard, *The Rudiments of Drawing Cabinet and Upholstery Furniture*, London 1822.

Buckler, J., and J.C., *Views of Eaton Hall*, 1826.

Busby, C.A., *A Series of Designs for Villas and Country Houses*, London 1808.

Cabinet-Makers' London Book of Prices, The, 1788, 1793, (reprinted *Furniture History*, Vol. XVIII, 1982), 1863.

Chippendale, Thomas, *The Gentleman and Cabinet-Maker's Director*, 1762.

Condy, Nicholas, *Cotehele*, London c.1840.

Dictionary of Architecture, The, Architectural Publication Society, 1853-92.

Eaton Tourist, The, published by J. Seacombe, Chester 1825.

Gillow Cost and Estimate Sketch Books, c.1790-1830.

Gillow Decorators and Upholstery Estimate Book 1817-24 from the Gillow Archive at the Westminster City Library Archives Department, No.344/142.

Hepplewhite & Co., A., *The Cabinet-Maker and Upholsterer's Guide*, 3rd edition, London 1794.

Hofland, Mrs., *A Descriptive Account of the Mansion and Gardens of White Knights*, London 1819.

Hope, Thomas, *Household Furniture and Interior Decoration*, London 1807; *An Historical Essay on Architecture*, London 1835.

Hunt, T.F., *Exemplars of Tudor Architecture*, Adapted to Modern Habitations, London 1830.

Ideas for Rustic Furniture, c.1790.

Ince and Mayhew, *Universal System of Household Furniture*, 1762.

Jacques, D., *A Visit to Goodwood*, Chichester and London 1822.

King, Thomas, *Designs for Carving and Gilding*, c.1830; *The Modern Style of Cabinet Work Exemplified*, 1829, 2nd edition 1839; *Modern Designs for Household Furniture*, c.1830; *The Cabinetmaker's Sketch Book*, 1835-6; *Fashionable Bedsteads with Hangings*, n.d.; *Upholsterer's Sketch Book of Original Designs*, n.d.

Library of Entertaining Knowledge A Description and History of Vegetable Substances, The, Used in the Arts, and in Domestic Economy, London 2nd edition 1832.

London Chair Maker's and Carver's Book of Prices, The, 1803, 1808.

Loudon, J.C., *A Treatise on Forming, Improving and Managing Country Residences*, London 1806; *The Encyclopaedia of Cottage, Farm and Villa Architecture*, London 1835; *The Suburban Gardener, and Villa Companion*, London 1838; *The Architectural Magazine*, 1834-1838.

Lugar, Robert, *Architectural Sketches*, 1805.

Martin, Thomas, *The New Circle of the Mechanical Arts*, 1819.

Moses, Henry, *Designs of Modern Costume*, 1812; *A series of twenty-nine designs of Modern Costume*, 1823.

Nash, John, *Views of the Royal Pavilion*, 1826.

Nicholson, P., and M.A., *The Practical Cabinet Maker*, 1826.

Nicholson, Peter, *The Architectural Dictionary*, 1812-19.

Papworth, J.B., *Rural Residences*, London 1818; *Hints on Ornamental Gardening*, London 1823.

Parker, Thomas Lister, *Description of Browsholme Hall*, London 1815.

Pugin, A.W.N., *The True Principles of Pointed or Christian Architecture...*, London 1841.

Pyne, W.H., *History of the Royal Residences*, 1817.

Repton, Humphrey, *Designs for the Pavilion at Brighton*, London 1808.

Robinson, P.F., *Designs for Ornamental Villas*, 1836; *Vitruvius Britannicus*, London 1827, 1833, 1855.

Rutter, J., *Delineation of Fonthill and its Abbey*, 1823.

Shaw, Henry, *Specimens of Ancient Furniture*, 1836.

Shearer, Thomas, *Designs for Household Furniture*, 1788.

Sheraton, Thomas, *The Cabinet-Makers' and Upholsterers' Drawing Book*, 1791-4; *The Cabinet Dictionary*, London 1803; *The Cabinet-*

Maker, Upholsterer, and General Artist's Encyclopaedia, 1804-7.

Smith, George, *A Collection of Designs for Household Furniture and Interior Decoration*, London 1808; *A Collection of Ornamental Designs*, London 1812; *The Cabinet-Maker's & Upholsterer's Guide*, London 1826.

Stokes, J., *The Complete Cabinet Maker, and Upholsterer's Guide*, London 1829.

Tatham, C.H., *Etchings of Ancient Ornamental Architecture drawn from the Originals in Rome and Other Parts of Italy during the years 1794, 1795, and 1796*, 1799, 1800; *The Gallery at Brocklesbury*, 1811; C.H. Tatham to Henry Holland, A Collection of original letters and drawings, 1794-1796. Victoria and Albert Museum, Print Room (D 1479/1551-1898).

Taylor, John, *The Upholsterer's and Cabinet Maker's Pocket Assistant*, c.1825; *Modern Designs for Household Furniture*, c.1830.

Tracings by Thomas Wilkinson from the Designs of the Late Mr. George Bullock 1820, an album in the collection of Birmingham Museum.

Whitaker, Henry, *Designs of Cabinet and Upholstery Furniture*, 1825.

Whittock, Nathaniel, *The Decorative Painters' and Glaziers' Guide*, London 1827; *The Art of Drawing and Colouring Flowers, Fruit and Shrubs...Painting on Velvet*, London 1829.

Workwoman's Guide, The, By a Lady, London 1840.

DIARIES, LETTERS AND MEMOIRS

Bamford, Francis, and Wellington, Duke of, (eds.), *The Journal of Mrs. Arbuthnot 1820-1832*, London 1950.

Edgeworth, Maria, *Letters from England 1813-1844*, (ed.) Christina Colvin, Oxford 1971.

Farington, R.A., Joseph, *The Farington Diary*, (ed.) James Greig 1924.

Fremantle, Anne, (ed.), *The Wynne Diaries*, Vol. 3, 1940.

Granville, Castalia Countess, (ed.), *Lord Granville Leveson Gower (First Lord Granville), Private Correspondence 1781 to 1821*, 1916.

Hare, A.J., (ed.) *The Life and Letters of Maria Edgeworth*, 1894.

Lewis, Lady Theresa, (ed.) *Extracts of the Journals and Correspondence of Miss Berry* from the year 1783 to 1852, London 1865.

Lewis, W.S., (ed.) *The Yale Edition of Horace Walpole's Correspondence*, Vol. 33, 1785.

Minto, Countess of, (ed.), *The Life and Letters of Sir Gilbert Elliot, First Earl of Minto, 1751-1806*, Vol. 1, 1874.

Papworth, Wyatt, *John B. Papworth, Architect to the King of Wurtemburg: A Brief Record of His Life and Works*, London 1879.

Pückler-Muskau, Prince, *Tour in Germany, Holland and England* in the Years 1826, 1827, 1828, London 1832.

Simond, Louis, *Journal of a Tour and Residence in Great Britain*, London 1817.

Southey, Robert, *Letters from England: By Don Manuel Espriella*, London 1807.

Treffry Dunn, H., *Recollections of Dante Gabriel Rossetti and His Circle*, London 1904.

von la Roche, Sophie, *Sophie in London*, 1786, trans. by Clare Williams, London 1933.

CATALOGUES AND INVENTORIES

Art Journal Illustrated Catalogue of the International Exhibition 1862, The.

Catalogue of the contents of Attingham Hall, July-August 1827.

Mss. Inventory of Chiswick, 1811.

Christie's Sale Catalogue of 'the stock of the late Mr. Bullock at 4, Tenterden Street, Hanover Square', May 3-5 1819.

Conner, Patrick, (ed.), *The Inspiration of Egypt*, Catalogue of the exhibition, Brighton Museum, 1983.

Henry Holland, Catalogue of the exhibition at Woburn Abbey, 1971.

Horace Walpole and Strawberry Hill, Catalogue of the exhibition at the Orleans House Gallery, Twickenham 1980.

Humphrey Repton Landscape Gardener 1752-1818, Catalogue of the exhibition by George Carter, Patrick Goode and Kedrun Laurie at the Sainsbury Centre for Visual Arts, Norwich 1982.

Catalogue of the contents of Lee Priory, 11-21 August, 1834.

Catalogue of the contents of Newstead, October 1815.

Phillips of Hitchin (Antiques) Ltd., *Patent Metamorphic Furniture 1780-1830*, 1978.

Sale Catalogue of the contents of Speke Hall, 1-3 September, 1812.

Index

NOTE: page numbers in italics refer to picture captions.

Photographic Acknowledgements

The illustrations on the following pages are reproduced by gracious permission of Her Majesty Queen Elizabeth: 33, 37, 143-4, 176, 198
The Avery Architectural Library, Columbia University, 307
Messr. H. Blairman & Sons, 13, 46, 54, 75, 83, 94, 98-9, 107, 110, 112, 115, 117, 133, 145-7, 171, 202, 204, 206, 218, 225, 269, 298, 317, 325
Messrs. Bonham & Sons Ltd., 24
The Bowes Museum, 25, 97
Messrs. Christie, Manson & Woods, 16-17, 30, 63, 67, 84, 190, 244, 255
Country Life, 10, 36, 38, 40, 42-4, 47, 69, 206, 264-6, 268, 270, 272
Messrs. T. Crowther & Son Ltd., 232
The Fitzwilliam Museum, 241
The G.L.C. as Trustees of the Iveagh Bequest, Kenwood, 48
The Guildhall Library, 223
Messrs. Hotspur Ltd., 66, 78-9, 81
The Hunterian Museum and Art Gallery, 242
Leeds Art Galleries, 61
Messrs. Mallett and Son Ltd., 58
The National Portrait Gallery, 240
The National Trust, 208, 211, 213, 217, 311
Private Collection, **Plate 3**; 169, 261
R.I.B.A. Drawings Collection, 263
Messrs. Sotheby & Co., 14, 20-1, 28, 33, 62, 113, 133, 188, 197, 236-7, 243, 245, 249, 260, 263, 310, 324
The Marquess of Tavistock and the Trustees of the Bedford Estates, 34
Temple Williams, 12, 15, 23, 45, 64, 77, 95, 103, 105, 108, 134, 137, 141, 154, 175, 179, 207, 210, 214, 216, 269, 318, 323
The Victoria and Albert Museum, **Plates 1-2, 4-40**; 10, 17, 22, 25-7, 30, 35, 47, 51-5, 58-9, 67, 70-6, 87-90, 92-3, 95-6, 99-101, 103-4, 106, 108-9, 114-6, 118-28, 130-1, 134-6, 138-9, 144, 150-3, 156-7, 159-60, 164-6, 168-70, 172-5, 178, 181, 183-8, 191-3, 198-9, 201, 205, 215, 219-21, 226-31, 233, 235-6, 238, 243, 245-8, 250-4, 256-7, 259-60, 271, 276, 298-301, 305, 309, 312-4, 316-7, 320-2, 327
The Worshipful Company of Goldsmiths, 161